I Survived Capitalism
and All I Got
Was This Lousy T-Shirt

I Survived Capitalism
and All I Got
Was This Lousy T-Shirt

EVERYTHING I WISH
I NEVER HAD TO LEARN ABOUT MONEY

Madeline Pendleton

Doubleday   New York

www.doubleday.com

DOUBLEDAY and the portrayal of an anchor with a dolphin
are registered trademarks of Penguin Random House LLC.

Jacket photograph by Lizzie Klein
Jacket design by Madeline Pendleton and John Fontana

Library of Congress Cataloging-in-Publication Data
Names: Pendleton, Madeline, author.
Title: I survived capitalism and all I got was this lousy t-shirt :
everything I wish I never had to learn about money / Madeline Pendleton.
Description: First edition. | New York : Doubleday, 2024. |
Includes bibliographical references.
Identifiers: LCCN 2023025110 (print) | LCCN 2023025111 (ebook) |
ISBN 9780385549783 (hardcover) | ISBN 9780385549790 (ebook)
Subjects: LCSH: Pendleton, Madeline, author. | Internet personalities—
United States—Biography. | Businesspeople—United States—Biography. |
TikTok (Electronic resource).
Classification: LCC PN1992.9236.P46 A3 2024 (print) |
LCC PN1992.9236.P46 (ebook) | DDC 302.23/1092 [B]—dc23
LC record available at https://lccn.loc.gov/2023025110
LC ebook record available at https://lccn.loc.gov/2023025111

MANUFACTURED IN THE UNITED STATES OF AMERICA
1 3 5 7 9 10 8 6 4 2
First Edition

This book is dedicated to the Tunnel Vision team.

Camila, Kenna, Kelsey, Story,
Sarah, Lizzie, Fern, Babylungs,
Marcella, Aya, Ria, and Leeanna—
teamwork makes the dream work.

Or whatever.

Capitalism: an economic system based on private ownership of property and business, with the goal of making the greatest possible profits for the owners

—CAMBRIDGE DICTIONARY

It is not from the benevolence of the butcher, the brewer, or the baker that we expect our dinner, but from their regard to their own interest.

—ADAM SMITH

Contents

Preface

Summer in Los Angeles is idyllic, with bright blue skies that seem almost painted on, like the city built a movie set just for you to live out your best California dreams, act by act. I woke up to the warmth of the Southern California sun on my face. The room was quiet around me; I kept my eyes closed, hoping to stave off the day for a few minutes more. Beside me, Mo-Dog rustled.

"That's weird," I thought to myself, and opened my eyes. The bedroom came into focus around me, with the floor-to-ceiling windows that opened up to the backyard where a waterfall gently trickled from the hot tub to the swimming pool and koi swam about in a pond, creating the faint sound of running water in the distance. Mo-Dog shook the blankets off her and walked up to me on the bed, wagging her tail and licking my face. I laughed and pushed myself upright. Time to get up, I guess.

"What are you doing here?" I asked her. She was rolling around on her back now, the comforter all scrunched up around her; she had one foot in her mouth. She was an unusual sight in the house that early in the day. Most mornings, she woke up with Drew—early with the sunrise. He'd walk around the house, talking gently to Mo-Dog in an upbeat chirping voice while he went through his morning routine. She'd bounce beside him, the tags of her collar jingling softly, while he made me coffee in the kitchen. Then, he'd leave a coffee by my bedside, kiss me on the forehead, and take Mo-Dog out for a morning hike in the canyon by our house. This morning, though, there was no coffee to be found and Mo-Dog was still there, looking anxiously at me like she was waiting for something to happen.

"I'm not taking you on a hike," I whispered to her. "You know I'm not much of an outdoors person!" She stared up at me, her big black eyes wet with anticipation, her tail wagging behind her.

"I will not be pressured!" I said to her playfully.

I walked to the kitchen to make myself coffee, Mo-Dog bouncing along beside me. Most days, I sipped my coffee in the kitchen and waited until Drew and Mo-Dog came back from their morning hike. He'd open the front door and she'd run in, full force, straight up to me to lick my leg and spin around in circles, a ball of excitement and frenetic energy. He was always a few steps behind her, already taking off his sweaty T-shirt, ready to kiss me good morning and ask me how I slept. We took our morning shower together, every single day, a ritual. He washed my hair and we talked about the upcoming day, laughing at inside jokes and already planning dinner. Sometimes, after he got out of the shower, he wrote notes for me on the bathroom mirror, things like "I love you" with big hearts drawn everywhere. I wondered if he'd left me a note there this morning. I walked back into our bedroom, past the closet he'd built for me and into the bathroom, with its huge walk-in shower and wall full of mirrors, but there was nothing. "Hm," I thought to myself. Strange.

Back in our bedroom, the old smelly boots and ripped-up jeans he wore every day were thrown onto a chair near my side of the bed. I picked up his jeans and folded them, keeping the belt on like he always did. They smelled like him, a mixture of tangerines and incense and our soap, and I smiled.

An hour or so passed with no sign of Drew. I wondered if maybe there'd been an emergency at work. He'd been running into some issues at the business, money issues mostly, and was in the process of completing a Chapter 11 bankruptcy, selling the business to a friend. There were papers to submit and forms to file and reports being constantly run. I ran out front to check the driveway to see if maybe he'd gone to a meeting I'd forgotten about. But his big blue pickup truck was still there, parked in the driveway where we'd left it when we came home the night before from my birthday dinner. I texted his friend Paul.

"Have you seen Drew?" I asked.

Almost instantly, Paul replied, "I'm coming over."

I furrowed my brow. Coming over? What did that mean?

I looked at Mo-Dog, who was starting to seem a little thrown off by our lack of morning routine as well. What if something had happened to him, I thought, on his morning run. What if there was an accident and he was hurt? I clipped Mo-Dog's leash to her collar and we left the house, walking to the end of the corner and turning right, heading past the heavy traffic of Mulholland and down into Fryman Canyon. There, a police car was parked, with the entrance to the hiking trail blocked off with yellow tape. A police officer stood guard at the top of the canyon. I walked up to him, Mo-Dog in tow.

"Excuse me," I said. "Has a hiker been injured? My boyfriend hasn't come home and I'm just wondering if maybe he's stuck at the bottom of the canyon?"

"There's been an injury," the police officer said curtly.

I felt a wave of relief wash over me. It must be him, I thought. Maybe he sprained an ankle. The canyon was steep and full of uneven terrain at the bottom. It would be easy to do, and hard to climb back up it without a working foot. Every time I tried running with him down there, I fell on a rock or tree root there at the bottom.

"Can you tell me if it's my boyfriend?" I asked. "He doesn't bring his phone when he goes out for a run. I could describe him maybe to you?"

The police officer shook his head. "I'm afraid I can't identify anyone, not properly—but if you show me a picture, I can let you know if it resembles the injured hiker or not."

"Yes," I said. "Perfect. One second." I pulled out my phone and opened my photos. The most recent photo in the camera roll was us together the day before, making a funny face into the camera. We sent it to my friend. I decided it looked too strange to show the officer, so I swiped backwards a few, finding a photo I'd taken of Drew just a couple of days before, in front of a piece of graffiti that read "It's a long way to the top if you want to rock and roll." His long hair was hanging in his face and you could see his tattoos in it, covering both arms. I spun my phone around and showed the police officer.

"Here," I said. "This is him."

The officer squinted for a second before nodding. It was a match.

"Great," I said. "Okay, perfect. I live just around the corner. Can I wait there until he's brought back up? Will you come let me know?"

The officer nodded again, grimly, and I gave him our address.

"Thank you!" I beamed, before turning around and walking Mo-Dog back to our house.

Back at the house, Paul was just arriving, with a woman I'd never met before. She seemed like a new girlfriend. They were somber and quiet.

"It's okay," I told Paul, smiling. "He was injured, I think, on his morning run. I'm sure it's just a sprained ankle or something. The hill is just so steep, you know?"

Paul winced, then tightened his lips. "We'll wait anyway," he said, "just to be sure."

We sat together in the living room. I tried my best to make small talk with Paul's new girlfriend, but she seemed strained in a way I couldn't quite make sense of. I drank coffee and made jokes, but her face contorted into a strange grimace each time. A few minutes later, there was a knock at the door. Paul jumped up to get it, and when he opened it, the police officer from the canyon was there. They spoke quietly, in hushed tones to each other. I craned my neck to see past Paul at the door, watching the police officer speak.

"He was having money trouble," I overheard Paul say, and the police officer nodded. A few seconds later, he closed the door.

Paul turned to face me. "Madeline," he said, softly but with resolve, "Drew is dead."

I felt the breath leave my body, my chest tightening as I exhaled, and I fell to the floor.

"You need to hear this," he told me, as I clutched the cool tile floor trying to find my breath. "He killed himself this morning. A hiker found his body on the trail and called the police."

In the canyon near our house, the same canyon where Drew played me songs on his guitar and we went on long evening walks and made plans for our future, Drew—overwhelmed with financial stress and unsure of a way out—shot himself in the heart. Everyone saw it coming but me. That day, I learned a horrible lesson: capitalism is a matter of life and death. The stakes are high, and if you lose, it might come for you in ways you'd never expect.

I Survived Capitalism
and All I Got
Was This Lousy T-Shirt

INTRODUCTION

At the age of twenty-eight, I was earning $19,000 per year in Los Angeles and barely scraping by. I had $65,000 in debt—student loans, maxed-out credit cards from emergencies like my 1997 Saturn breaking down all the time, and a car payment for a newer 2001 Volvo that I financed when I finally realized the Saturn might never stop breaking down. The Volvo was supposed to be a more reliable car. Spoiler alert: it wasn't. Interestingly enough, though, it did have a spoiler on it—right there on the back above the windshield—which should have been my first sign that it was not a good year, make, or model for Volvo.

The year was 2014. Median rent for a studio apartment in Los Angeles was $896 per month, or well over half of my income before taxes. The United States Housing and Urban Development Department says paying anything over 30 percent of your income towards housing makes you cost-burdened, and anything over 50 percent makes you severely cost-burdened. I was in the severe range. I woke up in the middle of the night, nearly every night, gasping for breath and shaking. In my nightmares, I saw credit card bills and eviction notices. The anxiety seemed to flow through my veins, itching and scratching just under the surface of my skin. Sometimes I'd hyperventilate. Other times I'd cry. Often I'd do both.

Money is both a practical and deeply emotional thing. On the one hand, it's a math problem. You add up your expenses and subtract them from your monthly income. It's cold and calculated and precise. On the other hand, if the numbers don't add up quite the way you'd like, it feels less like a math problem and more like a *you* problem. We carry with us the fear of not making ends meet, the shame of not earning more money, and the guilt over how we're spending the money we have. We carry generational trauma from the financial mistakes of our families before us, and we project our own financial mistakes out into the world around us, influencing the lives of everyone with whom we come into close contact. Financial issues are the fifth leading cause of divorce in the United States, as well as a leading predictor in instances of depression. In 2021, 73 percent of Americans ranked financial issues as their number one cause of stress—above politics, work, or family—and these numbers are highest in Generation Z and Millennials, with over 80 percent of people born after 1980 reporting that they find their finances to be a source of stress.

I never wanted to write a book about money. I wanted to read a book about money, a book that acknowledged the financial reality that our generations were born into. What I found instead were books written by men much older than me about how to survive in a world that didn't seem to exist anymore. Adages that might have sounded sagacious and wise in the past—like only spending 25 percent of your monthly income on housing—seemed ludicrous and out of touch by the time I became an adult. In 2022, the U.S. minimum wage is still stuck at $7.25 per hour or $15,080 per year, meaning you would have to pay just $314 per month to fall under that 25 percent rent threshold. Median rent in the United States is currently $1,253 per month, or roughly four times that. It's been the longest stretch in history where we haven't seen an increase in the federal minimum wage, meaning the real value of a minimum-wage worker's paycheck is worth 17 percent less than when it was implemented ten years ago.

If we look back at the minimum wage prior to that, the data is even more sobering. The minimum wage today is worth 31 percent less than it was in 1968. By contrast, housing prices have more than doubled when adjusted for inflation.

Millennials and Generation Z are currently contending with an unprecedented financial reality in the United States. Housing is more expensive compared to wages than ever before in U.S. history. CEO compensation has grown 1,322 percent since 1978, compared to just 18 percent for the average worker—creating the largest income gap between the rich and poor since 1928, before the Great Depression began. College has increased nearly 169 percent in cost since 1980, nearly 10 times the increase in typical workers' wages during that same period, making a college degree more expensive now than ever before. The number of Americans who have medical debt is up to an all-time high of 50 percent as of 2020. In short, life is getting more expensive by the day, but pay for most people in the United States isn't rising to meet those increasing costs. The financial worries of Millennials and Generation Z are not the same as the worries of our parents. We're facing increasing pressure to do more with less, and the old guidebooks written by generations who came before us are not helping.

This book is the story of how I learned to navigate finances in this unprecedented time and went from sleepless nights gasping for air to owning my own home, running a multimillion-dollar business, and sharing the profit and wages from that business equally among myself and every employee to ensure a better quality of life not just for me but for everyone there. It's the story of my own struggles to understand class, money, financial literacy, business ownership, and monetary planning, all while acknowledging this system is so deeply flawed that it makes survival seem nearly impossible. This is a book about my life, but it's also a book about so many people in my age range who have also lived a life marked by debt, low incomes, high costs, class identity struggles, and a hopelessness about their own financial future.

This is the story of how I came to understand the rules of money, a game we are all forced to play, and how I learned to bend those rules just enough to create a life where the people around me are happy, safe, and secure. This is a story about capitalism, and how—if we're lucky—we might survive long enough to see a better system, a brighter future, take its place.

CHAPTER I

No Place like Home

"Hey, this song is about us!" my cousin yelled, turning up the stereo in the dining room at my mother's house.

It was 1998, and the New Radicals' song "You Get What You Give" was everywhere on the airwaves. My cousin, three years older than me, was dancing around the dining room singing along with the words. My aunt, who was living with my mother at the time, walked into the room. She had dyed black hair and wore jangling jewelry, a gothic vision floating by the dining room table.

"Is this song about us?" my aunt asked, speaking over the music.

"Yeah!" my cousin yelled. "That part about being flat broke but doing it in style? That's totally us!"

I looked around my mother's house, a little old house built nearly a hundred years prior, filled with thrift store knickknacks spray-painted gold and black. Were we broke? I couldn't tell. I'd never met anyone with money before.

My mother's house was in a neighborhood called the Tower District in the city of Fresno. Fresno is a sprawling city of over half a million people, situated in the middle of two long, straight, boring highways that cut up through the middle of California—the I-5 and the CA-99. The highways run up the outskirts of town, meaning you could drive by Fresno every single day and have no clue that it was anything other than a few orchards and cow pastures. I'd say Fresno is a hidden gem, but I'm not sure how many people would consider it a gem at all. Nearly a quarter of the people there live in poverty, which makes it one of the poorest cities in the country last time I checked. The concentrated poverty level is so high that Fresno is widely considered the poorest city in California. The thing about growing up in a poor place, though, is that you don't really notice it like you might somewhere else. It just feels normal. A friend told me once that Fresno can best be described as having a "lifeboat mentality": the ship had sunk a long time ago, and we were all crammed into a tiny little lifeboat just doing our best to stay afloat. It wasn't great, but at least we were all in it together.

The year I was born, 1986, Ronald Reagan was in the middle of his second presidential term. I grew up with Fresno experiencing the real-time effects of "trickle-down economics"—Reagan's idea that cutting social programs while decreasing taxes for the wealthy would somehow help the poor—all around me. It wasn't always so bad in Fresno. In 1958, Visa launched the first trial run of credit cards there. It seemed like an all-American town back then, with a thriving middle class and all. For decades, in the middle of the century, so many people were moving into Fresno that the city had to subsidize building projects to keep up with the housing demand. In 1980, most neighborhoods in central Fresno were experiencing a poverty rate of under 20 percent. By the year 2000, when I was a teenager, that figure had roughly doubled, with aggressive increases in concentrated poverty rates hitting hardest throughout the late 1980s and early 1990s following Reagan's economic policies. Crime rates sky-rocketed, too. Today, Fresno has a crime index of 9, meaning it's safer than just 9 percent of other U.S. cities. In a few short decades, Fresno had gone from being an All-America City to something of a laughingstock nationwide.

Now, when you tell someone you grew up there, there's a

good chance they'll respond by saying "I'm sorry." It's a weird feeling, because on the one hand you're like "Yeah, for sure—it's a crime-riddled shithole with twice as many McDonald's as there are public parks." On the other hand, Fresno is *your* crime-riddled McDonald's-filled shithole and who does this asshole think they are to judge it? Growing up, I felt safe with the neon lights of the fast-food chains all around me. They felt as much like home to me as anywhere else in Fresno did.

When I was in the sixth grade, a new girl moved to town from Philadelphia and we became friends. I went to her house sometimes after school or for weekend sleepovers, and the only food she ever had in her refrigerator were frozen McDonald's burgers. She and her sister heated them up in the microwave and ate them for every meal, even breakfast. Their dogs ate them, too, sometimes, instead of dog food. Back in the 1990s, McDonald's ran promotions where on Mondays and Wednesdays, hamburgers were just 29 cents and cheeseburgers just 39 cents. Her dad, a single father who worked in construction, piled the kids and dogs into his pickup truck every Monday and Wednesday to go through the drive-thru. I went with them once and watched as he ordered dozens of discounted burgers at a time, then pulled back in through the drive-thru to do it all over again. We went in a loop like that through the parking lot and into the drive-thru line three or four times. There was a limit per car, he told me, but they usually wouldn't remember your car until the fourth or fifth round through. If you played your cards right, you could get close to a hundred burgers for around $30, which meant the family of three could eat for $1.80 per day if the kids got free lunch at school. In a world that seemed to desperately try to forget that places like Fresno—full of poor people just doing their best to survive—existed, companies like McDonald's seemed to be looking out for us. Sure, they paid their employees minimum wage and contributed to keeping the masses in poverty, but at least they gave us 29-cent hamburgers four times a month to make up for it.

To understand poverty in Fresno, you have to start with a

street called Shaw Avenue. Shaw runs east-west through town, bisecting the city: there's the half that's north of Shaw, and the half that's south of Shaw, where I grew up. Shaw Avenue is what a 1970s city planning document referred to as Fresno's "Mason-Dixon Line," the line that divides the whiter, more affluent parts of town from the poorer communities of color. In a country like the United States, which is built on a history of racism, it's not surprising that segregation persists. However, it is a bit surprising that it persists to the extent it does in Fresno, considering it's what's called a "majority-minority" city. If you travel north of Shaw, you can find enclaves of these few wealthy white residents, whose average life expectancy is a staggering ninety years, which is a full two decades longer than the life expectancy for residents who live on the south side of town.

I imagine most cities have a street like Shaw, which sequesters the wealthy away from the harsh realities of the poor. In my town, we even had rock bands named after this effect—one was called South of Shaw, in honor of the side of town I called home. In Fresno, Shaw Avenue's division was so extreme that in 1973, the United States Department of Health, Education, and Welfare found that segregation in Fresno schools violated the Civil Rights Act. To this day, schools north of Shaw feature higher concentrations of white students compared to schools located south of Shaw, and those schools north of Shaw are also widely considered to be "better" schools.

By the 1990s, poverty in Fresno was soaring south of Shaw and the city earned a reputation for hard-drug addiction. We were dubbed the "meth capital of America" one year due to the inordinately high incidence of methamphetamine abuse in the region, and instead of feeling shame, the general consensus among Fresnans was that it felt good to at least be known for something. In 2009, a famous British reporter came to Fresno and filmed a whole documentary about methamphetamine use in the county. He squatted in deteriorating buildings in neighborhoods south of Shaw like the Tower District, where my mom's house was. He stopped people on the street and made them show their rotting teeth to the camera. He made the city look more squalid and seedier than any of my memories had. Still, I sometimes show the documentary to people, pointing eagerly at the street signs in the background with a "Look, Ma, I'm on TV!" energy.

"I used to walk to that gas station all the time," I say, pointing at the screen. "It was in a documentary! In *England*!"

In 2019, that same gas station I pointed at in the background of the British documentary went viral on the internet. An employee made videos of the gas station regulars, people who just seemed normal to me. When I read the comments, though, I finally saw my hometown the way other people saw it: a sad place where poor people struggled to get by. Viewers donated money to help buy people in my old neighborhood lottery tickets and potato chips, and even RVs so they wouldn't have to sleep on the street anymore. I sometimes held up my phone to show the videos to my friends from Los Angeles or New York or San Francisco.

"Look!" I'd say. "This is the gas station on the street where I grew up!"

They'd watch for a few seconds then look at me, their faces scrunched up into a pitiful grimace, as if to say "Oh, honey, I had no idea."

One year, when I was a kid, there was a nationwide commercial about the future of electric cars. At the end of the commercial, the crisp condescending voice of the narrator said something about a bright shining future where you'd never have to stop for gas in Fresno. The local news station ran a report about the commercial. They interviewed people on the street to see how they felt about the ad. The Fresnans on the TV screen all had that knowing look.

"Well, yeah, Fresno's not the greatest place," they conceded, "but did they have to be so mean about it?"

If capitalism is a joke, maybe Fresno is the punch line. For decades, I couldn't tell why. It just felt like home to me.

. . .

My friends from other places—Los Angeles or New York or San Francisco—often tell me that I think more about money than any other person they've ever met, which is interesting when you consider that I don't have much of it. It is true, though, that my preoccupation with money guides nearly everything I do in life, including social interactions. As I get older, I find this happens a lot with people who grew up in Fresno. One day, when I was in my mid-twenties, an old friend of mine from Fresno called me. We both were living in Los Angeles, forced to move there after the Great Recession to look for work. She was living down the street from me in a small apartment in Koreatown.

"I don't think I can talk to people who aren't from Fresno," she told me over the phone. "I don't think I'll ever understand them, or they'll ever understand me. Do you ever feel that way?"

I thought about the time I had a boyfriend with wealthy parents from Portland, Oregon, who owned a three-story home, or the time I made friends with a girl from New England whose family paid her rent.

"I do," I told my friend.

"I met a girl the other day," she said. "She had Louis Vuitton luggage. And that part, that part wasn't surprising. I know rich people exist, right? But the thing that blew my mind is that she said her family was middle class. Do middle-class people just buy Louis Vuitton luggage? I thought I was middle class. I can't afford any luggage, let alone Louis Vuitton luggage."

I knew what she meant. Growing up in Fresno, surrounded by people who were mostly the same as me, I assumed we were all middle class, too. The kids north of Shaw, they were rich. The rest of us, we had a roof over our head most of the time, even if sometimes we had to live with family members to make it happen, so we must have been middle class. Now, in retrospect, I can see it for what it was. Those kids, the ones who lived north of Shaw, they were middle class. The rest of us, we were just poor. The poverty was all around us, though, so we couldn't see it. It just felt normal. Even now, I think if I told my mother that I grew up poor, she would shake her head and laugh.

"Oh, Maddie," she'd say. "Stop being so dramatic."

There's a joke I think about a lot. It's a Chris Rock joke, and he says, "If poor people knew how rich rich people are, there would be riots in the streets." I think that speaks to our understanding of wealth and money: we don't know what we don't know. How rich are rich people, really? What is a billion dollars? It might as well be the same as a million dollars. I couldn't imagine either of them. It's the same muddied, strange worldview that sometimes stops us from acknowledging that we ourselves are poor. We mythologize the idea of poverty, and it's easy to do because there is always someone who has less than us. As long as there is someone with less, we imagine ourselves in the middle, doing just fine. "The Poor" in our cultural mythos are Dickensian paupers, wretches of the earth, one morsel of food away from complete starvation—it's the most extreme image we can conjure of a person in destitution, who certainly might exist, but who doesn't reflect the way poverty tends to look in contemporary American society.

It's hard to imagine that we ourselves might be the poor—people from working-class backgrounds who are just one paycheck away from complete financial ruin. If we're unhoused, we're unhoused in a different way than the people who are *actually homeless*. If we're hungry, we're hungry in a different way than people who are *actually starving*. If we're broke, we're broke in a different way than people who are *actually poor*. I run into this issue, too, assessing my own life. Was I really homeless those nights I had nowhere to sleep? Was I really starving that day all I could find to eat in my cupboard was expired popcorn and leftover cake frosting? Was I really poor that day my bank account was overdrawn and I had to slip in the back door of the bus because I couldn't afford bus fare to get to work? It seems like the words are too big to apply to my life, as though poverty were a limited classification and using it to label my life might mean I was taking it away from someone who deserved it more.

What I do know is that my childhood, my upbringing, influenced my relationship with money from an early age. Now, when I talk to other people, I find myself wanting desperately to know about their parents and their upbringing, too. It's a way to gauge if we can relate to each other, if we come from the same kind of place. I stare at people's shoes in public and ask what kind of car they drive. I ask about their parents, if they still work, or if they've ever been on EBT (food stamps, it's sometimes called). The questions might be about parents and families and houses and money, but really they are all different ways of trying to figure out the same thing. In a world where people born into fortunes of over $100 million still get branded as "self-made" in the media, or business moguls start out with a "small loan" of $1 million from their parents and tell us to pull ourselves up by our bootstraps, asking questions about someone's parents is really a way to ask one question: "Can I trust you?" Can I trust you to know where I come from? Can I trust you to give me realistic advice? Can I trust you to guide me from the point I'm starting at now? Can I trust that you've been here before too?

When I think about my childhood, it's divided in half, one event cutting it right down the middle, much like Shaw Avenue cuts through Fresno. One half, the first half, is the years I lived mostly with my father, up until the age of twelve. The second half wasn't really a half at all—more like a period of five years where I lived with my mother, from the ages of twelve to seventeen, after my father's financial situation deteriorated so badly that he couldn't afford to take care of me anymore. To understand me, to understand my relationship with money, you have to start with my dad.

DUANE

My dad is a big guy, maybe six foot three, covered in tattoos from knuckles to neck. The knuckle tattoos read GAME OVER

DOLL FACE, the DOLL FACE letters right below the GAME OVER letters, separated on the finger by a single knuckle. The joke is it's the last thing you see before he punches your lights out for getting too rowdy at the bar. He worked as a bouncer sometimes.

My dad had always been wild, reckless, and fun. He tells me he graduated high school, but just barely. He was a scrappy punk kid in the '80s with a gap in his front teeth. I inherited the gap. When I try to stick my tongue through my two front teeth, it's an homage to him. When he was in high school, my grandma used to cut his mohawks herself in their front yard. She had a photo of him his senior year skateboarding down an unfinished on-ramp for the freeway that went through town. That same freeway would later expand, tearing down the house my grandparents lived in for years. My dad looks happy in the photo on that freeway, like he knows he's breaking some sort of rule but doesn't care. It was printed in the local newspaper. I'm not exactly sure why.

My dad is the kind of guy everyone in town knows. In the Tower District, we have a term for that: "Fresno Famous." It's the word we use for local characters like Amy the Hearse Queen or Poetry Lady or Fat Jerry the Satanic Body Piercer. My dad is Fresno Famous, but it's not exactly a paying gig. If you say his name in the Tower District, inevitably someone will say "Duane?! I love that guy! He owes me twenty dollars." I think that says a lot about just how likeable he is. How can you still love a guy who owes you money? My dad might be the only person on the planet to have figured that one out.

For years, when it was just him and me, we lived off and on in a series of tiny little apartments across the street from an arcade. Sometimes, he took me to play Skee-Ball and Ms. Pac-Man and House of the Dead on old-school arcade machines that broke all the time and ate your tickets. Inside the apartments, we had that gross brown carpet that everyone seemed to love in the late '80s and early '90s. It was stained and had cigarette burn holes in it here and there, but I always had my own bedroom with a hand-me-down waterbed and a place to store my dolls. It was a rowdy apartment building, where our neighbors threw parties most nights and it seemed like once a week we'd go outside only to find my dad's pickup truck—an '80s thing with red and purple and silver triangles painted all over it—had been stolen. They always found it within a few days. The paint job was too unique to hide for long.

Sometimes, my dad took me to a weird old diner called the Silver Dollar Hofbrau, with giant burger plates on the cheap. He'd bet me $20 I couldn't finish a whole plate by myself. I'd take the bet every time, but only actually won once. While we waited for our food to come out, he'd turn his hand into a little creature we called Thor. Thor stood on four legs, made from his thumb, index finger, ring finger, and pinky. His middle finger stuck out like a neck and a head for the creature. He'd use it to smell around the table—sniffing noises and all—and try to steal things for Thor to eat. If you weren't careful, after your food came, Thor would steal all of your fries. As adults, both my dad and I were diagnosed with attention deficit/hyperactivity disorder, ADHD. If I think about it long enough, most stories from my childhood illuminate our shared inability to just sit the fuck still for a minute. If the food took too long to come out, my dad would start mixing together all of the condiments at the table into a creamer pack to create disgusting concoctions. He'd mix the creamer with salt, pepper, ketchup, and relish, then stir it together with a toothpick, making "Mmmmmm" noises while I squealed. When it was all mixed together, he'd offer me money to drink it.

"Twenty-five cents?" he'd ask. "No? Okay, how about fifty? It's so small! Okay, okay. A dollar!"

He always had at least a little cash on him, which probably had a lot to do with the aimless car rides we took around town stopping at "friends'" houses where he'd run inside—for just a second!—while I waited in the car and listened to music. I didn't know what he did inside his friends' houses, and it never occurred to me to ask. Years later, though, I'd ask my mother about it.

"I think maybe Dad was a drug dealer?" I said, searching through broken memories, trying to super-glue together a narrative of some kind.

"Who wasn't a drug dealer?" she replied with a laugh. "I think we were all drug dealers back then." The answer satisfied me. Who was I—Nancy Reagan? The War on Drugs was a war on the poor, on people of color, on anyone who didn't fit in with the moral majority; the War on Drugs was a war on us.

I'd sit in the car while my dad ran into the strange houses, and I'd turn the radio up as loud as possible. It only took two or three songs before my dad came back out, and afterwards we'd go to Tower Records or Sam Goody and he'd let me buy some tapes or CDs. Once, he bought me a keyboard and a drum pad machine. Things like the keyboard and the drum machine came and went in my life. We moved a lot—often abruptly for reasons I couldn't understand at the time, and things would disappear in the transitions. Usually, we'd move in with my grandparents after leaving an apartment. We'd stay there a few months: my dad in the spare room, and me sleeping on the pull-out couch in the living room with my dad's pit bull, Caesar, guarding me at the foot of the bed, growling at anyone who dared to get up in the middle of the night to use the bathroom or get a glass of water. Then, whenever luck struck, we'd be back out in our own place again, usually a different apartment in that same complex across the street from the arcade, somehow always with the same stained brown carpet.

Eventually, my dad married a woman who was fixated on the idea of upward mobility, which to her meant a new tract home in a subdivision built on the ruins of old orchards on the outskirts of town. Fresno liked to sprawl, building out as far as possible, with housing developments that dotted the old countryside. The tract homes had five or so models. You could visit the model homes and pick the layout you liked, then choose the floors and countertops and cabinet colors all on your own, and they'd build it—just how you wanted it—

to your liking. Every fifth house or so on the street had the same layout, but they'd flip them, mirror-image style, to try to make them look different. At day care, I told all of my friends that my parents were buying a house for $139,000 and I was moving to a brand-new school on the other side of town. It sounded very impressive. We were all used to living in tiny, cramped apartments or sharing houses with our grandparents—multi-generational dwellings built more on survival than cultural tradition.

We lived at the new house for four years, until my dad lost his job and he and my stepmom got a divorce and eventually the house was foreclosed on by the bank. When my stepmother left, she took the furniture with her, and in the time between her leaving and me moving in with my mom, the only furniture my dad and I had in the house was the inflatable furniture from my bedroom—'90s things in purple filled with glitter. We sat on the inflatable furniture in the living room and played video games on my little TV, set right on the floor. One day, as we sat on my inflatable chairs playing Donkey Kong, I looked around at the house. It felt like I was really seeing it for the first time, that way sometimes you wake up to your everyday reality, like a stranger looking in on it, and it doesn't seem so normal anymore. We were eating cereal every night for dinner. Sometimes, the power was shut off.

"I don't think you can afford me anymore," I told my dad. "Maybe I should go live with Mom for a while."

That's where the dividing line in my childhood takes place, right there, in that moment, when I called my mom and went to live with her.

KAT

My mother has always been a beautiful, well-dressed person who drifts in and out of my life doing nice things for me in the wrong way. In the 1990s, her hair was dyed black in a chin-length bob with short bangs, and she wore Dr. Martens with long dresses and crocheted cardigans with little mirrors stitched into them. She played the Cure and the Smiths and Cocteau Twins and Concrete Blonde in the house, dancing and singing along like she might enchant me. Sometimes, I'd walk around her house looking for a book to read. All I found was *American Psycho* and the complete works of Anne Rice.

I stayed with her some weekends even as I lived with my dad, but on Mondays when those weekends were over, packing me lunch for school was always a struggle. She didn't have much in the fridge. Sometimes, I'd get hacked-together meals of leftover sushi and strange stews. She'd write me little love notes to go along with my lunches, which humiliated me to open. They had skeletons drawn on them, and she'd kiss them with her bright red lipstick, leaving a mark at the bottom of the page. I'd read the notes quickly, then crumble them into a ball and toss them into the bottom of my bag. I didn't want skeletons and bloodred lips. I wanted to fade quietly into the background, with a nice normal mom who shopped at Old Navy and gave me Lunchables like the other kids' moms did.

When I was born, my mother worked in an art store making minimum wage, which was $3.35 per hour in California. She tells me I was a "welfare baby"; government assistance paid the medical bills for my birth, which would have otherwise been something like $2,500 in 1986—or 746 hours of work for her. As I got older, she switched to a job working in insurance claims. It was a good job you could get without a college degree and it paid the bills. After that, she dyed her hair a sensible blonde color and started wearing cardigans and pencil skirts to the office.

"It's called work for a reason," she sometimes said. "You're not supposed to enjoy it."

As she became the mother I always wished I'd had, it felt a bit depressing, like a part of her had died. Eventually, though, she worked enough hours at the boring insurance job that she was able to buy a small $80,000 house in the Tower District. The down payment must have been around $2,800 for it then, or a little under the price of two months' rent on that same house today. The house had three bedrooms technically, but one was so small you could only fit a twin-sized mattress in it comfortably. That's the room my aunt sometimes lived in. Other times, my mother set up a divider in the living room and put her bed in the back half of it, right by the front door, making a makeshift bedroom in the space. In the summertime, when Fresno heat skyrocketed, she ran the swamp cooler. We didn't have air-conditioning, and the swamp cooler was noisy and shook the whole house as it ran, all while barely producing airflow of any kind. It was unbearably hot and loud, but unlike my father, my mother was prudent with her finances and seldom lived too far beyond her means.

Her financial reality was still contingent upon credit and debt, of course, like most low-income people. She likes to tell me that my first full sentence as a baby was "Charge it!" I apparently said it to the cashier at Macy's department store one day when he asked how she was going to pay for her purchases. However, unlike my father, she always paid her bills on time. She viewed the system as something you "worked" to survive, and from an early age, I was taught that credit scores—something that didn't get developed and implemented in the United States until she was twenty-three years old—were important tools to navigate that system.

"Whatever you do," she told me once when I was a teenager, "never damage your credit score."

"Got it," I replied. "So, debt is like membership to a special club. As long as you pay the monthly dues, you can get whatever you want. And your credit score is like the password to the club."

My mother agreed. Despite participating in the monthly debt club, she tried to live as frugally as possible. Her house was decorated with furniture we sometimes found on the side of the road and took home to spray-paint different colors. There was a coffee table spray-painted metallic gold, and an old chest of drawers with the handles switched out to be faux-crystal knobs instead. Despite being low-income, my mother would not have called herself poor—not with the "good job" and the house. Still, she was creative in that way poor people often are—taking little bits of discarded nothings and recycling them into something new. She was resourceful, and it didn't stop with furniture. We thrift-shopped for clothes to dye different colors back at home, using the little cardboard boxes of Rit Dye that came from the grocery store. We kept old cottage cheese containers to use as Tupperware. We sewed triangular strips of fabric into our old jeans to make them look like newer, more fashionable bell bottoms or flares.

Right before I moved in with her in the summer in between seventh and eighth grade, my mother married a new man—a respectable, reasonable man who also had a steady job. He drove a brand-new bright red Pontiac Grand Am and listened to bands I'd never heard of before, like Crosby, Stills, and Nash—a far cry from the punk rock and goth tracks of my youth. Where my mother was eccentric and artistic, he was straitlaced and conservative. She told me later that she was never sure if she even liked him; she just thought marrying him was the responsible thing to do. It was time to grow up, she thought, and surely this conservative buttoned-up man must know a few things about what it meant to be an adult. He wore his shirts tucked in with a belt on the weekends, for god's sake. What could be more adult than that?

Just before the wedding, however, she seemed to find out that the responsibility was all a mirage. She told me that he had mountains of credit card debt and cardboard boxes full of unpaid bills, which would become her problem, too, the day she said "I do." She sat at the dining room table for weeks, painstakingly going through boxes of paperwork, calling creditors to negotiate payments. The lesson, she explained to me, was to always pay your bills on time. I internalized this lesson, which along with the lesson about credit scores was the only thing either of my parents ever taught me about money. Years later, my own credit report would show me that at some point, my mother had opened an American Express card account in my name when I was a child. When I asked her about it later, she told me it was to help set me up with a good credit score myself from an early age. I'd be lying, though, if I said I didn't wonder if maybe, all those years ago, taking out a credit card in her child's name wasn't a way to help alleviate some of her own financial pressures.

Our childhoods set up our relationships with money, for better or worse. We absorb lessons about class from our surroundings. Our cities and towns shape our perceptions of normal, forming the basis for the scale we use to judge everyone around us moving forward. If you grow up in a town with more poverty, your scale slides just a little to the left—where normal is a little more broke. If you grow up in a town without poverty, your scale slides just a little to the right—where normal is a little better off. Similarly, our parents' incomes set the foundation for what we think an average income is— anyone with less than us is poor, anyone with more is rich. These are arbitrary standards that only make sense to us and people who are like us, with similar backgrounds and upbringings. We speak to each other and throw out these phrases— rich, poor, a good job, a bad job—as though they are terms with real meaning. In reality, when we use these words, we're describing our own lives rather than concrete things about the world around us.

Most of the things I learned about money were indirect, absorbed as I heard information pass me by in the moment. I'd heard enough to know my dad was bad with money, and that while my mother was better with money, neither of them was great. From my father, I learned that money comes and goes, and you should always try to have enough cash to make life fun enough to be worth living. I also learned that you should never get too comfortable or attached to material possessions because your financial situation can change in an instant. To survive this world, you needed to be flexible and roll with the punches. My father's motto was "adapt or die," and in that pursuit, laws were merely suggestions. The rich were doing whatever they wanted, so why shouldn't we?

From my mother, I learned to view money as a more practical tool. A job was a necessary evil, because money was a necessary evil. A credit score was important. With a credit score, you could get things like credit cards and loans to ease your short-term financial struggles. I learned how to negotiate debt down and argue with bill collectors. I learned when to hang up the phone if you weren't getting your way and try again another day. I learned to not fear debt because debt made life easier to live. Years later this mentality would leave me drowning in debt, yet somehow with an 820 credit score and pre-approval notices from banks eager and willing to raise my credit limits and give me more credit cards so I could end up in even more debt and perpetuate the cycle forever. It was a fake-it-'til-you-make-it mentality, maybe, but there was faith there that one day, if you kept your nose down and did your work, everything would fall into place.

The world around us is difficult to explain. It's chaotic and constantly changing, and within it, capitalism is a game of survival with higher stakes than ever before. There are rules to follow if you want to make it to the end, but we all start in different positions on the board with different tools by our side. The story of my childhood is the story of where I'm starting on the board: on the broker side of an already broke town, in a post-Reaganomics world where the money never quite trickled down. This is where my relationship with money began.

How to Build Credit

Credit scores are a digital measure of your ability to repay debt. Often, they are used as indicators of how financially sound you are. In reality, though, credit scores don't measure your financial health—they just measure your track record of paying back debt. Wealthy people can have bad credit scores or no credit at all. Broke people can have great credit scores. Having debt is generally not considered great, but having a good credit score will make it easier for you to do things like rent an apartment or get a loan to buy a house or a car, and usually you need debt to have a good credit score. It's a messed-up system, right? Here's everything you need to know about your credit score:

1. You don't have just one credit score. There are three main credit bureaus in the United States: Experian, Equifax, and TransUnion. They keep track of your credit history. There are also two main credit modeling systems used in the United States: FICO and VantageScore. You probably have a slightly different credit score with each of the three main credit branches, and your credit score will be a little different based on which model is used.

2. Credit scores are usually between 300 and 850. Some models allow for scoring to go up to 900, but those are rare. 300–629 is considered a bad credit score. 630–689 is considered fair. 690–719 is considered good. 720 and above is considered excellent. Not to toot my own horn, but my credit score is usually between 810 and 845 when I run it, so I think I'm a pretty trustworthy source on how to get a good score.

3. Credit scores take into account how many open debt accounts you have (more is better), how long your debt accounts have been open (longer is better), how many on-time or late payments you have on debt (on-time is obviously better than late), how many times you've applied for new credit accounts in the recent past (fewer is better), and how much of your total available credit you're using at any time (under 30 percent is best).

4. Most credit scores will be calculated using only debt accounts, meaning loans or credit cards. Experian has begun to experiment with including rent payments, utility payments, and subscription services in its model, but you have to sign up for that feature with them directly.

5. For the most part, using your debit card will not help you build a credit score, even if you run it as "credit" when checking out at a store. A designated credit card is different than your debit card, and will help you build credit.

6. A credit card is a debt account. The bank who gives you a credit card will give you a monthly "limit," or amount you're allowed to spend up to. At the end of the month, they will send you a bill for everything you spent, and you will need to pay it off, either in full or in installments of lower payments every month. For best credit, never spend more than 30 percent of the total available limit.

7. Some credit cards give you perks, like free airline miles, for using their card. Shop around for the best credit card reward systems. My credit card airline miles paid for me to take a free trip to Spain—my first time ever leaving North America!

8. If you're new to credit, you might need to look into something called a "secured credit card"—that's where you prepay a few hundred dollars on the card in advance of charging anything. It will help you build credit, and if you can afford it, it's a good place to start.

9. When taking out a loan or credit card, always pay attention to the interest rate, sometimes called the APR. You want the lowest percentage possible. Any month where you don't pay off the balance in full, that interest rate will get tacked on to what you owe. If the interest rate is high, it's easy for your debt to balloon out of control. I consider anything over 20 percent to be demonically high and a sure sign of predatory lending. Anything between 10 and 19 percent I consider not great, but manageable. Anything under 10 percent I consider pretty good. Interest rates are usually based on figures set by the U.S. government, along with your credit score.

10. People with good credit scores get lower interest rates on things like credit cards and loans. This means that if your credit score is high, things like cars and houses will actually be cheaper for you. The difference between a high and low credit score can cost you thousands of dollars when buying things like vehicles, too, so a good credit score is helpful when you (like most people) don't have enough cash to just go around buying cars and houses outright.

11. Sometimes, paying off a loan might actually lower your credit score. That's because when you pay off a loan, it closes the account. Remember that having more open accounts is generally viewed as a good thing. Additionally, if it was an account you've had open for a long time—like student loans—closing the account could bring down your average age of credit, which might additionally reduce your score. It's a weird gnarly game that doesn't always make sense.

12. Downloading a credit monitoring app is free and will help you keep track of what's going on with your credit score. I swear by them.

13. Checking your credit score does not lower your score. However, having lots of "hard inquiries" on your account does. Hard inquiries happen when you apply for a new line of credit, and they fall off your credit report in two years. You have to authorize them, which usually involves you signing a document saying someone can run your score. I try to keep my hard inquiries below three in a two-year period.

14. If you see errors on your credit report, you can dispute them with the credit bureau. Usually, there's a place to do it on their website. You never have to pay someone to help you dispute an error. It's pretty easy to do yourself, but there are a lot of predatory credit repair services out there who will try to claim you need them when you don't.

15. Banks take a calculated risk when lending to you. It's their job. If you find yourself in a position where you cannot repay your debt, it doesn't mean you failed. It means they did. They took a risk lending to you—they know that. They gambled and lost. Don't feel bad about owing money to a bank. They're evil bloodsucking mega-corporations and they don't care about us.

CHAPTER 2

Working for the Weekend

The weather in Fresno is terrible year-round. In the summer, temperatures soar to 110 degrees; heat rises off the asphalt in waves so thick you can watch them roll up towards the sickly still blue cloudless sky. The city parks out-of-service buses on the side of the road with air-conditioning running inside just to give pedestrians a reprieve from the brutality of the sun. When I was in elementary school, a teacher died of heat stroke in the middle of recess—falling down on the hot asphalt while the kids looked on in horror. In the winter, temperatures drop to around 30 degrees, but the conditions aren't right for anything as charming as snow. Instead, the cold air is so dense that a heavy fog descends upon the valley. It sits there for days sometimes, immobile, shrouding everything in a freezing cloud-like haze so thick that nobody can drive to work or school. There's a name for it apparently: tule fog. It's a special kind of fog that only exists in California's Central Valley, and it's just as miserable as Fresno's reputation.

One night in the year 2001, I found myself caught in the middle of the unrelenting tule fog as it descended over the city. I was thirteen years old, trudging down the street away from my mother's house, wishing I'd somehow had the foresight to be wearing a sweater when she kicked me out this time. At least I had shoes on. I wrapped my arms tight around my body in a futile effort to keep warm as I walked. Getting kicked out of my mother's house was nothing new, but I still hadn't figured out exactly how to deal with it—especially on a night as cold and foggy as this one. I stared at my phone in the darkness, trying to figure out where exactly I was going. The obvious choice would have been my father's house, if he'd had a house anyway. In my teenage years, my dad was often in between homes, sometimes for months at a time. My grandparents lived in a small town nearby with atrocious public transportation, which complicated my ability to get to and from their place. It was too late to call my friends, whose parents would surely not be excited to let their kid's weird buddy crash at their house for an indefinite amount of time. I scrolled through the contacts list in my phone, growing more pessimistic with each name I passed. I'd need to pull an all-nighter wandering the city or seek help from the Tower Rats.

Resigned, I sighed and turned the corner, walking south towards the heart of the Tower District—Fresno's haven for weirdos of all kinds. There, broke artists and gutter punks roamed the streets selling poetry or spanging—asking strangers for spare change. The Tower Rats, a roving pack of homeless street kids, paraded through the neighborhood at night, singing on the sidewalk in front of bars and laughing as they broke into abandoned buildings to sleep. They once showed me how to finagle free pizza and beer from the local pizza parlor. If you sat quietly in the back, the employees looked the other way when customers left so you could scurry over and finish their pizza crusts and alcohol pitchers. The Tower District was like that—a bunch of down-on-their-luck odd-balls helping each other get by. If anyone could help me figure out where to go on a freezing foggy night, I figured, it was those kids.

The Tower Rats were full of short-term solutions, but as I walked down Palm Avenue into the foggy darkness, I realized that I needed to come up with a long-term plan fast. More and more, I was butting heads with my stressed-out mom and her new husband, whose own relationship was on the rocks; relying on my family for shelter was proving to be unsustainable. I had to take matters into my own hands.

"I have got to get a job," I muttered to myself.

It never would have occurred to me in high school that both my father and I were homeless. In my head, homelessness was reserved for people who consistently slept on the streets, for whom not having a house was some sort of permanent condition they would have to contend with their whole lives. In reality, there are four different types of homelessness: chronic, episodic, transitional, and hidden. My father and I fell into the "transitional" or "hidden" categories, and if you ask around, you'll probably find that a lot of people you know have, too. People like us are often resistant to calling ourselves that, though—"homeless." It feels like a lie somehow, as though the term should be reserved for someone more vulnerable than us—someone dealing with disability, addiction, or social circumstances that make it impossible to participate in the harrowing world of a capitalist exchange of labor for survival.

It always felt like modern-day eugenics to me—those not able to work are left to die. How can you pay rent if you can't work a job to earn money? How can you file for government assistance if you don't have an address or a phone or access to a computer? The average life span for an unsheltered homeless person is 17.5 years shorter than the life span for the general population. This group—the most at-risk group—tends to be the group we think of as being "actually homeless" in our minds, which perhaps speaks to that tendency we have to assume that we can never be struggling if someone has it worse than we do. The chronically unsheltered, though, account for just 17 percent of the homeless population in the United States, which means that 83 percent of homelessness does not look like the vision many of us have in our heads.

The reality of homelessness is more complicated than that. I didn't know it as a teenager, but approximately 40 percent of unsheltered unhoused people have jobs. Having a job just isn't enough nowadays to make sure you don't end up on the street, even if it seemed like a good place for me to start.

In truth, people experiencing hidden homelessness are often people like I was: young people who needed to turn to friends, family, and neighbors for shelter after experiencing trauma or challenges in life. When I first read about hidden homelessness, I instantly recognized my own experiences. "Oh, that's like me," I thought with a laugh. Then the reality set in. The more I talked to people in my life, the more I learned that like me, they, too, had experienced homelessness without ever considering themselves among the unhoused. I have multiple friends who lived in their cars for durations of time ranging from weeks to months. I've known countless people over the past couple of decades who have casually mentioned that they are "couch surfing." I've had friends who stayed out going to bars and parties and after-parties all night not because they loved the nightlife, but simply because they didn't have a home to go back to. I've met people who jokingly referred to themselves as "hobosexual," meaning they were so poor they would date whoever would let them stay at their house for the night. I've had friends meet people who went on dating apps and engaged in hook-up culture just to have a place to sleep. None of these people would be included when we talk about the more than half a million people in the United States experiencing homelessness, though. When we expand our understanding of homelessness to include all facets of it and not just the cases that are the most severe, we begin to see the housing crisis take shape in the United States. Capitalism has crafted a world where "normal" is just not sleeping on the sidewalk for *too many* nights in a row.

In retrospect, my relationship with my mother was something of a "perfect storm" for creating the conditions that led to me wandering the streets with nowhere to go so many nights in my youth. In my teenage years, I was what adults call a "problem child"—too loud, too opinionated, too inquisitive, too much in general. While my mother was there for me in ways that sometimes surprised me—helping me dye my hair bright purple, buying me a pair of jeans I'd been coveting at the mall for months, or even standing up for me when I got into trouble at school—she was argumentative and headstrong, too, just like I was, and explosive arguments were common in our home. My mother was dealing with her own sources of stress and frustration; at just thirty-three years old, she was stuck in a relationship she loathed but worried that leaving would be financially irresponsible. Life was, after all, easier on two incomes. The house was something of a war zone and I tried to remain a conscientious objector—staying away from the house completely or hiding in my bedroom with the door closed, hoping if I was quiet enough everyone would forget I was there. I was seldom that lucky, though. It was just a matter of time before my mother and I would argue, and it was all too common for those arguments to end with me out on the street until things cooled down enough for me to return home—a process that could take hours or weeks depending on the severity of the conflict.

As a teenager, I saw my mother as a villain in the same tired cliché way most teenagers view their parents. Now, over twenty years later, I see her as a victim of the same system as the rest of us—one that tells you the stakes are high and one wrong move might leave you out on the streets for good. When I remember my teenage years now, as an adult, I know she felt alone and overwhelmed, struggling with how to cope in a relationship that was awful for her but provided a level of financial comfort and stability she would not otherwise have. Her house barely felt like a home to her, and it rarely felt like a home to me. Instead, my idea of home became bigger—stretching from Shaw Avenue to Belmont Avenue sandwiched in between West Avenue and First Avenue, encompassing all of Fresno south of Shaw—and everyone I knew there became a bit like family.

I avoided sleeping on sidewalks those nights due to the kindness of people in our community. The Tower District was a neighborhood where everyone seemed to know your name, and if they didn't know me, they at least knew my dad. Just like my father before me, I spent my teenage years in the punk and hardcore scenes of Fresno. South of Shaw, punks put on DIY shows in rundown old warehouses, which were aggressively targeted and shut down by the police. We fought it as best we could, clawing at every scrap of community we managed to build in those deteriorating walls. A girl named Mackenzie once jumped on a cop's back and started a "Fuck Police Brutality" chant when one venue was shut down. We all joined in, circling the cops to catch Mackenzie when they shoved her off. Mackenzie was in a local punk band where nobody knew how to play instruments; their best song was called "Let's Make Out." She made up new words for it every time they played, right there on the spot, yelling "you just got mono" or "I just got bailed out" or "this party is boring," and the crowd yelled back "let's make out!" Our local bands were all like that, terrible and fun. My friend Dirty Travis had a band called Capitalist Catastrophe or Capitalist Chaos or maybe Capitalist Conundrum. Every song was about how the government cared more about the military budget than about its own citizens. Their whole set was around ten minutes long. It was within these scenes that I found community, and first started to look critically at the system that put me and my family in the precarious financial positions we were in.

In the world of punk rock, politics were just as important as the music. Punk rockers made zines—small DIY magazines—simplifying complex political theory into digestible concepts: money is a middleman that complicates our ability to give people the things they need to live; people who do the same amount of work should earn the same pay; all labor is skilled labor and every job is important, otherwise the job wouldn't exist; you cannot convince rich people to care about the poor because caring isn't profitable. We read longer-form pieces, too, about things like radical workplace restructuring, advocating for workplaces to be run through unions or councils or co-ops rather than a typical top-down boss structure. Every book we read seemed to ask the same question: why should the people on top make the most money when the people on the bottom do the most work? Years later, one of my friends said with a laugh, "Back then, I thought the worker revolution was going to come tomorrow. I tried to recruit my cousin."

I read about the Black Panther Party's "Free Breakfast for School Children" program and helped out with the closest thing we had: Food Not Bombs, the local chapter of the anarchist organization where punk rockers fed the unhoused in a park downtown. A progressive Tower District church, the Big Red Church, let us use their kitchen to cook the meals— terrible stews made with produce we stole from the nearby grocery store, filled with too much cabbage and not enough seasoning. I got good at the stealing, often walking out with whole cartons of Kool-Aid and armfuls of carrots. Sometimes, I asked the security guard to help me with the door on the way out. They'd do it if you were confident enough, I learned. They probably weren't getting paid enough to care anyway. The punk kids in our town were redistributing the wealth, one pot of soup at a time.

The punk rockers helped each other out, too. When one of my friends found himself living in the country with no way to get to work in town, a few of us decided to steal an abandoned van from the side of the road. It had been parked there forever, months maybe, and we passed by it every time we drove him home from a show. The keys were in it, or maybe we hot-wired it, connecting the brown wires to the red. The answer is probably there, somewhere in the chasms of my memory, unless years of falling down at punk shows knocked it out of me. We spray-painted the van black with tiny cans of craft spray paint from the dollar store, getting high off the paint fumes and laughing until our faces hurt. The next day, my fingers were sore from holding down the tiny nozzles. Our friend drove that van for years, though, still covered in splotchy black streaks of paint.

Meanwhile, news of my precarious housing dynamic crept through the Tower District slowly; adults around me did their best to pitch in. My friend Rio had parents my dad's age who were in the punk scene with him back in the '80s. One night, Rio's mom—a vintage seller named Joy with curly bleach-blonde hair and a collection of ripped-up band Ts—let me stay at her house in Rio's old bedroom. Rio lived with her dad now, but Joy left the room just as it was. I walked around my friend's old bedroom like the ghost of her, touching her jewelry boxes and looking in her mirrors.

"You can stay here tonight," Joy told me as I haunted Rio's room, counting the band stickers on her dresser. "But tomorrow, I promised the room to your dad."

My father and I bounced around the Tower District in orbit around each other, crashing on the same couches a few nights before or after one another. I asked Fat Jerry, the neighborhood's local satanic body piercer, if I could help around the shop in exchange for being able to sleep in the waiting room some nights. He gave me odd jobs to do and taught me how to pierce nostrils and lips. Fat Jerry had grown up in the same '80s punk scene as my parents, too. He had a strained relationship with both of them, I think, and a sagacious wisdom about how the world worked.

"You know, Maddie," he told me once, using the nickname only my mother and father used for me, "you're the only kid I ever met who had to raise their parents."

I didn't understand what he meant at the time, but now I see what he saw: my father, equipped with all the paternal love necessary to be a good dad but none of the practical financial skills, and my mother, equipped with the responsibility to be financially stable enough but lacking the patience to really pull it off. In the middle, there was me—a scrappy teenager just doing my best to survive.

The Tower District did its best to raise me, but resources were limited. The thought of getting a job played over and over in my mind. A job meant income, and income meant having control, and control meant a chance at stability. I counted down the days until I turned fourteen and qualified for a work permit in the state of California. At long last, my fourteenth birthday came—right in the middle of summer break—and I started off my sophomore year of high school making a plan. My goal was to get off everyone's couch and onto a couch of my own. In class, I scribbled out a to-do list:

Step 1: Work Permit

Step 2: Get a Job (underlined twice in purple glitter gel pen)

Step 3: Get an Apartment (?????)

As I wrote, I sang "This couch is your couch, this couch is my couch," to the tune of the old Woody Guthrie track "This Land Is Your Land." Woody Guthrie hated capitalism too, it turned out. It struck me as odd that "This Land Is Your Land" somehow became a tribute to America rather than the critique he intended. The lyrics openly mocked the idea of private property, for starters, and took a jab at the idea that people would go hungry in the richest country on earth.

As I wrote down my list, the kid sitting next to me looked over and laughed.

"Get a job?" He giggled, as though it were a joke.

"What's so funny about that?" I asked.

"Any job you can get isn't gonna pay you enough to be worth it," he said.

"Well, what else am I supposed to do?" I asked.

The kid shrugged. "You could steal cars," he said. "My brother does it, it's good money. Way better than Burger King or whatever."

I'd only ever stolen one car myself, and I don't think I was very good at it. Burger King or whatever would have to do. I went to talk to my high school guidance counselor about a work permit that day.

"Your grades are good enough, that's for sure," she said, "but I hear you've been hanging out with those Tower Rat kids. Those kids are a bad influence. Why are you spending so much time with them?"

"They help me sometimes," I told her with a shrug.

There was a general understanding around school that my housing situation was unstable at best. However, most of the adults knew that calling Child Protective Services would have made a bad situation worse. I knew kids in foster homes or group homes—where other kids stole your shoes while you slept and threatened to stab you if you got in their way. If my house was a war zone, those houses were the apocalypse. My teachers talked in hushed tones with one another.

"Madeline is smart," they conceded. "She'll figure it out."

Years later, a friend of mine called this process the "adultification of Madeline." It was more convenient to view me as an adult. Adults figured things out for themselves.

After a bit of back-and-forth, I left my guidance counselor's office with a signed work permit and embarked upon my journey into the labor market, eventually getting a total of four jobs in my teenage years.

MADELINE'S HIGH SCHOOL JOBS

#1: Concessions

- The task: Sell concessions from a giant box around my neck at a stadium

- The struggle: Carrying something that weighed as much as me up and down stadium stairs in the hot Fresno sun
- The end result: Fired for making customers uncomfortable because I looked too young to be working
- The lesson: Optics are everything.

#2: The Office

- The task: File papers and enter data into a computer system
- The struggle: Getting made fun of by my adult coworkers constantly
- The end result: Quit so I could work somewhere with a better "company culture"
- The lesson: Sometimes grown-ups act like they're in high school too.

#3: Hot Topic

- The task: Sell body jewelry and fake punk T-shirts to teenagers at the mall, all to make some multimillionaire named Orv Madden even richer
- The struggle: Trying to earn the coveted regular position after my seasonal employment ended
- The end result: My boss hired a guy who was stalking me instead.
- The lesson: Your boss is not your friend.

Three days after losing my job at Hot Topic, I got a job working in a one-hour photo lab inside a Target department store. My manager there was a woman named Tamara who lived in a nearby trailer park with her two kids; her boyfriend was in prison. It was a much dorkier job than the mall, but I got to wear all black at least, and my coworkers were charmingly jaded.

"The best thing about this job," Tamara told me during

my first week of training, "is that nobody knows how these machines work, so if you ever get tired of the customers, you can just put up the machine's 'out of service' sign and nobody will get on your case."

"What if customers get mad?" I asked her.

"They don't pay us enough to care about that," she said, shaking her head.

Tamara realized a long time ago that you should never work harder than your paycheck warrants. The photo lab, despite being inside a Target, was not owned or operated by Target. It was a now-defunct different company entirely, called Qualex, which meant that the Target managers had no control over us. We relished the freedom and spent our time reading books and drawing pictures at the counter. I knew a boy in a band from San Luis Obispo who worked at the Qualex inside the Target there. We faxed each other funny drawings all day at work. During peak hours, when Target was overrun with customers, frenzied Target managers would ask us to help ring their customers up—as a favor or something.

"Can't do it," Tamara would say, shaking her head. She'd always follow it up with an excuse.

"We're dealing with a situation with the paper bleach," she said one day.

"What's the situation with the paper bleach?" I asked after the Target manager disappeared in a huff.

"No situation," she said. "That's not our job. Let them figure it out."

Sometimes, there would be situations, though—the machine would spurt and spit chemicals everywhere, rejecting the film as we tried to load it in. More than once, I found myself covered in thick pink chemical ooze, from head to toe, with it dripping from my hair all over my black work uniform. One day, an OSHA inspector came by for a surprise workplace safety assessment. I showed him our machine chemicals in the back.

"Looks good," he said. "But you need to put these stickers on them, especially the paper bleach."

He handed me a stack of stickers, one for each chemical, that said CAUTION: CONTACT WITH BARE SKIN CAUSES CANCER.

"Is this real?" I asked him.

"It's real," he said. "But you should be fine as long as you're wearing gloves when you work."

"Gloves?" I repeated back, perplexed. "I've literally swallowed this stuff before."

"You should . . . get that checked out," he said, grimacing.

When I told Tamara later, she shrugged.

"Did you know this stuff was a carcinogen?" I asked her.

"Nobody ever told me," she said. "Makes sense we'd all get cancer from this place, though. Perfect ending to a perfect job. This company doesn't give a fuck about us."

While I struggled to find my place in the world of the teenage labor market, the U.S. military did its best to convince me that they were my only hope—in ways that were both direct and subtle. The military had a strong presence at my school, a 70.9 percent Hispanic school south of Shaw in the Tower District where 60.4 percent of students came from families living in or near poverty. At a nearby school north of Shaw and just down the street, they had college fairs—events where colleges came to school and talked to students about their future educations. My school, though, only had the military—coming into class to try to convince us to sign up every few months. One day, they pulled me out of my class during a demonstration to speak with someone higher up in recruitment.

"We wouldn't send someone like you to fight," the recruiter told me with a smile. "You're intelligent. We've seen your test scores. You're valuable. You'd be used in strategy."

"Oh, so you just send the stupid ones to die?" I asked, confused and angry. "Isn't that eugenics?"

The man didn't have an answer. They didn't try to recruit me again, but huge military banners still hung in our cafeteria, plastering the walls as if to remind us teenagers on the south side of Shaw of our rightful place as wartime fodder. Meanwhile, the military budget grew each year, along with CEO salaries for private weapons manufacturers like Lockheed Martin and Raytheon. My friends and I joined the antiwar movement in town, attending protests and rallies on our days off school and work. As I struggled to earn enough while working minimum wage to afford the two months' rent necessary to move into my own apartment, I was acutely aware of the message: the U.S. government told me every day that there was money for war, but there wasn't enough money to help people like me.

According to Columbia University, in the year 2000 the United States saw 245,000 deaths due to low levels of education, 176,000 deaths due to racial segregation, 162,000 deaths due to low social support, 133,000 deaths due to individual-level poverty, 119,000 deaths due to income inequality, and 39,000 deaths due to area-level poverty. We were told it was simply not in the budget to care about those lives. The country we lived in seemed far removed from the type of place we all deserved, and as early as high school, I wondered if things would ever get better. My punk rock friends all assured me the revolution was on the horizon. What if they were wrong? I struggled with how to reconcile my belief that we deserved a better world with my need to survive in the one we have now. In the end, those years in high school led me to three simple guiding concepts for my life:

1. Hope for the best but prepare for the worst.

2. If you want to survive, remember to secure your own oxygen mask before securing the oxygen masks of others.

3. Whatever you do, though, don't forget about the others.

Roughly two years into my teenage work journey and still employed at the photo lab, I found myself sitting in the principal's office at school one day waiting to be suspended. I had a tendency to violate dress code at school—sometimes showing up with my hair dyed bright purple or forgetting to take out my nose ring—and my dedication to working created a cycle of poor classroom attendance that was increasingly difficult for my instructors to manage. I sat in a chair in front of the principal's door, ready to be scolded for either issue or maybe even both, kicking my legs back and forth to stave off the anxiety. Suddenly, a message came over the intercom announcing me as a Class of 2003 valedictorian. I furrowed my brow, perplexed.

After a few minutes, the principal called me into his office.

"You guys made a mistake," I told him, setting my bookbag on the floor. "I'm a junior, class of 2004. I'm not graduating this year."

"About that," he said, tightening his lips. "You have enough credits to graduate, so we'd prefer it if you just left now."

It didn't sound like I had much of an option. At home, I told my mother the news.

"Why don't you go to Federico's?" she asked. "It's a hair school down the street! You'd be great at hair."

I'd been dyeing and cutting my own hair for years; she had a point. Still, it felt like with grades as good as mine, there ought to be something I could do that would set me up for a better future. I didn't understand how college worked, and from what I could tell, the more academic schools cost upwards of $100,000 to attend, which was definitely not in my budget. I knew, though, that the world around me seemed convinced that if only I could get a bachelor's degree, everything in my life would work out just fine. Just sixteen years old and unsure of how to proceed, I enrolled at the local community college to get my associate's degree. If nothing else, it would buy me some time to come up with a plan—all while saving me money.

I attended community college classes full-time at the cost of $10 per credit, and the increased flexibility in class scheduling meant I was able to take on more hours of work at the photo lab. Finally, I had enough money to start looking for apartments. The only trouble was that as a minor, I wasn't sure who would rent to me. Most minors require legal emancipation to sign a contract like a rental agreement, but to get emancipated you have to prove you have somewhere to live. I asked aunts and uncles if they'd be willing to let me move in with them to qualify for my emancipation. They looked at each other with wide eyes, considering it deeply, but in the end all said no. I understood why. I wouldn't want an argumentative teenager with dyed blue hair and fishnet tights sulking around my house either, if I had the option. Still, it felt like a Catch-22. I couldn't get emancipated until I had a place to live, and I couldn't get a place to live until I was legally emancipated. You also needed your parents' consent for emancipation, which felt like a minefield I wasn't ready to step into with my mother. Maybe, I thought, I could just say I was eighteen and nobody would check.

My best friend Ryan and I set to work looking to rent an apartment together, and after just a few weeks we found the perfect spot: a two-bedroom apartment on Olive Street, right in the heart of the Tower District. I filled out the rental application, changing my birth year to 1985 and writing down eighteen for my age. I prayed the landlord wouldn't need to check my driver's license. The landlord wasn't a corporation—that's something that wouldn't really pick up steam until five or so years later. Instead, it was just a regular-seeming guy who worked at the fire department.

"You remind me of my daughter," he said with a smile. "Did you do debate in high school?"

"I was the captain of the debate team!" I said, doing my best to brim with charm. It wasn't a lie. The debate team was something of a club house for all of the weirdos at my high school. With my punk rock zines and fighting spirit, I was a no-brainer for the coveted position of Captain of the Freaks.

Two days later, we got the news that we were approved for the apartment. I moved out of my mother's house in the middle of the night, throwing everything I could into Ryan's car, working quietly to avoid detection. That first night in my new apartment, I lay down on the couch and exhaled. I felt something I'd never experienced before: relaxation.

The next day, my mother sent me a text message: "Did you move out?"

"Yes," I replied with satisfaction.

Our apartment became something of a sanctuary for our friends who struggled with family dynamics of their own— kids who were too gay or not religious enough, kids whose parents didn't understand why they had weird piercings and listened to such angry music, kids whose parents wondered why their child couldn't be more *normal*, whatever that meant. We threw family-style board game nights in our living room, replacing the families that cast us aside with each other instead. We baked Funfetti cakes and let touring bands crash on our floor. We crowd-funded abortion costs for our friends with religious parents who would surely disown them if they knew they'd had premarital sex. Other kids in the local punk rock and hardcore scenes jokingly called us a cult.

"We're not a cult," I told them defensively. "We look out for each other. We're what a family should be."

I was repaying my debt to the Tower District, for the years it spent helping raise me. Community made everyone stronger, and there at the apartment on Olive Street we were giving back to the community that had given so much to us for so many years. I was still working a minimum-wage job, earning just $6.75 per hour. Most months, my income was around $600, and half of it went straight to rent. I struggled to pay my bills and put gas in my car, and many times, the only food I could afford was off the Taco Bell $1 menu. Still, the future seemed bright. I'd figured out how to survive; the next step was figuring out how to thrive. If everyone I knew was right, the first step on my path to thriving was to make it the fuck out of Fresno.

How to Rent an Apartment or House

Renting a house or apartment to live in seems to get harder and harder every year. It's increasingly competitive and landlords seem intent on making applicants jump through hoops. Here's everything you need to know about renting an apartment:

1. The more roommates you have, the cheaper rent usually is. Typically, a studio apartment will be a lot more expensive than renting a room in a house. If you're looking to rent a room in a house and save some money, you can either find prospective roommates to join in on your house hunt, or you can look online at places like Craigslist or Facebook for rooms available to rent in places that already have an active lease. These are sometimes called "room shares." Sometimes, an existing room share will be cheaper than going in with a bunch of friends on a new spot together, just because rent tends to increase over time, and existing spots were most likely locked in at a lower rent at the time the lease originated.

2. When moving into a new place, you'll typically need to have two or three times the monthly rent available. This is because landlords will want "deposit and first (and sometimes last) month's rent." The deposit is a fee that is usually one to two times the price of the rent itself, paid up front, in case of any damages to the property. Deposits are technically refundable when you move out, but most landlords are assholes and will find any reason they can to try to keep some or all of your deposit. If possible, when moving into a new place, take pictures of any damage in the apartment before you move in. That way, the landlord can't deduct it from your deposit when you move out.

3. When applying for a place, the landlord will usually want to see your credit score and verify your current employment. I recommend getting ahead of the game by creating something I call "the Packet," which consists of—

- **a.** An introductory letter describing everyone who will be moving into the unit, along with any pets, and photos of the pets looking very cute for manipulation purposes

- **b.** A generic rental application (you can usually google it and find one on the internet) pre-filled out for every person applying

- **c.** A screenshot of the credit score of everyone applying to move in—if someone has a bad credit score or no credit score, still include it and just add a note like "I'm a bit afraid of debt so I don't have much of a credit history, but I am very responsible and pay my rent on time!" Don't get too personal with it, but include some sort of explanation that makes you sound like a reasonable human being. The landlord would find your bad credit situation when running a report for you anyway. This way you can at least get in front of it.

- **d.** Three months' worth of pay stubs showing the income of everyone moving in. If you don't have this handy, ask the payroll or HR department at your work—they can help you access it.

- **e.** A letter from everyone's boss or HR department verifying employment. If they seem too busy to do this for you, ask if you can write one and have them just review and sign it. The letter should confirm that you are employed, state your pay rate, and ideally say that they are planning to keep you in your position for the future.

   f. A screenshot of the bank account or savings account of everyone applying to move in. This should show that you have enough to cover two to three times the monthly rent up front, meaning you can afford to pay the deposit and get the place.

4. If you make "the Packet," print out multiple copies and hand them to the person who shows you the apartment. They will probably be confused by it, but later when they have a chance to look it over, they will be impressed that you basically did their job for them. Even if your credit score isn't stellar or you have pets or you don't have much of a rental history, it will make you look prepared and responsible, which will make them favor you just a bit more!

5. Speaking of trying to manipulate people into giving you shelter, if you're applying for a room share and meeting people who already all live together, consider bringing them a sweet treat like cookies. Bribery will get you everywhere.

6. Remember that the landlord will probably call your current employer and potentially your previous landlord to inquire about your responsibility. If you've had trouble with a boss or former landlord and don't think they'll give you a good review, ask a friend to pretend to be your previous boss or landlord instead. Put their name and number on your paperwork, and tell them in advance about your plan. Make sure it's your most responsible friend, and tell them you'll do the same for them in the future. Housing is essential, and you shouldn't feel bad about anything you need to do to secure shelter.

CHAPTER 3

Making It Out

Growing up in a town like Fresno, you're bound to hear the phrase "making it out" thrown around a lot.

"Did you hear about Sandy?"

"Oh yeah, she moved to Portland. She made it out."

It was the idea that Fresno was a sinkhole where dreams and opportunity go to die, and if you wanted to do anything worthwhile in your life, the best thing you could do was make it out of the sinkhole—make it out of this town—before all of your dreams died too. There was this thought that a better life lay beyond the horizon, just past the threshold of California's Central Valley. If you could just manage to make it out of a place like Fresno, then surely your whole life would change for the better. I wasn't exactly sure what "better" meant, but this idea seemed to be so widely accepted as a universal truth that I figured everyone must be right.

I absorbed the lesson of "making it out" at an early age and set my sights on San Francisco. As a kid, one of my favorite movies was *So I Married an Axe Murderer*. It's one of those early '90s movies where Mike Myers plays multiple different characters, all dressed up to look like different people, with accents and everything. The main character, Stuart, is a beat poet in San Francisco looking for love; Stuart ends up dating a woman named Harriet who may or may not be an axe murderer. Stuart recited beat poems where he squawked like a bird and snapped in between lines. B-roll footage in the movie showed him driving all around the charming streets of San Francisco in his vintage Karmann Ghia. I watched that movie repeatedly in what I later learned is called an ADHD hyperfixation, and vowed that one day I, too, would live in San Francisco. I would make it *out*.

College presented an opportunity to make it out of Fresno. Moving to San Francisco would be—on its own—a frivolous waste of money. However, moving to San Francisco to *attend college* would be an investment in my future. Just like my apartment planning to-do list, I wrote out my next steps:

1. $ave money ☺

2. Move to San Francisco

3. Enroll in ♥ college ✳

It looked easy enough on paper. Actually *doing* it was a different story. The thing about "making it out" of Fresno is that nobody tells you where you're supposed to go, how you're supposed to do it, or what you're supposed to do when you get there. We were forced to guess for ourselves, and the people around me happened upon their own answers in a variety of different ways. One day, I stood in the middle of a parking lot in the Tower District and watched as a Volkswagen bus full of the Tower Rats pulled off headed north, waving their goodbyes out the window to the rest of us. They were moving to Portland, Oregon—a popular destination for Fresno escapees. Another day, I helped Mackenzie load her belongings into the back of a Toyota Echo. She managed to rent a studio apartment in Los Angeles—right there on Hollywood Boulevard, near L.A. party spots we'd snuck into many times as teenagers. One girl met a man on the internet and moved to the Midwest to start a family with him, someplace like Ohio. A friend of a friend went train-hopping with a group of crust punks across the USA. Ryan, whose parents were better off financially than mine, went to art school in Chicago. It didn't seem to matter where you went; all that mattered was that you left. Anywhere, we figured, would be better than Fresno.

I'd managed to graduate high school at sixteen, which meant by age eighteen I had an associate's degree from the local community college. That same year, the lease on Ryan's and my apartment came to a close. I researched apartments on Craigslist in San Francisco to plot my next move. Average monthly rent there, though, was $1,451 at the time, which was over twice my monthly income and a lot higher than the $300 I was used to paying. I was apparently too broke to even try to figure out how to *not* be broke anymore. Still, I mulled the idea over in my mind. There had to be a way to escape this town somehow.

A few weeks before wrapping up my associate's degree, I met the ex-boyfriend I usually refer to as "the Drug Dealer," although, admittedly, I'd end up dating many more drug dealers than just this one. He was a friend of a friend who drove down to Fresno from Santa Cruz a few times a month to sell drugs to the locals. He was a few years older than me and had grown up in Fresno. He still wore thrift-store clothes and had crooked hair that he cut himself, but he was glamorous in that way all outsiders were to us in Fresno. He had made it *out*.

One night, at a party after a show in town, three men from the touring headlining band cornered me and aggressively groped at me while I struggled to break free. I screamed and shrieked, slapping their hands off me while they tugged at my clothes.

"This is a compliment," one of them said. "You should be proud. You're like the coolest girl in *Fresno*."

They broke out into laughter as he said it. Everyone in Fresno was a laughingstock to a major band like them, I guess.

The message was that a girl from Fresno should be lucky someone like them would even notice me. As I squirmed and tried to shove their arms off me, a man came up from behind them and spun them around.

"I told you," he yelled, exasperated, "you can't do this again!"

Again. The word stuck out in my mind, echoing. These men were serial creeps. I took the opportunity to duck free from their clutches and ran into another room where the Drug Dealer was tending an illegal makeshift bar. I sat down on a stool in front of him, dazed.

"You want a drink?" he asked. We had mutual friends in town and had met before in passing.

"Nah," I said, shaking my head. "I need to get out of here. Any chance you're free to walk me home? I live close. I just don't want to go alone right now."

"Sure," he said. "I'm about done here anyway."

The Drug Dealer wrapped things up at the card-table bar and walked me home, the two of us wandering in the hot summer night through the boring grid-like streets that go from Downtown Fresno up north a bit to the Tower District, where I lived. I glossed over the run-in with the Boys in the Band—shortening it to the phrase "bad encounter" and avoiding the word "assault" outright. He told me stories about his own "bad encounters"—mostly run-ins he had as a teenager with the KKK in the nearby town of Clovis.

"I had to get out," he told me.

I nodded in understanding. When we got to my house, he came inside and stayed for a week.

"What are *you* still doing here?" he asked me one night. "In Fresno, I mean? Why haven't you left yet?"

"I don't really know," I said. "I'm finishing up my AA this week. The lease is almost up on our apartment. I guess it feels like . . . I know I'm supposed to go somewhere, but I don't really know where or how."

"What about Santa Cruz?" he asked. "You can live with me. I mean, I don't have a place right now—I'm just sleeping on couches, but I bet I can find us a room somewhere. I have friends there, other people from Fresno. You'd like it."

I'd been to Santa Cruz before. In high school, my punk rock friends and I went a few times. I ditched class to drive up with them, blasting the Adicts and Misfits as loud as the speakers in their shitty old car would go. We all pitched in our cash for gas on the way up—crumpled-up fives and ones that we threw in a pile. We never had enough money to make it back. Instead, we'd hunt for cardboard on the ground near the boardwalk, then write on it in big black marker: "Fotos With Freaks—$5!" My hair was dyed purple or blue or red and I had a giant ring through my nose. I wore ripped fishnets and a leopard print jacket and Dr. Martens—hand-me-downs from my mom. My friends wore their hair in liberty spikes or a devil lock like Jerry Only. Tourists paid five bucks to take family photos with us—them looking wholesome and friendly in pastel tones to our right and left, us with our strange hair and faces full of piercings wearing clothes covered in patches and studs and spikes. It had never occurred to me to move there, though. Still, it was north and near water, which meant it was closer to San Francisco than Fresno was. Besides, it was someplace else, and that's all that actually mattered.

"Okay," I told him. "I'm in."

A few weeks later, he found us a room for rent in a retro two-story house near the coast. Move-in costs including the deposit were $700 each. It was more than I made in a month. I offered to give my friends haircuts in my living room all week to earn enough cash for the move. I'd been cutting my own hair for years, I figured. How hard could it be to cut someone else's? My friends, most of whom didn't even need haircuts, lined up dutifully at my front door to support me—paying whatever they could from extra cash they had folded up in their pockets.

I sold my old sewing projects off—band Ts I'd turned into tight-fitting baby Ts, hoodies I'd altered to have puffy princess sleeves, things with zippers and lace sewn onto them in weird places. In two weeks, I came up with the $700 I needed to move. I crammed as much as I could into the back of my Saturn and drove the three hours north up to Santa Cruz. I passed through farmland and over rolling hills, and as I turned off the main freeway to get onto the CA-1 highway that runs along the coastline, I saw a man on the side of the road hitchhiking. The sun was sweltering and he was covered in sweat, sitting on top of his backpack with his thumb out looking miserable. I pulled over.

"Hey," I yelled out the window at him. "If I give you a ride, are you gonna kill me?"

"If I was gonna kill you, would I tell you?" he yelled back.

Fuck, I thought. He was right.

"Look, are you gonna give me a ride or not?" he asked. "I have to get to Santa Cruz by nightfall."

I moved the fast-food bag full of old French fries off the passenger seat and onto the floorboards, leaning across the car to open the door for him.

"Get in," I yelled. "I'm going to Santa Cruz, too."

We drove the last hour or so in relative silence with the radio turned up loud, playing old shitty punk rock like Crass and the Germs, then I dropped him off in the center of Santa Cruz's downtown.

"You need some cash for food or anything?" I asked him as he got out of the car.

"Nah," he said. "I'll figure it out."

I fished $5 out of my furry cheetah print wallet and thrust it into his hands.

"Here," I said. "This will at least get you some Taco Bell. Do they have Taco Bell here?"

"Yeah," he said. "It's the rockabilly kids' hangout spot. But it's okay, seriously. You gave me a ride, keep the money."

"Hey, man," I told him, "you don't know how many people in my life have given me rides and free food. I'm just payin' it forward."

He tightened his lips and nodded in understanding. We're all just doing our best to get by; sometimes you're on the giving end, other times you're on the receiving end. Today, it was my day to give.

The house the Drug Dealer found us wasn't in Santa Cruz at all, it turned out. It was in a nearby seaside town called Aptos, roughly a fifteen-minute drive away, and covered in retro wood paneling from the 1970s. We rented one of two small rooms downstairs next to the garage, covered in that same gross stained brown carpet from my youth. Upstairs, though, a huge deck wrapped around the house and afforded us beautiful views of the coastline running all the way up north to Santa Cruz.

Santa Cruz was full of gorgeous old houses, some in Victorian or Edwardian designs, some retro-modern like ours, and some simple ranch-style places tucked into the woods. If Fresno was a sinking ship, I thought, maybe Santa Cruz was the shore on the horizon I'd spent years trying to paddle to. It had houses painted bright colors with cute nicknames like "the Beehive" where people threw parties with live bands and you could roller-skate inside. It had bonfires at midnight on the beach most nights, and if your friends ever weren't there, you could crash someone else's group and they'd usually offer you a drink. It had a huge boardwalk full of my favorite arcade games, and right across the street was my favorite taco place in the world (or at least in the handful of places I'd ever been), Las Palmas, where they deep-fried their taco shells so they crunched and flaked every time you took a bite. It had interesting people—artists and academics and hippies and witches and a girl I met a party once who screamed instead of talking and told the police "I'm not drunk, I'm just obnoxious!" when they tried to give her shit about it. Santa Cruz felt magical in a way that Fresno never had. That first night in town, I unpacked my things in the closet in the little room downstairs and fell asleep fast, eager to start what would surely be a better, brighter life. I had finally made it *out*.

But life anywhere costs money. I needed to figure out how to make some more of it fast. The next morning, I woke up at six and put on a collared shirt and a pair of trousers. It was a far cry from my usual look of studded belts and baby Ts and striped pants with Dr. Martens.

"What are you wearing?" the Drug Dealer asked, still in bed and rubbing his eyes.

"Office clothes," I told him. "I have to find a job."

"Why don't you just like apply at Urban Outfitters or something?" he asked.

"What is that, like a grocery store?" I asked.

"It's a clothing store," he said sleepily, "downtown."

"I was kind of hoping to make more than minimum wage," I told him. "Six bucks an hour was barely enough to live on in Fresno, it's definitely not enough to live on here, and I'm down to my last twenty dollars."

He shrugged a bit and went back to sleep. I left the house and made the drive an hour south around the bay, heading towards the city of Monterey. Before leaving Fresno, I'd searched on the internet and in phone books and managed to find a temp agency there, the closest one to Santa Cruz or Aptos. The website boasted pay up to $20 per hour. I had made résumés at my community college's library and printed out twenty of them, packed safely into a folder that I kept under the seat of my car the whole drive up.

"This," I thought, as I pulled into the parking lot of the temp agency, "is where life starts to get better."

Inside the agency, I was greeted by a professional-looking woman who politely directed me towards a row of computers lining the wall. I took proficiency tests in Microsoft Word, Excel, and PowerPoint. I did basic literacy and mathematics tests. I tested my typing speed. The computer spit out a number: 100 words per minute. The advisor looked pleased with my scores.

"Have you taken typing classes?" she asked.

"No," I told her, shaking my head. "I just grew up in chat rooms and message boards on the internet."

"Well," she told me, smiling, "you should never work for less than fifteen dollars per hour. Your skills are in demand."

I beamed, excited. "Does that mean you have a job for me?"

"I do," she said. "It's fifteen dollars per hour but it's about forty-five minutes south of here. I assume that won't be a problem?"

My heart sank. Forty-five minutes south of Monterey meant an hour and forty-five minutes away from Santa Cruz, or nearly four hours of driving every single day for work, accounting for traffic. My dilapidated little Saturn had already started to have engine malfunctions, overheating every thirty miles or so. It wasn't suited to make a regular drive of that size, and public transportation in the area was limited.

"Do you have anything closer by?" I asked. "Maybe even further north, up towards Santa Cruz?"

"Not at the moment," she said. "Monterey Bay isn't exactly a huge job market. It's more seasonal jobs, tourism stuff, and we're in the off-season. Do you want to think on it and let me know tomorrow? The position starts Monday."

Crushed, I drove back to Santa Cruz, weaving in and out of the nice expensive-looking houses painted bright colors all around town. With houses this big and beautiful, there had to be money to be made here, but where? Defeated, I stopped in the downtown strip and dropped off my résumé at Urban Outfitters, as well as a few other clothing stores down the street. Mostly, though, they ignored my résumé and looked at my outfit—a sad mismatched business casual look intended more for an office than a cool clothing shop. After a few failed attempts, I went home to change clothes and try again, piecing together the hippest and most "fashionable" outfit I could from my handmade and thrifted wardrobe. Back on the downtown strip, my new outfit worked. One store manager looked me up and down, pleased, and asked when I could start.

"I'll start right now!" I blurted out, too eagerly. "I really need a job!"

She grimaced a bit and took a step backwards away from me. I had come off too desperate, I realized instantly. Everyone knows the best person to hire is someone who doesn't need the job. Needing a job means you're not in high demand, and that must be for a reason. It's hard to catch a break: the longer you've gone without a job, the less likely someone is to hire you. In 2011, UCLA did a study about it and everything.

"We'll call you if something opens up," she said with a strained look on her face.

Later that day, I went through the clothes I had packed for my move and picked out my nicest pieces, then drove them to a secondhand clothing store downtown to sell, earning around fifty bucks and ensuring the day wasn't a total loss. Afterwards, I wandered around the city, looking for the transcendence and opportunity at a better life that making it out of Fresno was supposed to grant me. All I found were multimillion-dollar homes inhabited by smiling faces who claimed to be progressive with their rainbow murals and free libraries out front, but whose demographic makeup painted a different story. Later that evening, I turned to the Drug Dealer and asked, "Where do you guys keep the poor people?"

"What do you mean?" he asked. "There are poor people around, my friends are poor."

"Yeah," I said, "but that's just, like, one house—and it's mostly just people from Fresno. How about the other ones, the ones that aren't your friends? Where do they live?"

"Huh," he said, stopping to think. "I guess they're in Watsonville."

Watsonville was a small city twenty minutes or so outside of Santa Cruz, and the two cities had sweeping demographic differences between them. In Santa Cruz, the Latino population was just 24 percent. In the nearby city of Watsonville, it was three times higher—72.8 percent. I'd experienced segregation in Fresno, but nothing as extreme as the Watsonville and Santa Cruz Divide. The median annual household income in Watsonville was $55,470—nearly half of that in

Santa Cruz; the poverty rate in Watsonville was 31 percent higher than Santa Cruz next door. The Drug Dealer was right. If the Santa Cruz area had poor people anywhere, it probably wasn't in Santa Cruz at all. It was probably in Watsonville. There in this picturesque seaside town that was supposed to make me feel like everything was right in the world, everything felt wrong. The hypocrisy of the town's faux counterculture hippie visage plastered onto a whitewashed upper-class population of people who surely aligned more with the power than those fighting it felt violent to me and dishonest. It felt like I'd fallen for a scam.

That night, the Drug Dealer and I went to his friends' house: a big old place right on the harbor in Santa Cruz called Harbor House, one of the few places in the entire town where poor people lived, evidently. The house was a landing pad for former Fresnans—all a few years older than me, but some of whom I recognized.

"Congrats," they all told me. "You made it out!"

I smiled and thanked them, but I wasn't quite sure why. So far, Santa Cruz was seeming even harder to have a good life in than Fresno.

"I'm having trouble finding a job," I told them. "I applied at like twenty places today, but it seems like there's not a lot of jobs here?"

"It's a small town," one of the Drug Dealer's friends told me, nodding. "The best way to get a job is through someone you know. It's competitive, and there aren't a lot of jobs really out there even."

He was right. Up to 50 percent of all hiring in the United States is done by referral.

"Where do you guys work?" I asked. "Are any of your jobs hiring?"

"Our main office is," one guy said. "I work at a photo lab. Do you have any experience in photo labs?"

"Does the film stabilizer always turn pink?" I asked with a laugh. I was in.

The following Monday, I started my first shift at the pro

photo lab in town. It was a huge sprawling office, filled with people fielding international calls from photographers all around the globe. My job was customer service. I made minimum wage, but it was a job. Customers called to ask questions about pricing or film processing or prints, and I'd thumb through documents looking for the best ways to answer their questions. Sometimes, they'd yell at me about things I couldn't control. Other times, they'd confound me with questions that seemingly had no answer. One day, after being on the receiving end of a particularly scathing diatribe from a customer about something I had no control over, I locked myself in the bathroom at work to cry. My boss, though, just smiled an insincere smile and flashed a thumbs-up as I walked out of the bathroom wiping away the tears from the corner of my eye.

"You're a rock star!" she said, beaming.

I didn't feel like a rock star. I felt like a minimum-wage worker in a call center who was being verbally abused all day by customers. What was rock and roll about that? I imagined climbing up onto my desk at work and smashing a guitar into pieces. Instead, I climbed up onto my desk and fought with the printer, covering my hands and face in ink as it sucked paper back and forth, spitting out smeared pages and making noises that sounded like a dying robot.

One day, I leaned over to the woman who sat next to me. "What's the best paying job in this building?" I asked her.

"Probably image retouching," she told me. "But you have to know Photoshop. Other than that, I guess Laura's job."

Laura sat two desks down from me. She did customer service, too.

"Laura?" I asked, shocked. "Why Laura? Doesn't she do the same thing as us?"

"Yeah," she told me, "but when Laura first started, she looked up what makes someone low income in Santa Cruz, like from HUD's data, on their website. She figured out that you have to make like twenty dollars per hour to not be considered low income here. So, when she applied for the job, they asked her what she'd like to make, and she said twenty dollars per hour. She wrote it right there on the application and everything. They told her it's usually a minimum-wage job, you know, like six bucks or whatever, and asked why put down twenty dollars per hour. And she told them—get this—'Well, I just assumed you're the kind of company that doesn't want your employees living in poverty, and the price to be not considered poor here, according to HUD, is twenty dollars per hour for full-time work for a single person, which is what I am. Was I wrong? Is the company intentionally setting its employees up to live in poverty?' And you know, what can they say? They can't say they want their employees living in poverty, right? It looks bad. I mean, they don't actually care, but they can't say that out loud. So, they say yes, she is totally right, and they hire her on the spot, starting pay, twenty dollars per hour."

"You can *do* that?!" I exclaimed.

"I guess." The girl shrugged. "It's a way of negotiating, you know. But nobody else in customer service is making twenty dollars per hour, I know that for sure. You know our boss? The one that keeps calling us rock stars? I think she makes like fifteen dollars."

I had already blown the salary negotiation part of the job and I didn't know how to use Photoshop, but it was invigorating to know that under the right conditions, the budget was there to pay us more. Maybe, I thought, I could work so hard that I'd earn a raise. I vowed to become the best worker in the building. I memorized our training documents and worked on perfecting my customer service skills. Soon, I was able to turn angry customers into happy ones, cracking jokes to get them on my side while I blamed invisible catastrophes for intervening in our otherwise perfect workflow. I taught myself Photoshop on an old secondhand laptop I found at a pawnshop, complete with an illegally downloaded version of the program I got from a file-sharing website. When there was down time, I jumped up from my chair at work in a dramatic show of team-oriented-ness and asked what else I could help with.

"What a rock star!" my boss exclaimed.

One of my coworkers, Lee, pulled me aside one day as I volunteered to break down boxes in the shipping department.

"Look," Lee said, "the thing to know about this job is that you should never try to learn how to do anything, and especially not anything outside of your job description."

"Why?" I asked, confused.

"The more you learn how to do," he explained, "the more they're going to make you do."

"I'm trying to make more money here," I said. "I need to get a raise."

"They're never going to pay you more," he told me flatly. "They're going to be happy you're doing all that extra work for free so they don't have to hire someone else to do it. Trust me, I've been here years. The key to getting by in this place is to just act really, really stupid."

I didn't want to be stupid. I wanted to be smart—a hard worker, an asset. I ignored Lee's advice and took on more unpaid extra labor in the shipping department. Meanwhile, the regular shipping staff staged a mass quitting, walking out all together in the middle of the day. Only I stayed behind.

"I guess Madeline is managing our shipping department now," my boss said with a smile. "What a rock star!"

"Managing!" I gasped. "Do I get a raise?"

"You're so funny!" my boss said with a laugh. "No, no. It's just a figure of speech."

My heart sank. Maybe the company couldn't afford to give me a raise, I reasoned. Maybe I could find a way for them to save enough money in shipping that it would offset a pay increase for me, though. I made spreadsheets showing the cost efficiency of shipping different products with different mail carriers and presented them to my boss and the company owner, an eccentric ex-hippie who drove a fancy BMW into work and was rumored to have a massive house in town. Selling out had got him far, apparently. Santa Cruz was beginning to show me why punk rockers all hated hippies so much.

"If we follow this plan," I told them, "we can save over two hundred thousand dollars per year in shipping costs compared to how we ship now."

"You made this?" the owner of the company asked, looking over the data.

"Yep!" I said proudly. "I started implementing the plan last week, and it's already saved us over three grand."

"Excellent work," he told me, nodding in approval.

"I was thinking," I said, "since I'm the shipping manager now, maybe with these changes there will be enough money to increase my pay? You know, to a more managerial level?"

"Maybe," the owner said with a laugh. He turned to look at my boss. "We've gotta keep our eye on her! One day, she'll have our jobs!"

I couldn't pay my rent with "maybes." I left the meeting feeling even more confused, and started spending my weekends lugging furniture from my house to a nearby pawnshop to make ends meet. I also developed a side hustle where I snuck a seam ripper into the dressing room at secondhand clothing stores and "tried on" designer garments, only to seam-rip their labels out once in the privacy of the fitting room. I smuggled the detached designer labels out in my pocket then went to a thrift store, where I bought the cheapest Forever 21 and H&M fast fashion garments I could find. Back at home, I diligently replaced the fast fashion labels with designer ones. A worthless Forever 21 top suddenly became a collectible Marc Jacobs rarity. I sold the fake designer goods back to the higher-end secondhand shops to subsidize my low wages at the photo lab.

Meanwhile, the Drug Dealer was struggling, too. He lost his night job as a server after the owner of the restaurant caught him on security camera footage doing drugs with the manager—a friend of his—one night during closing. As the due date for rent approached, I asked him how much he had.

"I'm close," he told me. "I have a little under three hundred dollars."

"What are you going to do for the last fifty bucks?" I asked him. "I don't have enough to cover you."

"I think I'll just go out and, like . . . try to find it," he told me.

"I don't understand," I said. "You're going to *find* it? What does that mean?"

"I'll just, like, walk around town and . . . find it. Like on the ground," he said.

Later that night, he came home with around $60 in his pocket.

"Did you spange?" I asked him.

"No," he said. "I just found it, like on the ground. I got us some bread from the bakery's dumpster, too."

I'm still not sure where he came up with the money he claimed to have "found." A few months into my stay in Santa Cruz, I was skeptical of a lot of things. I had made it out of Fresno, but nothing seemed any better. The town was prettier, sure, but it's not like I could afford to do anything. The only thing I could really afford to do was play old arcade games on the boardwalk, just like I'd played old arcade games across the street from the apartment my dad and I lived in as a kid. Where was the promise of a better future that "making it out" was supposed to afford me? I had the same carpet in my room as I'd had in Fresno, nearly the same job, and the same hobbies, too. Only here, I had to pawn my belongings to pay rent on top of working my crummy photo lab job.

One day, I came home from work and found the Drug Dealer crouched over the floor, combing through the gross brown dirty carpet, depositing tiny bits of dirt and grime on the linoleum of the attached bathroom.

"What are you doing?" I asked him.

"I think I dropped some coke here last week," he told me, not bothering to look up.

Then he formed the filth from the carpet into a line and

snorted it off the linoleum floor as I looked on, shocked. I'd made it out of Fresno, but now it was seeming like I'd probably need to make it out of Santa Cruz, too.

It's true that Fresno has unique considerations that many other places don't have: the unusually high rates of concentrated poverty, the egregious segregation along Shaw Avenue, and the isolated nature of the city, situated in between major highways. However, the more I saw of places outside Fresno, the more I realized that the greater issues we faced there were the same issues people faced everywhere in the country. People weren't earning enough at their jobs to survive, while their bosses earned more than they needed. People couldn't afford comfortable living arrangements, let alone access to things like healthcare and reliable transportation. Job opportunities were few and far between in most places, with increased competition for the few good jobs that existed and an "it's not what you know but who you know" hiring mentality. Class mobility wasn't as achievable as people acted like it was— getting to college alone could be cost-prohibitive.

The more I saw of Santa Cruz, and the more I talked to my friends who'd moved other places, the more I came to understand that these were universal issues when existing in a system of capitalism. My friends in the Midwest who had children early and settled down in a traditional family were struggling to find jobs that paid enough for them to secure proper childcare; they were forced to stay home with their children instead, making them a one-income household and flinging them into poverty. My friends in Portland, Oregon, seemed to have traded whatever low-paid service industry job they had in Fresno for the same type of low-paid service industry job there—working at bars or coffee shops just like they had back home, struggling to make rent and survive all the same. My friends in Los Angeles were adjacent to glamour and wealth, but the side of town they lived in looked no different than Fresno most days: endless strings of strip malls and concrete and fast-food places and check-cashing services and payday lenders sandwiched in between cockroach-infested studio apartments. The places with the jobs were more expensive to live in. The cheaper places to live didn't have as many jobs. Santa Cruz had the unique charm of being both expensive *and* having limited job opportunities. If you lived in a cheaper place and commuted to a more expensive place, you'd have to contend with the travel expenses and quality of life issues that come with spending so much time driving. Where exactly was I supposed to "make it out" to?

My grandfather used to tell my aunt "Everywhere you go, there you are." I think it was supposed to mean something about not running from your problems, but it seemed like capitalism was my problem. Everywhere I looked, companies were being incentivized to cut costs to raise profits, and workers' pay was a cost to be cut. Landlords were incentivized to raise rents, and tenants' incomes couldn't keep up. No matter where I went in the United States, there capitalism would be. I'd always have a boss whose primary goal was to pay me as little as possible for me to get the job done. I'd always have a landlord whose primary goal was to get as much money out of me every month as possible for rent. Beyond that, there would always be banks trying to lure me into high-interest credit cards and loans to help me survive the conditions that low pay and high expenses created in my life. There was no town or city in the whole country I could run to where these issues would not apply. I was beginning to learn that surviving capitalism was more of a question of "how" than "where."

A few months after moving to Santa Cruz, I drove back down to Fresno for the weekend and walked into a tattoo parlor. The woman working had a thick European accent, a rarity for Fresno. She'd moved to the city from a place like Switzerland or maybe the Netherlands—I can't remember which.

She said she was trying to decide between San Francisco and Los Angeles, but couldn't choose. Instead, she looked on a map and saw that Fresno—a major city of over half a million people—was perfectly in between the two.

"Great," she thought. "I'll move there! They'll have a high-speed rail that will take me to Los Angeles or San Francisco, and it will be a big enough city that I'll enjoy being there."

When she arrived in Fresno, though, she was horrified to see that the city—a dirty, grimy, ugly place where meth-amphetamine use ran rampant, and temperatures rose to 110 degrees in the summer—didn't have a high-speed train anywhere in sight. She got a job at a local tattoo shop and tried to figure out how to earn enough money to move back home.

When I walked into the shop that day, I told her I wanted a Fresno tattoo, right there on my arm, prominently displayed.

"No," she said, shaking her head. "I'm not giving you that. Have you ever left Fresno?"

"Of course," I told her. "I live in Santa Cruz right now."

She looked at me, shocked. "And you still want a Fresno tattoo?" she asked.

"Yes," I told her, nodding decisively.

"Why?!" she asked, perplexed.

"I grew up here thinking it was the worst place on earth," I said. "Now, what I'm realizing is that every place is awful in its own little way. At least here, it's all on the surface so you know what you're getting. It's honest, and there's integrity in honesty. Ink it."

She sighed and drew up the artwork: an outline of California with a mark in the middle, right where Fresno is. It was the shop minimum price—just $50—but it was a lot of money to me at the time. Still, it felt important, like I had realized something that many people never realize at all. Everything I learned about survival, I learned from the people around me in Fresno. There was beauty in the way that we had struggled together, and I wasn't sure that I would ever find that kind of community anywhere else again. Making it out hadn't been enough to change anything in my life. I was just broke in a different place.

"After I graduate from college," I thought, "everything will get easier."

I didn't know then how fucking wrong I was.

How to Get a Job

Getting a job is a necessary evil. When looking for a job, there's a few things to know:

1. Put together a résumé. Your résumé should have your contact information at the top, followed by your work experience, education, and technical proficiencies. The goal of your résumé is to highlight your best traits, so put whichever category looks most impressive at the top. You can google *résumé format* to get an idea of how they should look, and Google Docs has a free template you can use to get started.

2. If you don't have much work experience, get creative. Remember that things like babysitting or doing yardwork for your neighbors count as work experience. If you have gaps in your résumé, put your work experience for that period as something freelance. Nobody's gonna know. Say you worked for yourself trying to start a business in one of the fields of your hobbies. It looks better than having a huge space where you didn't work.

3. Never forget to include your technical proficiencies. This includes the computer and even phone applications you're familiar with. Even social media platform knowledge can be an asset when you're job hunting, especially when applying at small businesses. You never know what skills might come in handy for someone hiring, so don't be shy about including things like Photoshop, Excel, and even TikTok or Instagram.

4. If your résumé is looking a little empty, take an online typing test to determine the words per minute you can type. It's a great résumé padder. Also, look online for free certificates for things like Excel and Word.

5. If you speak more than one language, include that. It's a major asset on the job!

6. If you're good at school, include your GPA in your education section. If you're not, leave it off.

7. Your résumé should fit on one page unless you are an expert with, like, a decade of experience in a specialized field. Keep it simple, and avoid using obscure flowery "résumé speak." When possible, use simple and clear results-oriented descriptions of your work experience. If you worked retail, instead of saying "operated point of sale system and maintained accuracy in manual accounting while facilitating in-person customer service during checkout process," say "met sales goals for six months in a row" or "increased average transaction value by 15%." Try to use facts and figures to show that you're good at whatever job you're applying for.

8. When job hunting, don't keep it a secret. Tell everyone you know that you're looking for a job. You never know who will have a connection with an opening.

9. If applying for a job online, don't skip the cover letter. Cover letters should be short and sweet—three paragraphs maximum—and they should be personalized to whatever job you're applying for. The first paragraph should introduce you and say where you found out about the job. The second should say why you think you're a good match for the job. The third should thank them for their time and give them a way to contact you. It doesn't have to be long, but try to use keywords from the job listing whenever possible. Yes, it's time-consuming and annoying, but it can really help you stand out.

10. Sometimes, when applying for corporate retail jobs, you'll have to apply using their fill-in forms. It's good to have your résumé handy, though, so the information is convenient for you to input. If there's a personality quiz, try googling it to see if someone has posted the desired results from the test. Personality quizzes are bizarre and pretty unethical in my opinion, so don't feel bad about cheating on them.

11. If you get an interview, remember to smile as much as possible, even if it's a phone interview. People can hear a smile in your voice. You want to come across as eager, hardworking, and humble. Google *frequently asked interview questions* beforehand and ask someone to practice with you. It's nerdy but useful.

12. If you're ever in a pinch and need work fast, look for temp agencies or hiring agencies in your town. They often take a cut of your pay as a fee for placing you in a position, but sometimes they can place you in a job as soon as the same day. It's a good short-term fix when you need cash coming in the door.

13. If you find yourself in a position where you have two job offers, you can often use them to get yourself a higher wage. Tell the job that offered you less money something like "I'm so happy you think I'd be a great fit for your team! I feel the same way. However, I have been offered a position at (wherever the other company is) for (whatever the pay is). Is there any way you'd be able to beat their offer?" You have nothing to lose. If they say no, you can go with the higher offer at the other company. If they say yes, you can take that new higher offer to the first company and say the same thing. Don't get greedy—only do this one time at each place, but often you can up your salary offering quite a bit with this technique!

14. During an interview, they will probably ask if you have any questions. It's always good to research the company a bit beforehand and ask a generic question about their mission statement or customer base. However, if you want to be a bit bold, you might consider asking what company turnover is like at their business. If a lot of employees are leaving the company frequently, it's a sign that it's a pretty bad place to work. Sometimes, you're desperate and need a job—any job. However, other times, you might have the luxury of holding off for a better offer, and knowing about employee turnover is a useful tool in determining if the job you're applying for is the right fit.

15. When going to an interview, dress in a way that makes sense for the job. If you're applying to work at a "hip" company, wearing business casual might not be the right move. However, if you're applying to work at an office, you might want to err on the side of caution and dress more conservatively for your interview process. When interviewing, you will get a sense of what the company dress code is like by observing the clothing of people already on the job, and you can use that to help shape how you'll dress in the future.

CHAPTER 4

Student Loan Debt, Here I Come!

I was seventeen years old the first time I ever spoke with a college recruiter. While the public high schools north of Shaw in my hometown had college fairs and guidance counselors to help students with post–high school planning, living south of Shaw meant taking research for college into your own hands. Neither of my parents had a college degree, so I turned to the internet for guidance. I figured the best chance I had for a nice life was to get a job doing something I was really good at. I just had to figure out what, exactly, that was.

In high school, I'd won two of those silly awards they put in the school newspaper and yearbook at the end of the year, where everyone in your grade votes on them. I think they call them "superlatives." I'd come out with "most intelligent" and "best dressed." "Most intelligent" didn't seem to mean much. The same standardized tests that ranked me in the top 0.01 percent of all academic performers had been created from a system originally developed by the eugenicist Carl Brigham to help separate test-takers by race and economic background. I was smart enough to know that school didn't measure intelligence; it just measured how good you were at school. Try as I might, I couldn't figure out how being good at school could ever possibly translate into anything tangible in my life, and especially not a career. I didn't realize then that academia was a whole field of its own, with job opportunities at every turn for someone like me who excelled in a school setting. Certain careers are gate-kept from the lower class by virtue of exposure alone, and I'd never been exposed to the world of academia. In the big game of life, I was missing half of the rule book and didn't even know it.

What I did know was that people designed clothes for a living, and that I appeared to have a knack for putting together outfits that other people liked. As a teenager back at my mom's house in Fresno, I once logged on to our dial-up internet to search *fashion design schools in San Francisco*. Three schools popped up. The first was a private non-profit art school that had existed for nearly a hundred years. Annual tuition in 2005 was around $25,000 per year, and only 66 percent of students who attended even graduated. Their fashion program was more focused on textiles and less on apparel design, and notable alumni seemed to be the types of people who made multimedia sculptural artwork you saw in museums rather than regular people working regular jobs. It felt like a place rich people sent their kids for fun. I needed more than an art-based summer camp, so I scrolled on to the next result. The second school I found was a private for-profit art school founded by a family with a net worth of $800 million. The school had a 100 percent acceptance rate and was one of the largest property owners in all of San Francisco. Annual tuition was just $14,000 per year, but only 10 percent of attendees graduated. It seemed a bit like a money-making scheme to me, so I passed.

The last school I found stood out among the others. It was a private for-profit art school, but unlike the previous one, it took a career-focused approach to apparel design, viewing it more as a skilled trade than an upper-crust art form reserved for the wealthy. Where the last for-profit art school had an acceptance rate of 100 percent, this one had an acceptance rate of just 42 percent. I didn't know much about college, but I knew the harder you had to work to be accepted, the better it usually meant the school was. They had an entire section called "career services" dedicated to getting their graduates actively employed in the field. Their website featured news about industry conferences and graduate success stories in employment. Tuition for a bachelor's degree in fashion design was around $27,000 per year, but they boasted high graduation rates and even higher job placement rates after college. A pop-up window on their website invited me to attend an open house in my area to meet with a recruiter.

At seventeen years old, I met with a recruiter for the school in a small conference room in a hotel in Fresno, where a handful of recruiters sat at round tables interviewing students. There, the recruiter asked me what I was looking to gain from a college degree. I told him in no uncertain words that I wanted a job after college, a good job—a steady job— where I could earn enough to live. He opened a folder and showed me pie charts and graphs about the school's alumni, showcasing high employment rates in the field within the first five years after graduating.

"All of our instructors," he told me, "are actively employed in the field they are teaching, so you are always getting up-to-date industry training. And we all know that when it comes to getting hired, it's just as much who you know as what you know. You'll be networking every day with real-life people in your field."

"What about the cost to attend? Is there financing?" I asked.

"Are your parents helping?" he asked.

"No," I said, shaking my head. "I don't have . . . they don't . . . uh, it's just me."

"We can help you figure it out," he assured me. "Whenever you're ready, visit our admissions office in San Francisco. We'll see what we can do."

To my right, a recruiter was telling a girl that this school would not be the right fit for someone like her. Dejected, she gathered her things and left. I turned back to the man in front of me.

"Do you think this school would be the right fit for *me*?" I asked.

"I think you're the *ideal* candidate for a school like ours," he said, smiling.

Assuming he was referencing my stellar grades and high school achievements, I smiled back. Years later, looking back on this moment, I see it differently. When he looked at me, he saw a kid from a poor town whose parents didn't have a college degree, and who didn't know much about how college was supposed to work. He must have known that I was putting my faith in a college degree to be the one thing that made my future fall into place, and that there was nobody in my life to make me question whether or not this school was the right place for me to get it. I can't help but wonder if, as we sat there—him with his very mature-looking suit jacket and mountains of manipulated data on employment rates and job fairs, and me with my funny dyed hair and hacked together wardrobe made from thrift store clothes—he smiled because he saw a mark.

One year later, I stood in the tiny bedroom with the Drug Dealer in Aptos, California, watching him snort dirt off the floor, and thought about the recruiter. If I ever wanted a life better than this, I thought, I'd have to go to college. The next day, I called in sick to work and drove an hour and a half to San Francisco to meet with the admissions department at the school. The drive to San Francisco from Santa Cruz goes over CA-17, also known as "the Most Dangerous Highway in California" or sometimes just "Blood Alley." The 17 cuts through the coastal mountain range, twisting and turning around the face of a mountain with switchbacks flanked by steep cliffs. The first time I pulled into the city after surviving the treacherous journey on the 17, I felt a wave of relief wash over my body. I'd survived something dangerous, and now it felt like I was coming home.

The school itself was in a gorgeous old building in the heart of San Francisco, right there on the busiest street in town with a subway stop and trolley car out front. It was the opposite of the strip malls and neon lights to which I'd grown accustomed in Fresno, and it was hard not to feel wrapped up in the magic of it all. Inside, the admissions department gave me a tour of the campus, taking me up to the fashion department on the second floor. I peeked in the windows of classrooms where students drafted patterns on big worktables and sewed on rows of industrial machines. It was everything I'd ever dreamed of. The only question was if I could afford it.

"How much will this all cost me?" I asked the admissions advisor.

"That depends," she said.

It was a strange concept to me, the idea that the cost of things might be subjective. She handed me pamphlets with labels on them like "Understanding the FAFSA" and "Which Student Loans Are Right for Me?" On the computer back in her office, she opened up a dark screen with empty lines laid out in a grid.

"We use a quarter system here," she said. "That means that if you attend school full-time all three quarters we offer classes, you can complete a bachelor's degree in three years instead of four."

"I already have an associate's degree," I said. "So, that means I'd just need a year and a half, right?"

"If your credits transfer over," she replied.

"If?" I asked. "Shouldn't an AA cover all of my general education?"

"Sometimes," she replied with a smile.

She plugged numbers into the computer and the screen populated with a tally of figures laid out in rows. She scurried over to the printer, then brought back a long sheet of paper on the school's letterhead with numbers laid out for tuition and living expenses. The final figure at the edge of the page was nearly $100,000.

I balked, taken aback: "I can't afford this."

"That's okay," she said with a reassuring smile. "Let's figure out what you *can* afford."

It felt more like buying a used car than planning my future.

"Well, we can start here," I said, pointing to the line for living expenses. "I pay all of that on my own, right?"

"I thought you said your parents weren't helping you?" she asked.

"They're not," I replied, confused. "But like, I have a job. I'll just keep paying for my living costs on my own, right? With my job?"

"Oh," she said, surprised. "I mean, yes, but then you won't be going full-time to school, right?"

"No, I will," I told her. "Do people not usually do that?"

"Not typically," she said. "A shared room in the dorm will cost you around $1,200 per month. Will you be able to work enough to afford that?"

"Twelve hundred a month to share a room?!" I exclaimed. "You can rent a studio apartment on Craigslist two blocks from here for eight hundred dollars a month."

"Most people pay for the convenience and experience of dorms," she said.

"I can't afford conveniences or experiences," I told her, shaking my head. "Get a pen. I have a feeling we'll be crossing a lot of things off this budget."

We filled out the FAFSA—the Free Application for Federal Student Aid—together. With my parents' low income and my favorable academic performance in high school, I managed to qualify for an array of Pell Grants and scholarships. In the end, as long as my credits all transferred over from my community college associate's degree, I'd only need to take out $27,286 in student loans in total to complete my bachelor's degree.

"This is the lowest I've ever gotten a loan here," the advisor said, staring at our handiwork.

I breathed a sigh of relief. I wasn't sure how much college

was supposed to cost, but it felt reassuring to think I was getting a good deal at least.

"Now," she said, "we just need a parent to co-sign on your student loans. Your credit is fine, but you don't have enough of a credit history to qualify on your own."

My heart sank. My father couldn't qualify as a co-signer, and my mother wouldn't do it. In the end, my financial aid advisor entered me into a lottery based on my academic achievement. There were only a few winners each year, she explained, but if I won, the school would agree to be my co-signer on the loans. A week later, she called me to give me the good news: I'd won, and, with a little bit of finagling on my end, they'd agreed to transfer all of my credits from community college over into my new degree. I drove back up to San Francisco the next day to sign the paperwork and officially enroll. As I signed the documents for my student loans, I felt momentary trepidation. How much was $27,000? Was it a lot of money? Was it a little? I knew it was a lot less than my peers at this school were paying for the same education, but still a teenager, I didn't have a reference point for how much or how little it truly was. The associate's degree from my community college had been basically free, coming in at just $10 per credit. For the student loans I'd need to complete my bachelor's degree, the interest rate set by the Fed was 6.8 percent. Was that high? Was it low? What even was the Fed? How did interest rates work?

"Don't worry," the advisor told me. "College graduates earn over half a million dollars more in their lifetime than people without a degree. Twenty-seven thousand dollars isn't much compared to the five hundred thousand more you'll be earning. By the time you have to start paying them off, six months after you graduate, you'll have a great job and those monthly payments will feel like nothing."

It sounded reasonable to me. I signed the paperwork with a smile on my face, imagining my future: an apparel designer living in the big city, making a six-figure salary, working for a great stable company for many years to come.

. . .

Back in Santa Cruz, I tried to figure out how to make college in San Francisco fit in with my life. I couldn't afford to move to San Francisco on my own right away. Instead, I'd have to commute the hour and a half each way every day for school, all in my rickety 1997 Saturn that overheated every few miles. If I could squeeze my classes into two days, I figured I could continue working full-time at the photo lab in Santa Cruz and do my homework at night. Then my only extra expense would be the gas it took me to get back and forth from San Francisco twice per week.

At the photo lab, I talked to my boss about changing my days in the office.

"Are there any positions here that work on weekends?" I asked. "I'm starting school in January."

"There's one," she said. "It's from four a.m. to one p.m., Wednesday through Sunday. You have to collect and organize all of the film for the developing team to work on for the next week."

The hours sounded brutal, but it would be a lot easier than finding a new job.

"Is there an opening in that department?" I asked.

"For you?" she said. "Why not. You're our favorite rock star, after all!"

The one thing that working harder than everyone else in the building had got me for nearly a year was the privilege of working at four in the morning on weekends. It was hardly a desirable gig for anyone else, but for me, it freed up Mondays and Tuesdays to attend classes in San Francisco, which we just referred to as "the City." Lee, the person who had tried to train me to act stupid at all costs, was moving to the City himself. I offered him $100 a month to crash on his couch every Monday night once he got there, minimizing my drives back and forth over "Blood Alley." He agreed.

"Who am I to turn down a couch to a friend in need?" he said with a smile. I gave him the $100 a month in cash. I later learned he never told his roommate I was paying them at all.

Come January, I settled into my weekly routine for school, which included 3 hours of commuting, 24 hours of class, 33 hours of homework, and 40 hours at the photo lab. It was a grueling schedule with no days off, made worse by the stress of the drive. I needed to figure out how to move to San Francisco fast, but I knew I couldn't do it without getting a job there first. At work, I sifted through customer accounts in our database, taking note of photographers located in San Francisco. Maybe, I thought, I could cold-call them to see if anyone was hiring. Before I had the chance, though, I heard the familiar voice of my boss ringing through the office.

"I need a rock star to help fill in with customer service today!" she called out. "Laura went home sick!"

"I'll do it!" I yelled, jumping up from my chair and hurrying over to my old desk. "I'll do it, I'll do it. I'm pretty much done with film prep for the day."

My boss looked at me and smiled, then mouthed the words "rock star" while pointing at me with both hands.

I knew that hopping on the phones meant talking to clients, some of whom lived in San Francisco. I popped on my old headset and got to work answering calls. Today was the day, I decided, that I was going to find a new job, and I'd use my current job to do it. It was the least they could do, I figured, for all of the time I went above and beyond for nothing. Anyway, wasn't this what people usually call "networking"? For the next three hours, I scanned the addresses of every customer service phone call I received, hoping to find someone from "the City." When I found a winner, I'd perk up instantly and recite some version of the same routine.

"San Francisco!" I'd say, smiling through the phone. I read somewhere once to always smile on the phone. The person on the other end can hear it in your voice. "Isn't that something! I'm moving there soon. You've gotta help me find a good job up there—I don't know anything about the area!"

Without fail, their curiosity would be piqued.

"Oh really," they'd say. "Huh . . . Someone from your company would really be an asset up here. You've got all the inside info on how things work at the lab! Say, I know it's a bit strange but you wouldn't be interested in meeting up with *me* for an interview, would you? I could always use a new assistant!"

By the end of the day, I had four interviews scheduled for the following week with photographers in San Francisco. Now all I needed was a place to live.

Working at four in the morning meant going to sleep every night at eight, a schedule that wasn't exactly compatible with the Drug Dealer's lifestyle. Some nights, he'd still be out by the time I woke up for work. Other nights, he'd come in drunk and high at 2:00 a.m. We started fighting, an inevitable development given the incompatibility of our schedules and growing incompatibility of our lives. My patience was wearing thin and the situation was growing less tenable by the day. I needed out.

One night, my friend Ross from Los Angeles texted me.

"I know it's short notice," the text read, "but my band is playing tonight at Rickshaw Stop in SF if you want to come. I'll put you on the list."

Growing up in Fresno, I'd spent a lot of time in Los Angeles—going to parties or shows, and sometimes even sneaking into nightclubs and bars. I'd managed to make a fair number of friends there, all of whom wondered why—in exasperation—I didn't just move there for school.

"We have the fashion jobs here," they'd tell me, their eyes wide and hands outstretched. "You can go to the big fashion school here, FIDM! You can get a job working for a designer down here for sure, or at the very least a styling gig! I'm friends with Jeremy Scott! I mean, I met him at a party once and he gave me his number anyway. I bet I could get you an internship! Why don't you just move here already?"

It was a question that I never could fully answer. My

grandmother was from L.A., a small neighborhood on the east side called Eagle Rock. Long before my grueling jam-packed college schedule, Los Angeles was something like a second home to me. I'd been going out in Hollywood for years, befriending bouncers at places like Star Shoes—a now-defunct bar that back then bordered on being a club, with long-haired DJs spinning electroclash while hipsters danced alongside gangsters and nobody ever bothered to check your ID. I knew the best way to skip the line at Teddy's nightclub inside the Roosevelt Hotel, and my friends and I found solace away from the abrasive DJ nights of a then up-and-coming Steve Aoki by sneaking away to a dive bar called the Cha Cha Lounge to take photo-booth pictures and drink cheap beer. We went to shows and dance nights at Spaceland in Silver Lake during the peak of what would later be renamed the Indie Sleaze era, and we crashed multimillionaires' house parties at mansions in the Hollywood Hills. Illegal raves popped up in abandoned buildings downtown, years before property developers had dreams of "revitalizing" the area, and we'd sneak through the parking lots giving passwords to random men who led us through a maze of back alleys to the official location of the rave. We went to independent fashion shows filled with drag queens in three-foot-high wigs in an area that would later be called the Arts District, but back then was just an old industrial part of town where people rented out entire floors of old factories with crumbling walls covered in hap-hazard caution tape.

Los Angeles was comfortable and safe, but I knew enough about the area to know that everyone there was talented, creative, and tenacious. In San Francisco, I could be a big fish in a small pond. In Los Angeles, I was just another minnow hoping I didn't get swallowed whole by a shark. Everyone seemed to be a fashion designer there—a thousand well-dressed and likeable people competing for the same three fashion internships every year. Los Angeles felt like a place where the big dogs went, and I didn't feel like a big dog. I felt more like a small, frightened chihuahua.

The college options in Los Angeles seemed even worse than the options in San Francisco for someone like me. Bachelor's programs for apparel design in Los Angeles had 1.1 percent graduation rates or tuition that soared to nearly double that of the programs I'd looked at in San Francisco, and none seemed focused on helping you land a job. Still, when times in Santa Cruz felt especially depressing, I texted my Los Angeles friends just to check in on the life I could have had.

"Where are you going tonight?" I'd ask them, just to hear them name off some of my favorite places. Sometimes, I'd scan the Cobra Snake website—a collection of Los Angeles party photos posted online for the whole world to see—looking at pictures of my friends from the night before, throwing drinks on each other and sharing cigarettes in tight-fitting bodysuits or sequined bell bottoms with lots of scarves. If only I could be in two places at once, I often thought to myself. I was sacrificing my friendships, my weekends, my sleep schedule, and more for the chance to get the college degree that would surely set me up for life. The world around me seemed to constantly push a narrative that said sacrifice is all it takes for things to fall into place, and that hard work always paid off. It was biblical in a way, a parable of self-immolation to the gods of commerce and finance. If you just kept the course—slow and steady— you'd come out on top. I tried hard to remember that every time I saw an L.A. nightlife party photo pop up on MySpace.

The night that Ross texted me, it seemed as if—for one moment—I truly *could* be two places at once. My Los Angeles friends were coming to San Francisco, a place where I spent nearly forty-eight hours every single week. I'd have to make it to the show, no excuses. I jumped into my beat-up old Saturn and started the familiar drive up the 17—in the pitch black of night—towards the Rickshaw Stop in San Francisco.

"What's up with your shoes?" Ross said, pointing at my feet the second I found him outside of the venue.

"Don't ask," I said with a groan. "I sold all my clothes the first day I got to Santa Cruz."

"I can tell," he said with a laugh.

"Who can think about fashion at a time like this?" I asked him. "My life right now is an endless cycle of pattern drafting and organizing rolls of film into tiny little bags and sleeping on someone's couch and being angry at my boyfriend and nearly dying on the 17 freeway."

"It sounds like you need a change," Ross said, concerned.

"I do," I agreed. "I need to move to San Francisco. The rent here is just so expensive. I've heard the rent control is great, though. If I could just find a room in a place where someone's already been on the lease for a while, I think maybe then I could afford it. I just need to find a roommate."

"You should ask around," Ross said, gesturing at the crowd. "There's a lot of cool people here. Someone's gotta know of a room opening up."

He was right. You don't get anything you want in life by keeping what you want a secret. If Laura in customer service had taught me anything, it's that it never hurts to ask.

"You're smart sometimes," I told him with a laugh. "All right, watch my drink and wish me luck. I'm gonna go find a new roommate."

"Are you even old enough to be drinking this?" he teased, taking the drink from my hands. We both knew I wasn't.

As a kid, I had been painfully shy and afraid of the world. My dad had affectionately nicknamed me Spock; I was full of information—things learned from books and television shows—which I rattled off at length in lieu of conversations. As I got older, learning how to socialize became a bit like studying for a test. I spent time studying how other people did it—what people responded well to, what they didn't. I wondered if studying socialization in this way made me a bit of a phony—one of those L.A. "networking" types everyone seemed to hate, or if it was just me trying to figure out how exactly being human worked. I wasn't great at it. I was a little too eager and a little too loud, a little too talkative and a little too pushy. I was earnest, though, in my interest in other people and their lives, and my concern for their well-being. I learned that if you compliment a stranger's shoes, they'll usually talk to you for a few minutes at least, and if you overstep your boundaries, apologizing profusely while calling yourself an idiot goes a long way. I walked around the Rickshaw Stop, staring at strangers' shoes, looking for someone to compliment. What I found was a guy about three drinks overboard being propped up against a wall by a friend.

"Are you okay?" I asked.

"I'm fine," the drunk guy stammered. "I just hate her so much."

"Breakup?" I asked.

"No," the drunk guy mumbled. "Roommate."

"What happened?" I asked.

"She just moved out," he said, gesturing wildly with his hand. "Who does that? Rent is due in like two days. How am I going to find a roommate in two days?"

My eyes lit up.

"How much is rent?" I asked.

"Six hundred dollars," the drunk guy said.

"What's the deposit?" I asked.

"No deposit," the drunk guy said. "I kept her deposit. Fuck that, you know? She screwed us."

"Listen, I have six hundred and three dollars," I told him, "and I can move in tomorrow."

"Are you serious?" the drunk guy asked.

"Dead serious," I said. "Give me your phone number."

Just like that, I'd found my first apartment in San Francisco. A few days later, I quit my job and a fellow Fresno escapee from the Harbor House named Blaire helped me pack all of my stuff up into the back of her van and drove it to the City. The apartment was cute, a two-bedroom spot in Lower Pacific Heights that had been converted into an awkward three-bedroom like most places in San Francisco by setting up partitions in the living room to create an extra place for a bed. My room was a proper bedroom, though, with windows and hardwood floors and crown molding. I didn't have a mattress, so I plopped an old futon pad straight onto the floor to use as a bed. I had a small TV that I put on a chair beside it, and a few trash bags plus a suitcase full of clothes and random books and documents.

Later that week, I met up with the four different photographers I'd chatted with at the photo lab to apply for a job. I took a job with a peculiar man who looked a bit like John Waters and worked out of his house in Bernal Heights. Minimum wage in San Francisco at the time was $8.82 per hour. He offered to pay me $20 an hour for 40 hours per week of work, which meant moving to San Francisco had cut four hours of driving off my weekly schedule and earned me a pay increase of over $2,000 per month.

My rent was nearly double what it had been in Santa Cruz, but the rest of my bills—gas, internet, phone, car insurance, and food—stayed relatively the same. I'd heard my whole life that living in a high-cost-of-living city was a bad idea if you were broke, but what I found was the opposite. Rent may have been more costly, but rent control in the city was amazing and allowed people to sign on to existing leases while still under the protection of rent control. People held apartments in their name for decades—even after they'd moved away from the building—with new roommates moving in and old roommates forwarding the rent to the landlord on their behalf as a sort of community service to keep the rent control going and prices low. It was an unspoken rule of how the city worked back then; housing was viewed as a civic service provided by the people who'd lived there the longest to people who needed it the most. It was "from each according to their ability, to each according to their needs," all playing out on Craigslist around us in real time.

This communitarian ethos flowed throughout San Francisco, a holdover element from the glory days of the Golden

Gate Park and Haight-Ashbury hippies from the 1960s. It had been forty years since revolutionary Abbie Hoffman and his disciples had set up a Free Store (everything is free!) on Haight Street, but in some pockets of San Francisco, it may as well have been yesterday. Haight-Ashbury had long since been commodified—there was a Gap on the street corner after all—but to some of the residents of San Francisco, keeping its original spirit felt like a torch they were destined to carry. Ronald Reagan might have killed "peace and love" in most of the country, but here in San Francisco, some people were fighting to keep it alive. An old roommate who now served as a "master tenant" to keep everyone else housed with cheap rent, even though they'd since moved away, was just one example. You could find other examples in the people who gave away free homemade pot brownies in Dolores Park, or the crust punks who played banjo on the sidewalks with their dogs howling along beside them. For my part, I kept Abbie Hoffman's Free Store vision alive by posting everything I didn't need on the "free" section of Craigslist. We take a little, we give a little back, even if what we have to give doesn't seem like much.

Moving to San Francisco did wonders for both my finances and my scheduling. However, my early days in the City presented one new challenge I hadn't prepared for: What the hell was I supposed to do with my car? Cars were expensive, and it hardly seemed like a good idea to just get rid of mine. Still, the City was not exactly conducive to a car-centric lifestyle, and a slew of new challenges presented themselves in regard to my crummy little motor vehicle. I struggled to park my car in the block around my neighborhood each day, circling the same few streets in concentric circles just looking for parking spots, sometimes looking for hours on end. In the morning, when I walked out to my car, I had a three-point checking system for car comfort:

1. Is the car still there? If yes, that was a great start. It meant it hadn't been towed in the night because I accidentally parked in a spot I wasn't supposed to.

2. Was there a parking ticket on the windshield? If not, I could breathe a sigh of relief knowing that parking the night before hadn't cost me hundreds of dollars due to accidentally violating a street sign's notoriously inscrutable directions.

3. Were the windows still in place?

In San Francisco in the early 2000s, there was an epidemic of car break-ins. They were simple enough, smash-and-grab style, where someone would break the passenger-side door window, open your glovebox, and root around in it looking for something good. For me, though, a broke person barely scraping by, this usually meant they rummaged through the Taco Bell hot sauce packets in my glovebox and threw them around my car—leaving empty-handed—while I had to try to figure out how to pay to replace the window the next morning. Each time the window broke, it was $100 to get it replaced. I'd find the window broken on my car at least once per month, and dutifully I'd drive down to the local glass shop on my lunch break to get it replaced.

One morning, the day after fixing a broken window, I came out to find that the window had been shattered again—twice in two days. I had $60 to my name and four days until payday. Fuck. Exasperated, I sat down on the steps of my neighbor's front porch and started to cry. A man in a suit leaned his head out of the window of the house, looking down at me.

"Hey," he said. "Are you okay?"

The house was beautiful, like most San Francisco houses are—an old Edwardian painted gorgeous colors and perfectly restored. Houses like that cost millions of dollars each, even back then. It was nice, I thought, that a man like this—who had probably made a fortune only looking out for himself—actually felt human enough to care about *me*, a sobbing stranger on his doorstep, in that moment.

"I'm okay," I told him through the tears. "It's just that my car got broken into again, the second time in two days, and I can't afford to just keep fixing it, you know?"

"Oh," he said, looking around a bit. "Well, this is private property, so you can't do this here."

I stared at him for a second, then chuckled a bit to myself. So much for giving people in suits the benefit of the doubt, I guess. The tech industry was starting to infiltrate the City slowly but surely, and more and more, our streets became filled with well-off men who worked at tech-based start-ups and had little concern for the humanitarian and collective care culture of San Francisco. I packed up my sniffles and got in my car, lambasting myself for ever thinking this rich man in his beautiful Edwardian mansion would care about someone like me. Rich people never care about the problems of broke people. Maybe, though, other broke people would care. I fished around the inside of my car, going through my schoolbag and pulling out a Sharpie and an old piece of paper. I started writing.

Hello, car thief! I see you are breaking into cars, that's fine—I get it! However, you might have noticed I'm driving a shitty 1997 Saturn. That's because I don't have much money. There's nothing in here you'd be interested in taking, unless you like old Taco Bell hot sauce packets. This is a pretty nice neighborhood, so odds are I'm parked in between a Mercedes and an Audi. I was wondering if you could break into their cars instead of mine? That way, you have a better chance at getting something good, and I don't have to stress over trying to pay to fix my window, cuz it's pretty expensive and I don't have the cash. It's win-win for both of us! Thank you for your time!

I put the piece of paper into a clear plastic sleeve with cardboard backing that we used to pack photos at my job, and I propped it up into the lip of the car window. It was perfect. For the next year, I left the sign up in my window every single night. My car was never broken into again. I'd like to believe that whoever saw the sign respected the situation I was in, just like I respected the situation they must have been in to need to break into cars to survive. I remembered the kid in my high school who said he was going to steal cars for a living. I remembered the car we'd stolen for my friend off the side of the road. If you create a world that's nearly impossible to live in honestly, people will do dishonest things in order to survive. Smashing a car window didn't seem so bad. For all they knew, I reasoned, I was a rich kid whose parents were paying to fix it every month. You don't get anything without asking for it first, and my sign was a polite way of asking to be spared the expense. The neighborhood car thieves delivered on my request, granting me temporary respite from one-third of my car-related issues in the City. Eventually, though, my car reached an untimely demise when its engine melted on itself in a tragic display of defeat. To be fair, I'd never changed the oil in it once.

Having a car in San Francisco had been a burden and a hassle, and once I was free of it, the quality of my life improved even more. I traveled all across the city on a bicycle and with an illegal bus pass made by a kid from the graphic design program at my school for $20. With my car gone, I found myself saving hundreds of dollars per month on transportation expenses. The city found new ways to save me money every day, it seemed. Its investment in public transportation was an investment in the quality of life for everyone who lived there, myself included. I felt grateful every time I hopped on the MUNI or BART.

Meanwhile, my school schedule was slowly growing more hectic. I'd traded the hours I spent driving back and forth from Santa Cruz for more time in the labs to complete homework, hoping to raise my grades. I was used to being a straight-A student, and was shocked when I got my first B on an assignment: a garment I sewed for my construction class. Indoctrinated by academic pressure for years of my life, I hadn't yet realized that "C's get degrees" and that no future employer would be looking at my college transcripts. Devastated, I approached my teacher after class.

"What do I need to get an A?" I asked her, my face drawn. "Is there any way to fix this?"

"That?" she said, looking over my shoulder at my assignment: a dress still situated on a mannequin from our classroom presentation and critique. "There's not too much to fix. It's pretty good. Your seam allowance was just one-sixteenth of an inch off or so in a few places."

"Right," I said, nodding my head eagerly. "So, what do I do to improve the grade? Do I remake it?"

"Remake it?" She laughed. "The whole dress?! Not worth it. Take the B, it's a fine grade. Besides, in real life nobody cares what their clothes look like on the inside. It's what's outside that counts. And from the outside, you made a pretty good dress."

She packed up her bag and left the classroom, while I stood contemplating my garment. It was pretty good, sure. Pretty good, though, wasn't perfect. I became determined to sew a perfect garment. Over the next few months, I threw myself into my coursework with an unprecedented level of commitment—spending hours each day at class or work, only to then spend hours each night hunched over a machine in the sewing lab until campus security kicked me out at midnight and locked the doors. The harder I worked to make a perfect garment, the more I wondered how other people were pulling it off. To be sure, I only knew one other student who worked full-time like I did. She waited tables at an upscale restaurant in the nearby town of Marin every night after class, commuting across the Golden Gate Bridge each way to do it. It was worth the trip, she explained, because people had even *more* money in Marin than in San Francisco. She cleared $300 in tips most nights. Everyone else seemed to have taken out loans for their living expenses, living in overpriced dorms or expensive apartments with brand-new leases in nice parts of town. The thousands of dollars per month they paid for living expenses through student loans was set to accrue 6.8 percent interest each year, and I wondered if they considered it.

A year or so into the program, I finally met my goal of constructing a perfect garment. The piece—an elaborate hand-pleated wool ball gown—had been a painstaking effort. I spent weeks hand-setting micro knife pleats along the skirt alone. During critique, my instructor turned the garment inside out and showed the class. Not a single stitch was out of place. I collapsed onto the floor in a fit of laughter and relief while the other students clapped.

As I left the class that day, I wondered why it was so hard to get an A in these classes. Very few of the garments I owned that had been professionally manufactured were as flawless as the garments we were expected to turn in. On top of that, homework seemed nearly impossible to complete on time, and coursework easily piled up. It required constant vigilance to stay on top of everything. I was beginning to wonder if our college coursework was difficult by design. Students often failed classes two or three times, paying to retake them—another thing that got tacked on to their student loan debt totals in the end, driving amounts up even higher than they'd initially been quoted. The longer I stayed in the program, the more I saw students drop out of school entirely, overwhelmed with frustration as their student loan debt ballooned out of control. Many racked up six figures of student loan debt for a degree they never even completed.

The coursework, while challenging, was also hardly taught by leading industry professionals. As we grew more familiar with our instructors, we learned more about their lives outside of class. From what I could tell, most of the instructors there were teaching part-time because they were unable to secure full-time employment in the field themselves, meaning we were taught by the bottom rung of industry performers. At one point in time, the dean of the Fashion Design department had no fashion design experience at all; she had simply been a dollmaker in the 1980s.

As early as 2007, my second year of college, the school I went to was being hit with lawsuits alleging deceptive program costs and misleading advertisements of its job placement skills. The Career Services department that had appealed to me as an applicant turned out to be little more than one person at a computer reposting job ads they found on Craigslist, or subpar job listings they heard about through friends. The job fairs that had looked so appealing in promotional pamphlets were, in fact, attended by tech companies and startups without any budget or experience in the world of apparel design at all.

I didn't know it then, but by 2015 the corporation that owned my school would agree to forgive up to $103 million in student loan debt (my loans didn't qualify), as well as pay $95.5 million in restitution for participating in a student recruitment strategy that violated U.S. federal law with its predatory practices. By 2018, the school would lose its accreditation completely and the following year would officially close its doors for good.

Despite my growing mistrust in the school I attended, in 2008 I graduated on the dean's list with my bachelor's degree in fashion design. At just twenty-two, I was eager to transition into a lucrative career that matched my skill set. I knew it wouldn't be easy, and I knew I wouldn't start at the top. I was fully prepared to work my way up from the bottom, but I didn't realize how low the bottom would be. The first time I opened an assistant design job listing sent to me from Career Services, my heart sank as I saw the starting wage: $10 per hour, degree required. Shocked, I scrolled through more job listings on the college job board, open only to recent graduates, but they all read exactly the same. The degree that I'd fought so hard for had put me in a position where I was now expected to take a $500 per month pay cut and pay an extra $250 per month in student loans for the pleasure of being able to do it.

As I read the listings, my jaw clenched tight and my hands balled up into fists at my sides. I knew enough to be angry, but was still too proud to admit what I now know, over a decade later, was the truth: I had been scammed. In 2008, I became a part of the statistics about for-profit private colleges with high costs and subpar educations. I thought back to my classmates and peers, the overwhelming majority of whom came from lower-income backgrounds like me. I remembered the open house in my hometown, where I met with a recruiter and over-heard another recruiter beside me tell a girl she wasn't the right fit for the college. I wonder now what had made her the wrong fit. Was it because her parents had gone to college and would know better than to send their daughter to a place like this? There's no way to know for certain what made me the "ideal candidate" for this type of school, but I had a few guesses. For-profit colleges disproportionately enroll low-income students like me, eager for a chance at a better life but lacking the background and support to know exactly how to do it.

The teenage version of myself who signed up to take on those loans believed wholeheartedly that a college degree would be my path towards class mobility—the first step on a journey to a more stable future. When I think back on her now, working full-time at minimum wage while also going to school full-time, driving back and forth on "Blood Alley" in a barely functioning car on heavily compromised sleep—doing everything in her power, everything the world told her was the right thing to do, to work for a better future—I get angry. It's not that I ever believed the system was set up to help people like me. I knew better than that. I think, though, I believed that if I sacrificed enough, if I worked hard enough, maybe I would emerge on the other side into a world where I didn't have to worry about my checking account getting overdrawn just to pay for my insurance each month. I had fallen for the American myth of individual exceptionalism by thinking that if I worked hard enough, I would be the exception to the rule. In reality, the system didn't care how hard I worked. I wasn't an exception. In the end, I was just a frightened twenty-two-year-old girl clutching a worthless piece of paper with my college degree on it, wondering how the hell I was going to pay back all of this debt.

Navigating College

For most of us, college is the second most expensive thing we will ever spend money on in our lives, just behind buying a house (if we ever get to do that at all). It's not a decision to be taken lightly, and nobody should pressure you into attending college if you're not ready—it will just be a waste of time and money. Here's everything you need to know about college:

1. Some colleges are public, meaning they receive funding from the government and tend to be cheaper to attend. Others are private, meaning they rely more on student tuition to fund their expenses and tend to be more expensive. Private school tuition is around three times the cost of public school tuition in the United States.

2. Community colleges are typically extremely affordable public schools and usually offer two-year degrees, or "associate's degrees." If you plan on getting a four-year degree (a bachelor's degree), you can usually save money by going to a community college for the first two years of the degree, then transferring your credits to the four-year college you prefer. Some credits won't transfer over. Many times, though, you can contest credits your four-year college denies so you don't have to pay to take classes twice.

3. It's usually cheaper to attend college in your home state. This is because they figure you've paid taxes in that state to help fund the school. This means that on average, the cheapest way to get a four-year degree is to attend an in-state community college for the first two years, then transfer to an in-state public four-year university for your last two years.

4. College is not for everyone. Out of the three most successful people I've ever met in my life, two were high-school dropouts and one was a college dropout. You can have a good life without a college degree. However, 63 percent of people who earn six-figure salaries do have a bachelor's degree or higher. Only you can decide what path is right for you. A college degree is not a sure-fire path to financial stability, and not getting a degree doesn't mean you're relegated to a life of second-class citizenry.

5. It's very possible money won't be the primary motivating factor in which degree you choose. However, if you opt to go for a degree with a traditionally lower return on investment, consider being more mindful of your budget when deciding what college to attend. Getting a $100,000 degree for a job that pays $30,000 per year is setting yourself up for a life of financial struggle. However, getting a $15,000 degree for a job that pays $30,000 per year might be worth it to you, especially if you're passionate about the field.

6. Housing costs on campus are usually more expensive than housing would be if you secured it on your own off campus. Research off-campus housing costs before committing to live in dormitories whenever possible.

7. Approach loans for living expenses cautiously. Not everyone can work while they are in school. Only you know what you're capable of handling. Just make sure you're remembering that student loans are not free money. You'll have to pay it back, and despite what college recruiters might tell you, there's no guarantee you'll be fabulously well-paid and financially stable when it comes time to do it.

8. The average cost to apply to college in the U.S. is $50. Research colleges in advance of applying so you're not going broke from application fees alone.

9. Check out the U.S. Department of Labor's free scholarship search engine. It will help you find out if there's free money available to help you pay for college.

10. Remember that failing classes means you'll have to repay to take those same classes. It might be financially prudent for you to take fewer classes each term so you can focus on passing them. Keep in mind your school's cost per credit when deciding your workload each term.

11. It's not worth attending college to fill time while you figure out what you want to do with your life. College is expensive and time-consuming. Choosing to attend should not be taken lightly! It should be part of an overall plan for your future with a firm want and why—meaning you actually want to do it and you know what you hope to get out of it. Don't let your family pressure you into attending school if you're not ready for it! It could very well be a waste of money.

CHAPTER 5

When You're Here, You're Family!

If you work for a small business long enough, there's bound to be a moment when you look at your boss and realize "Wow, this person is completely and utterly out of their mind." Let's face it: the types of people who start their own businesses are often the types of people who, for better or worse, do not fit in a traditional work environment. This can be a good thing, sure—a realization that the ideas of "professionalism" and "work" often dehumanize us and deny the reality that we are complex, multifaceted creative beings in need of more than a strictly regimented 9-to-5 day job. However, it can be a bad thing too—wherein we're forced to contend with extreme emotional volatility at the hands of our employer in a place where we just want to show up, do our job, and get a paycheck so that we can put a roof over our heads and live our lives. A small business is usually an intimate reflection of the person running it, and because of that, they can be as good or as bad as any regular person can be. Like most people, they're usually a mixture of both.

The thing about people, though, is that we *love* to support an underdog. In the classic mythology of America, there's perhaps no greater underdog than the small-business owner. The small-business owner is a venerated piece of the

American story: hardworking, struggling in the face of all odds, innovating new ways to do business for the promise of a brighter future. In a place where we spend most days throwing our hard-earned money into the faceless void of a mega corporation who will use it to exploit their workers and siphon off as much profit as possible to make their already rich CEO even richer, it feels good to instead support a *small* business—to stand up for the "little guy" who is just fighting to put food on their table. What happens, though, when the "little guy" is just as evil and exploitative as the big guy, only with fewer resources and less accountability?

Moving to San Francisco marked the beginning of a long period of time in which I worked for small businesses—ranging in size from ten or so employees all the way down to just me and the owner. Each business was different, but what they all had in common was that they cultivated a "family-like" environment. After all, everyone worked closely with each other every day, getting to know each other on a deep and personal level, sometimes even working in someone's actual home. People tend to forget, however, just how dysfunctional families can be, and "work families" are no exception. Just like my own family back home, work families can experience bickering and squabbling, emotional outbursts, money trouble, and resentment.

When interviewing with photographers in San Francisco, I was often in the photographer's home, already blurring the lines between the professional and personal spaces we're used to in a more conventional work environment. I interviewed with one photographer—a man with a delightful British accent who'd just relocated from London—who informed me he wouldn't be able to test my computer skills that day because his computer had been acting up a bit ("cheeky bugger," he called it with a grimace), so he put it in the garden to teach it a lesson. I learned that day that "garden" is just the word British people use to describe any outdoor space attached to their homes. His "garden" was little more than a patch of overgrown weeds with a folding chair in the middle, atop of which his bulky '90s desktop computer sat, ostensibly in shame and punishment for having displayed the infamous Blue Screen of Death one too many times.

I interviewed with another man who informed me that I'd be starting work before he woke up each day, and since there was only one bathroom in the house, I'd need to get comfortable seeing him walking around in just a towel after his morning shower. I could feel free to pop in to use the bathroom if I wanted while he was showering, if I was comfortable with that sort of thing. The interviews themselves felt like auditioning to join someone's family, and these people's families might have been even more strange and complex than my own.

The job I finally settled on, working out of the house of the John Waters–esque photographer in the Bernal Heights neighborhood of San Francisco, seemed to be the most "normal" option available. However, after starting the job I began to see just how quickly even the most "normal" of small business jobs can devolve into a "family-like" atmosphere, whether you want it to or not.

"Did you take AP classes in high school?" he asked me one day.

"My school didn't offer a lot of them," I conceded, "but I did take the ones they offered, yeah. AP English Literature, AP Calculus, AP American History, and AP European History."

"I took AP European History," he said. "What did you get on the test?"

"I can't remember if I got a four or a five," I told him. "I remember on one of the essay portions, I used an example that was off by ten years or so from the prompt, so I got docked."

"I doubt you got a four or a five," he said with a laugh. "I was very good in school and I only got a three on that test. It was a hard one."

"Oh, I was pretty good at school, too," I told him offhandedly, continuing to work on the computer while we chatted. "I graduated as a junior and was valedictorian."

"What?" he replied, taken aback.

"Yeah, I'm a school person, I guess. It just makes sense to me," I said.

"That's ridiculous," he said.

I looked at him, expecting him to be teasing me or joking around, but his face was serious and annoyed. Was I now fighting with my boss—an adult man in his forties—because he was jealous that I had done better than him on a test in high school? I assured myself this couldn't be the case. I'd never had a brother, but it felt like the kind of thing a sibling might be upset with you over. This man was not my sibling, though. He was my employer, and because of that, I surely must have misread the situation.

From that day on, though, it seemed the Photographer and I had a rivalry. Or rather, the Photographer had a rivalry at me rather than with me, and I had to deal with it if I wanted to keep my job and pay my bills. As the months unfolded, he took delight in my failures—charging me for things I damaged while in training, or seeming to set me up for disaster at every opportunity, just to be able to hurl a snide remark about my general incompetence wherever he could. I struggled to maintain as professional a demeanor as possible, a hard task when working out of someone's house with them in close quarters every day. It all came to a head when tax season approached.

The Photographer had hired me at a rate of $20 per hour. The rate was the result of negotiation, since I'd been offered jobs with the other photographers I'd interviewed with as well. They'd offered me between $18 and $20 per hour each, and I settled with the Photographer because he seemed the most sane, and because he agreed to match my highest offer. He paid me in paper checks, amounts that came in short of the $20 hourly rate, which I had assumed was due to taxes being withheld. When tax season approached, I was shocked to receive a 1099 form in the mail instead of a W-2. The 1099 form is given to freelance workers, who are liable for their own taxes, which they are supposed to pay quarterly throughout the year. W-2 forms are given to proper employees, for whom most employers have already sent in a share of estimated taxes based on earnings throughout the year. I had been a freelance worker this whole time, and not on payroll like I had assumed. Even more shockingly, this meant that the discrepancy in my payments wasn't the result of taxes being withheld, but the result of the Photographer intentionally underpaying me. On top of that, I was now liable for taxes on the entirety of what I'd earned, since taxes hadn't been withheld and sent on my behalf like I had assumed. I would owe thousands of dollars, and I had absolutely nothing in savings. It was a fine enough job, but even still, I was just breaking even on my expenses. Furious, I brought the 1099 to work with me.

"Why did I get a 1099 instead of a W-2?" I asked him, brandishing it in front of me.

"Because you're a freelance contract worker and not an employee," he said casually.

"When did we decide that?" I asked.

"It's always been that," he said calmly. "Did I not tell you?"

"I work a set schedule, without my own equipment, which means I should be a regular employee according to the law. Plus, you told me I was earning twenty dollars per hour, and my checks worked out to more like fifteen dollars," I said, nearly shaking. "I assumed the remaining twenty-five percent was withheld for taxes. This means that you've just been shorting me?"

"You should have been smart enough to figure this all out week one." He laughed. "If there was a problem with your check, you needed to bring it up then."

"There wasn't a problem with my check if taxes were coming out of it," I said angrily. "How was I supposed to know taxes weren't coming out?"

"Well," he said, "you never saw a pay stub, did you? That should have been your first clue."

I was livid. I'd been robbed of 25 percent of my promised

income and was now on the hook for paying taxes on it out of pocket all at once.

"I'm not working for less than the twenty dollars you promised me," I told him.

We negotiated again and settled on $18 per hour, free-lance work, still at my same schedule. From that point on, though, we had become "family" in the worst sense of the word. We took to bickering nearly every day, arguing about everything from the best way to ship out prints to who was the king of Italy in the ninth century. We seemed to intentionally inconvenience each other with our work, getting in each other's way and snapping in harsh tones. I came into work one day to find his house filthy, just minutes before a client was scheduled to arrive.

"They can't see that you live like this," I exclaimed. "We'll never get their business. Give me a broom!"

I swept and tidied his house, fuming like an angry mother. I didn't even have time to clean my own house thanks to my hectic work and school schedule, and now I was cleaning up after an adult man who couldn't even be bothered to pay me what he promised. The small-business mantra, the one that says "we're like a family," had officially gone too far. I worked for a man who stole from me, condescended to me, and treated me with absolutely no respect. I didn't want a workplace that was like a family, not this family anyway. I needed out.

One day, the Photographer got a phone call from a friend, who was crying. She was a photographer, too—an eccentric woman in the Haight-Ashbury neighborhood of San Francisco. She was more successful than him, with a team of employees, and that day they'd all walked out on her at the same time and quit.

"I don't know where anything is," she told the Photographer over the phone. "I can't find anything. I need help."

"It's slow over here today," he told her. "I can send my assistant, Madeline, over if you want to pay her for the day? I'm sure she won't mind."

I was more than happy to get out of the Photographer's house for the day, and at any rate, it sounded like his friend might be in the market for more permanent help. I nodded enthusiastically while he wrapped up the telephone call, then made my way to Haight-Ashbury armed with her address written on a small slip of paper.

The new photographer, Toni, worked out of a beautiful old apartment that she'd converted into a photo studio. It still had its original layout—two bedrooms, a huge living room, a kitchen, and a bathroom—up a tall flight of stairs. The living room operated as the main office for her operation, with three workspaces laid out in a giant L shape curving around the perimeter. The largest of the bedrooms at the back of the apartment was the photo studio. Toni herself was a friendly chaotic artist type, with a pixie cut and colorful eyeglasses and a love of David Byrne. She was, objectively, just as unprofessional as the Photographer, but in a way that was charming and refreshing. When I arrived, she was panicked about the state of her office—which had been reduced to piles of boxes and scattered papers and she was struggling to make sense of the records her employees had left behind—but even with all of that stress, she was still kind and respectful in a way that the Photographer had never been with me. When I first arrived, she asked me if I'd like something to eat or drink. It wasn't much, but after months of fighting over every little thing with the Photographer, it felt a bit like a warm hug from a friend.

"I'd love a bite to eat," I told her.

"Good," she replied. "I never trust a person who won't take food from me."

Toni's employees had left—in unison, all together—not because of issues with workplace labor rights being violated or a toxic work culture or any of the usual suspects. They'd simply grown tired of her inability to catch up with the times. She was a film photographer, which made her something of a relic in the early 2000s, when all photography was converting to digital. She held fast to her old ways of doing things, much to her employees' chagrin, requesting paper copies of invoices that already existed in digital form, or requiring a specific hard-to-find paper to process film prints on because it retained the "warmth" a bit better than the readily available alternatives. She had frustrated them with her hard-headedness, she acknowledged. She was ready to make some changes and enter the future, no matter how uncomfortable the change could be.

I organized her invoices and paperwork, making sense of her upcoming billing and appointments. When I was finished, she looked at me as though she might cry.

"Thank you," she said, her eyes welling up. It was the first time I'd ever felt appreciated in a workplace.

Toni was an offbeat, fun free-love type. She seemed to embody everything good about the rich, flamboyant history of San Francisco from the 1960s to the 1980s. In a city where tech firms like Google and Facebook were eagerly working to build their offices on the ruins of San Francisco's vibrant past, Toni was a reminder of the hippie counterculture days. She wore feather boas and cracked dirty jokes. She went to the local street fairs and took pictures with leather daddies in bondage gear whom she seemed to know going back decades. She knew everyone on the block, where she had lived since she first moved to San Francisco in the 1970s. She bought the apartment from her old landlord, she said, back when you could still just buy housing that easily, and she lived there for years before eventually moving out and converting it into a photo studio full-time. She told me about the man on the corner outside of her building who mooed every day. It was his way of asking for spare change, she explained, so that he could buy some milk. She told me about the hippie café on the corner. She told me about the family that ran the corner store underneath her building. She told me that if you tell them what you like, they'll stock it for you the very next week. She loved the neighborhood, and San Francisco in general, and her positivity was contagious.

At the end of the day, when we'd sorted through all of her old invoices and calendars and created new systems for how to manage her workload, she turned to me and asked, "How much is the Photographer paying you over there?"

"Eighteen dollars per hour," I said, rolling my eyes a bit.

"I think we can do better than that," she said with a smile. "How would you like to work here instead? The Photographer is my friend, sure, but I think I need you. He'll just have to understand."

Toni was a beautiful, bubbly feather-boa'd angel, and I had just been saved.

Over at Toni's, we rebuilt her a team of four people, myself included, who together ran her office, retouched images, and handled sales. I made $25 per hour, plus commission on anything I could sell to clients. Toni was the top baby photographer in San Francisco, and her clients included some of the richest people the city had to offer. Real estate developers, famous rock musicians, big-time bankers, and people with old San Francisco money came in every day. From her office, I watched the wealthy buy multimillion-dollar homes over the telephone with their assistants, sight unseen. I saw stay-at-home moms with full-time nannies who loved nothing more than to shop and do yoga every day. I saw stay-at-home moms who seemed to resent both motherhood and their husbands, and came to sales meetings as a way to just escape their own family back home. I saw wealthy dads who barely remembered their kids' names. We sold them photos, sure, but we also sold them memories of their children's youth that they might not have otherwise had the time to notice.

Toni may have worked for the rich, but she never catered to them. She treated them like they were average, which both infuriated and appealed to them. At a certain point when you accumulate wealth, it becomes novel for someone to tell you no. When customers complained about not getting special treatment, she held firm to our policies and defended her staff.

"That person is just a pain in the ass," she'd say to us later in private, shaking her head. "You didn't do anything wrong."

In a world where "the customer is always right," it felt good to have a boss who knew that sometimes the customer was being an unreasonable and downright horrendous person, and we deserved better. Toni charged premier prices—with one-hour photo sessions costing what many of my friends back home would earn in a month. Privately, though, she offered free photo sessions to people who couldn't afford anything near what her rate was, scheduling photo shoots on her day off just to share her talent with young or struggling families, often people from her neighborhood and the nearby community. Like most small-business owners, Toni was not the kind of person who could have worked in a normal environment. Her office was abnormal in every sense of the word, but abnormal in a way that saw everyone's humanity first, and at the end of the day recognized that this was just a job and there was more to life than this for all of us. If anything, it seemed like Toni was more concerned about us finding and seizing the joy in life than even we were sometimes.

At Toni's office, it was easy to see what a small business could be. She did her best to service her community and pay her employees fairly. She set up commission systems so that when the business did well, we all did well. She gave us flexible scheduling and talked to us like people rather than cogs in a money-making machine. If small businesses were a family, Toni was one of the best family members I ever had. She was difficult, too—sure. She was still a bit resistant to digital technology and had a way she liked things to be done. She was regimented about her organization and disliked change. We did things in bizarre, antiquated ways sometimes to suit her comfort level. Sometimes, we'd end up in headstrong arguments about how to efficiently complete tasks, which usually ended with her throwing her hands in the air and proclaiming "Okay! Let go and let Madeline!" It was a reference to an age-old saying, "Let go and let God," and meant something about the faith and trust she put in me to look out for her. It was a push-and-pull relationship, with emphatic displays of "why this" and "why that" for seemingly everything we did. The trade-off, to work in a place where I felt truly valued, was well beyond worth it in the end.

By the time I graduated from college, Toni's office had in fact become a second home for me, more like a family than perhaps anywhere I'd grown up. The corner store stocked my favorite snacks, at my request, and let me just take things when I forgot my wallet in the chaos of the day. I carried change in my pockets to give to the mooing man on the corner so he could buy milk. I learned the names of everyone who worked at the café across the street and tried all of their tea latte concoctions, named after each one of them, written in chalk on a little board by the register. I babysat Toni's stepdaughter on the weekends, and talked with her husband about the early days when he and Toni had first met. When I got my dog, Toni was the first person in San Francisco to see her—running around the office on all fours alongside my little dachshund Mo-Dog yelling "Puppy, puppy, puppy!" while they played with a tiny squeaky ball.

"I'm alpha dog!" she told me, barking alongside Mo-Dog while they played.

To this day, Toni still feels like family to me. We talk every now and then, a decade later, catching up on life and sending each other photos. She still asks me if I ever plan on moving back to San Francisco, and says I'll always have a job with her if I want it.

Small businesses are a microcosm for the world at large. They reflect our cultural values and norms, but also the values and mindsets of the people who run them. They still exist in the capitalist machine—often set up in a way that maximizes profits for the owner at the top while exploiting the workers below them. At their worst, small businesses are just as cold, callous, and selfish as any major corporation, only with fewer protections and less oversight. At a small size, they're able to sneak by regulations. At their smallest size, with just one employee and the owner, there aren't even other workers to join forces with to ask for change. A small business might use guilt to manipulate and coerce workers into not recording overtime, into not taking days off, or into not reporting misconduct. Too often, the claim that "we're a family" is used to keep workers from asserting their rights or looking out for themselves. In fact, 79 percent of workers in a small-business survey reported being abused in their workplace, compared to 71 percent at major corporations. On top of that, over 15 percent reported a high level of abuse working at a small business, which is double the rate for large corporations. Businesses are not intrinsically any more ethical just because they are small. If anything, data shows they tend to be less ethical overall.

However, what Toni's office showed me is that there's an opportunity in small businesses, too—there's a chance to do things differently. You can carve out small areas of kindness within the traditional work structure. You can establish policies and guidelines that favor human beings over profit. You can build a workplace that offers you everything traditional workplaces out in the world failed to provide. You can make your own little world within four walls, and you can run it exactly as you'd like.

Today, though, too often we see even small businesses being established with the goal of creating "passive income" for the owner, creating a structure wherein the primary goal is for workers to remain at low wages to maximize earnings for the small-business owner in charge. The idea of business ownership seems to appeal to a type of person who sees existing in the world as a competitive sport, and they are determined to win. What this means is that everyone who works at the business underneath them is destined to lose.

. . .

There's this old business adage about how you should always pay your employees way more than they think they are worth. Then, they will feel extremely grateful for the job and work as hard as possible to keep it. If you pay a worker more than they think they deserve, they will be loyal to the company, they won't steal, and they'll always go above and beyond. You can tell it's an old business adage, rather than a current one, because it places value on loyalty and performance over company profits.

Today, 65.8 percent of workers believe that they are underpaid in their current positions, and this might correlate to why 85 percent of workers in the United States are unhappy at their jobs. If you pay people less than they need to live, or less than they think they deserve, they are going to look for ways to "earn" that money back. When I was a teenager in Fresno, I went to visit my friend Andrew at his job one day. He worked at a local arcade, and when I showed up to meet him, he was nowhere on the arcade floor. Finally, fifteen minutes later, he emerged from behind an EMPLOYEES ONLY door.

"Sorry," he said. "I didn't see that you were here. I was shitting."

"Oh," I said, a bit surprised by the candor. "Uh, okay . . . Yeah, that's fine. Bathroom breaks are . . . good."

"They're more than good," he told me with an intent look in his eye. "Madeline, tell me, do you shit at work?"

I pictured the bathroom at the photo lab I worked in, which was usually inexplicably wet, sometimes with vile things I dared not try to identify smeared across the walls.

"Uhhh . . . I'm more of a . . . privacy of my own bathroom kind of person," I said, a bit confused by the invasive bathroom questioning.

"Ah, Madeline, you should always shit at work," Andrew replied. "Sometimes, I have to go in the morning before work, and you know what I do? I hold it in until I get to work."

"Why?" I asked, truly perplexed.

"Because if I'm gonna shit, why not get paid to do it?" he said. "Like, I have to shit no matter what, why wouldn't I shit at work while I'm on the clock, you know what I'm saying?"

I didn't know it then, but Andrew's line of reasoning actually fell in line with a popular workplace rhyme:

> *Boss makes a dollar, I make a dime*
> *That's why I shit on company time*

The American workplace is so adversarial that workers schedule bathroom breaks out of spite to maximize their meager earnings. It's funny, of course, but also sad. Why is it so hard for workplaces to simply treat their employees with dignity and pay them enough money to live?

There had to be a balance between the extreme loyalty that businesses who insist they're like a "family" seemed to demand of their employees, and the combative nature of most employment scenarios that leads workers to feel like their workplace is the enemy. When I think about the small businesses I've worked for, what I really wanted was to be seen as human, the way a family or friend might see you, but to be provided with transparency and accountability the way a trustworthy institution might. I wanted to work in a place that I might develop my own sense of loyalty to over time, but not have that loyalty demanded of me or anyone else. What's in between a family and an enemy? It seemed to me the answer is being viewed and treated as a person.

If capitalism is the problem, like I suspected it was, small businesses operating on a capitalist model that still valued profit over people couldn't be the solution. However, with the right approach, small businesses could be the vehicle through which a different solution was achieved. First, though, someone would have to figure out how to create a workplace that valued workers' humanity without commodifying it as a tool for further exploitation—and if I knew anything for certain, I knew that person wouldn't be me. My experiences working for small businesses showed me that I never wanted to work for myself. It was messy and chaotic and unpredictable, and absolutely everything I didn't want. Instead, I just wanted a steady reliable job that paid me enough to have a decent quality of life.

Life has a funny way of working out, though. My graduation date from college was right in the middle of 2008, meaning I would be graduating college into the start of the worst global recession in generations—one that would significantly alter my life's entire trajectory, both professionally and financially, for decades to come. If my life were a movie, this would be the part where the camera zoomed in on my optimistic, hopeful twenty-two-year-old face while the soundtrack dropped the "dun dun dunnnnnn" of impending doom all over the frame.

Figuring Out How Hard to Work

One of the hardest things about working a job can be figuring out just how much exactly you're supposed to care. Caring too much can take a horrific toll on your mental well-being. Not caring enough can get you fired, which is all fun and games until rent comes around. Here's everything to remember when trying to figure out how hard you should work at a job:

1. Right away, remember that you should never care more than your boss does. If your boss doesn't think something is broken, you will run yourself ragged trying to convince them to change things around the office. If you think there's a more efficient way things could be done in the workplace, present an idea once to gauge their receptiveness. If they shut it down, adjust how much you care to meet their level. It's not worth the struggle.

2. Keep track of how many people at the company you work for are promoted from within. If your company has a good track record of promoting people, going above and beyond in your position may pay off. If they tend to hire people from outside, though, going the extra mile probably won't be worthwhile to you at all.

3. Talk to people who have worked there longer than you. Remember that you are legally allowed to discuss your salary for all jobs in the United States. Be open about your wages, and ask people about theirs. It will give you a good idea of whether or not hard work is rewarded in your workplace, and it will help you build unity with your coworkers. You're stronger together!

4. If anything unethical or illegal is going on in your workplace, be sure to make note of it in writing, ideally to HR (if you have it) or a higher-up. They probably won't fix or change anything, but it's good to have it in writing because it allows you the opportunity to pursue legal action later if you want. Reach out to labor attorneys. Many operate on a contingency basis, meaning they don't get paid unless you win or settle with your employer. However, it's going to be hard to win or even settle if you don't have documentation of the wrongdoing that's occurred in your workplace.

5. Always look at your federal, state, and local (city) labor rights and regulations. Your employer might be asking you to put in illegal overtime or go above and beyond without proper compensation. Your state might have different rules for overtime or paid time off than the federal government, and your city might have more protections than your state. Know your rights so you can know if they are being violated. A workplace that is knowingly violating your rights is adversarial and not one you should ever go above and beyond for.

6. Be wary of any language trying to convince you that a business is "like a family." While it's true that working in close quarters with people can sometimes produce close relationships that mirror family dynamics, companies that openly proclaim this are often trying to guilt people into doing more work than they are being adequately compensated for. Being told a workplace is "like a family" is usually a red flag, unless you truly believe your boss would go above and beyond to help you out in an emergency.

7. Remember that your coworkers are not your friends. Keep your private life private as much as possible in the workplace. The less they know, the less they can use against you.

8. Be mindful of talking to your boss and coworkers off the clock if you're an hourly worker. You're not getting paid for that time, and any boss who expects you to be "on call" should realistically have you on salary. You can bring it up in a cheery, positive way by saying something like "I've noticed lately that my role includes some communication beyond my hourly schedule. Can we plan a meeting to discuss converting me to a salaried position so I am in a position to better address these off-the-clock requests?"

CHAPTER 6

Funemployment

It's hard to explain the Great Recession to someone who wasn't an adult during it. It felt like standing on top of a hill watching a forest fire rapidly advance towards you, but being stuck—powerless to run away, and powerless to stop it. One by one, you watch the forest fire slowly devour other people's homes, and you pray that it won't come for yours. You stand there on the hill, your fingers crossed, just wishing—with all of your might—that you'll make it out okay. In the end, of course, the fire comes for your home, too. You survive, but just barely—singed, scorched, and burnt, but in a state of shock. In the state of shock, it hasn't really hit you just what's happened here today. You stand up, dust yourself off, and say, "Huh, well that wasn't so bad." You feel fine, maybe even good, but that's only because it won't be until years later that you realize how much you truly lost that day.

To understand the recession, we have to start back in the mid-1990s when I was just a kid—around nine or ten years old—and my father and stepmother were looking to purchase their very first house. From 1995 to 2006, a bubble was forming in the housing market in the United States. A "bubble" refers to something that's artificially overvalued, a price trend that seems to grow in an unstable fashion until the bubble eventually bursts. With a housing bubble, the value of houses grows far too quickly, outpacing things like household income. The thing about bubbles, though, is that it's hard to know you're in one until it pops.

Around the time that people like my father and step-mother were looking to purchase their first home in the mid-'90s, buying a house seemed like a sure way to make some money. Home prices were rising fast, and it seemed like if you could just get your foot in the door of home ownership, you'd be sure to come out on top in just a few years' time. Because of the supposed "sure thing" nature of investing in hous-ing, banks were introducing new types of mortgages geared towards "subprime" buyers. A "subprime" buyer might be someone who had a lower credit score, lower income, or rela-tively high amount of debt, coupled with a low or nonexistent amount of savings available for a down payment.

It's hard to know for certain if my dad and stepmother were subprime borrowers when they bought their first house in the mid-1990s. However, given the fact that the home was foreclosed on pretty soon thereafter, and we spent much of our time eating off fast-food dollar menus, it's not a stretch to think so. What I do know for certain is that the American Dream is heavily predicated on the idea of home ownership, and people want to believe that dream is within their grasp. For broke people who have struggled to maintain consistent housing their whole lives, buying a house means security and safety. We're desperate for it, and desperate people with limited financial knowledge are going to be easily sold on anything that promises them the future they know they deserve.

Now, you might be thinking: what could be wrong with making it easier for people to buy houses? The answer, of course, is nothing, as long as people can afford to keep up with their monthly mortgage payments. But these subprime loans created a system wherein it was nearly impossible for borrowers to keep up with their monthly mortgage payments once they'd taken out a loan for a house. Subprime borrowers were targeted with predatory lending practices, including the adjustable-rate mortgage—which meant that following an entry-level fixed amount of time, your monthly mortgage payment for your home might change suddenly based on the interest rate. Theoretically, adjustable-rate mortgages save people money over time. When it comes to how they play out in the day-to-day for low-income people, however, a wildly fluctuating monthly housing price is just a disaster waiting to happen.

By the beginning of 2007, the federal government was beginning to sense that this whole subprime mortgage issue could be a really bad thing. The housing market was slumping, and interest rates were climbing significantly higher, meaning more borrowers with adjustable-rate mortgages were having trouble keeping up on their new higher monthly payments and began defaulting on their mortgages. Average Americans were beginning to lose their homes. As the year came to a close, the National Bureau of Economic Research declared two straight quarters of economic decline and announced that the United States was officially in a recession.

By early 2008, fear was rising among Americans, and the consumer-spending portion of the economy—that thing we call its "backbone"—was suffering a metaphorical slipped disc. Brokerage firms and mortgage companies were beginning to file for bankruptcy. When an eighty-five-year-old brokerage firm called Bear Stearns collapsed in March 2008, I was twenty-one years old and in my final quarter of college. The Great Recession was in the air, but it wasn't something that seemed to be affecting my life or that of my fellow apparel design students yet. We saw industries beginning to crumble one by one around us—things like furniture stores and automotive suppliers and cement companies and airlines. However, it seemed that for the moment, the industries paying the bills in my life—fashion and photography—were unscathed. The primary clientele at my regular job with Toni were the wealthy elite—people with what we called "Old San

Francisco Money," which seemed to know no bounds. Our work was steady and consistent, and somehow—despite the inefficiencies of my school's Career Services department—I had managed to land a coveted six-month design internship at Levi Strauss & Co., based solely on the quality of work in my portfolio.

San Francisco may have been a big city in the eyes of America, but when it came to the apparel industry, it was small and insular, consisting of just two major companies: Levi Strauss & Co. and Gap, Inc. Getting a design internship at Levi Strauss was like winning the jackpot in the competitive lottery that was San Francisco apparel design. If I could prove my worth there, I could parlay it into a full-time job as soon as I graduated from college in June. I worked out a way to do my internship two days a week, take my classes full-time for two more days per week, and cram as many work hours at Toni's into the remaining three days as possible. The internship was paid—a rarity in the world of fashion—and provided me with $25 per hour. Teachers and classmates assured me that Levi's was a "good job" and that if I could hold on to it, I'd be set for life. In the midst of a recession, you wanted to get in with a company like Levi Strauss that had been around for over a hundred and fifty years. They'd weathered many storms and proven they had staying power.

The Levi Strauss & Co. offices were on a massive campus in San Francisco's North Beach neighborhood, with huge open windows that let in the sunshine and provided stunning views. Some days, I'd set aside a little extra money to buy a coffee at the coffee shop across the street, standing in line side by side with the other Levi's employees, all of us wearing our company lanyards with keycards around our necks. On the first floor of the main design building where I worked, there was a museum paying homage to the more than one hundred and fifty years of apparel Levi's had made. Upstairs in the design rooms, I bounced around from department to department, creating concept booklets and color stories and technical flats. I ran every errand and took on every task. Supervisors nodded their heads at me and smiled in approval.

"Keep this up," one said, "and departments will be fighting over who gets to keep you once your internship is up."

In hushed tones, I talked with design assistants in the cafeteria on my lunch breaks.

"What's starting pay like here for an assistant design job?" I asked.

The resounding response was something like $65,000 per year. That was good, I thought, but even better was the knowledge that there was room to move up with the company. The senior designers made something like $150,000 per year. Their bosses made over $200,000. If I could stay at Levi Strauss & Co., I thought to myself, my future would be set.

In June 2008, I graduated. My internship extended another three months beyond my graduation date, and after I completed my degree, my supervisors at Levi's began to increasingly assure me I'd be kept on as a full-time hire once the internship was up. They asked me questions about which departments I'd prefer and began increasing my creative input around the office.

Toni wrung her hands with mixed emotions.

"I'm so proud of you," she said. "You'll be so happy. But wouldn't you maybe just like to stay here instead? I know, I know! Never mind! You'll be so happy!"

"I'll always be here to help," I told her. "You know that."

Toni had truly become like family—the good kind of family—and I felt bound to her not from a place of guilt but from a place of community and concern for not only her well-being but the well-being of everyone else at work. I trained other employees in my daily tasks so that they could take over "when the time came." My internship was set to expire at the end of September, meaning I'd be offered a full-time position by one or more departments at the beginning of October. It was only a matter of months before my career would officially start.

The month after I graduated, the unemployment rate was up to 5.8 percent. Nearly 9 million Americans were unemployed, and all around us, more and more companies were failing. It seemed that everyone I knew watched the world with bated breath, reading the news every day to discover another company had gone under. News stations were filled with stories of families who had become homeless and lives that had been ruined. Slowly, the housing developer clients of Toni's stopped returning our calls. All that remained were the mysterious "old money" clients and aging rock stars, whose assets were so solid they didn't need to rely on a single industry to get by.

That same month, I wandered into a house party in San Francisco and was shocked to discover my dad there, hanging out with my older crowd of SF friends. We hugged each other warmly while our friends looked on amazed. My father, unbeknownst to me, had been coming up to San Francisco looking for work, crashing on one of my friends' couches. Our friends put the pieces together as they saw us embrace, having heard both of us talk about each other in abstract familiar terms ("my dad" or "my daughter"), but never realizing we were talking about each other. When I asked my dad why he came to San Francisco to find work, he explained that it was simple: he was trying to get his union card for stagehand work, and there was more of an opportunity to join in San Francisco—IATSE Local 16. It was grueling work, driving up and down from Fresno to San Francisco each week, but if he just stuck it out long enough, he might be able to get a good job, a union job, that protected him against the faltering economy. A union meant protection, he told me. A union meant that no matter how bad things got, you were never in it alone.

Meanwhile, I counted down the days until I could make my transition into the secure and stable "good job" of my dreams, which boasted a livable wage as well as benefits like health insurance and paid time off. Then, two weeks before my internship came to a close, an announcement dropped at the Levi Strauss corporate office: the company was on a hiring freeze. No new hires would be approved until further notice. I raced into my supervisor's office.

"What does this mean?" I asked him nervously. "Would I be a new hire? I'm not new, right? I've been here. I'm just . . . changing roles. I'm still set to go full-time and become a real employee, right?"

He tightened his lips and shook his head no with a sad look in his eyes.

"The hiring freeze includes promotions and changes in position," he said sadly. "Since your internship was on contract, it's set to expire at the end of the month, and we can't even retain you in that position since it would technically be a new contract at that point. I'm so sorry, Madeline. You can apply again when the freeze is up, though."

I tried to catch my breath, but it felt like my entire future had been crushed before my eyes in an instant. "How long do you think that will be?" I asked, defeated.

He sighed. "The hiring freeze is set to extend through the end of 2008, and all through 2009," he said.

I nodded solemnly. Well, I thought to myself, at least Toni will be happy.

A few days after my internship at Levi Strauss came to a close, Mervyn's filed for bankruptcy. Mervyn's was located in the East Bay, in a small city called Hayward roughly a one-hour drive away from San Francisco. Mervyn's was a lower-priced department store but had within it a relatively robust team of apparel designers. The closure of the Mervyn's corporate office flooded the small San Francisco design world with newly out-of-work apparel designers. By October 2008, designers with ten years of experience were applying for the few entry-level jobs that popped up online. For recent college graduates like me, not even a prestigious Levi's design internship could help me compete against seasoned design professionals who were desperate and willing to work for $10 per hour. The oversupply of laborers drove the value of design work down within the city limits, making applying for new design jobs completely fruitless. My student loans were set to kick in for repayment in March 2009. I needed something stable and consistent.

Fortunately, Toni was making it through the recession with minor losses. I watched as my fellow college graduates around me floundered, ending up in minimum-wage retail jobs or moving back in with their parents. I counted myself lucky to have a reliable job that paid me well enough to get by.

From October 6 to 10, the stock market in the United States took its largest ever weekly loss, causing Americans— whose retirement funds are typically invested in the stock market via 401(k) accounts and IRAs—to see the value of their life savings plummet. Panicked, some people made ill-advised stock sales, dumping their portfolios at a loss leaving them no chance of recovery. Meanwhile, financial pundits gained viewership on television shows across the country by stoking flames and encouraging this behavior, like Jim Cramer who on October 6 told viewers of the *Today* show to pull their money from the stock market if they needed cash for anything in the next five years. In fact, the stock market bottomed out the following March and began a bull market that lasted for ten years afterward.

The Great Recession raged on, sowing panic and chaos everywhere you looked. By the end of 2008, the federal unemployment rate was 7.2 percent, as small and medium-sized companies around the U.S. collapsed. People seeking unemployment insurance benefits were subjected to constantly busy phone lines, with no hope of getting in touch with anyone to discuss their options. My friends began filling out unemployment application forms and sending them to our state unemployment insurance department via regular mail, with no tracking available, just hoping that one day they might get a check back. In cities like New York, the number of people in homeless shelters jumped 40 percent compared to the previous year. People who had lost their homes due to the recession had no way to get back on their feet.

By 2009, the Great Recession had created a pattern we would all become familiar with. Smaller companies would fail. Bigger companies would get bailed out by Congress. Stock prices would plummet. Houses would get foreclosed on. Wealthy people would buy them for dirt-cheap prices to use as investment properties. The rich would get richer. The poor would become homeless. More people would lose their jobs.

In my world, I had a different problem to contend with. Toni suffered a severe and sudden injury to her back, rendering her unable to work. Without Toni taking pictures, work at the office ground to a halt. I spent the first few months of Toni's injury going through records of old clients. Toni had been working since the 1980s in San Francisco, meaning some of her earliest clients had children who were graduating high school or even college that year. I cold-called them, hoping their phone numbers hadn't changed.

"Hello," I'd say when they answered. "I'm calling from Toni's office. She photographed your baby seventeen years ago, and if my math is correct, that means they're set to graduate from high school this year! Can I interest you in the gift of a photo album of their childhood pics to help send them on their way into adulthood?"

Half the time, it worked. I drummed up as much money in sales as I could making keepsakes for older clients. After a few months, though, I'd been through nearly every old client I could reach, and Toni's injury wasn't improving. She helped me apply for partial unemployment and gave me enough busywork to keep me occupied for fifteen to twenty hours per week.

"Does the unemployment cost you money?" I asked. "I know you don't have income coming in right now. I don't want to be a financial burden. I can get a job at Taco Bell or Starbucks or something."

"Don't be silly," she said. "I've already paid for the unemployment. It comes out as like an insurance or something every paycheck for every employee."

I thought about my friends, some of whom had their unemployment claims denied by their previous employers.

"It doesn't cost businesses anything extra to honor unemployment claims?" I asked.

"No," she said. "Not really . . . maybe higher insurance premiums if it happens a lot. But mostly anyone who denies someone's unemployment claim is just an asshole."

It seemed there were a lot of assholes in the world.

With my new free time, I scoured Craigslist looking for any freelance jobs or gig work I could find. I designed clothing for video games and yoga companies and golfwear lines, often having to wait thirty days or more to get paid for my finished work, and sometimes not getting paid at all because the company ended up filing for bankruptcy. Eventually, I found myself scouring Craigslist looking for a new place to live, too. I moved into a three-bedroom house on the outskirts of town where between ten and twenty people lived at any given time. My rent was $300 per month, a triumph for San Francisco back then, and we put on shows in the basement sometimes to help with the cost of utilities. When that failed, our neighbor—a friendly drug dealer who liked our style—let us run a big orange extension cord from his house to ours so we had electricity.

The house was full of indie rock kids, but it felt more like a punk house than any punk house I'd ever been to. It sat at the edge of town and was a joint effort at survival. There was a revolving door of roommates, with new people seeming to show up every week. Sometimes you'd wake up in the morning and see a stranger in your kitchen—someone another roommate let crash there for $50 a month, sleeping on an old couch in the basement until they got back on their feet. We shared resources with each other the best we could to get by.

One of my roommates wrote a novella on my ten-year-old clunky laptop, hoping to create a new career for himself as a Great American Novelist. Another baked for us with groceries she stole from her work at a coffee shop. At night, we sat at the dining room table—sometimes by candlelight—playing board games and contemplating our lives. We struggled to imagine a future for ourselves beyond the Great Recession, but we were grateful at least that our rent was cheap.

At the not-punk punk house, my friends and I filed for SNAP—previously called food stamps. We spent our afternoons in the park, eating sandwiches we got for free with our EBT cards, lying in the sun and panicking about money. It was a weird feeling, being on what people then called "Funemployment." It was the first time since graduating high school that I'd worked less than full-time. In many ways, it gave me an understanding of the freedom that could come with having a more humane work schedule, one that didn't force me to be on the clock for sometimes sixty to eighty hours per week just to get by. Suddenly, I had time to take up more hobbies and cultivate better relationships with my friends and people around me. On the other hand, though, we all lived with a constant and pressing fear in the backs of our minds. What if this week the unemployment check just didn't come? What if the food stamps on our EBT cards didn't replenish? What if everything somehow fell apart even more in new and horrifying ways we couldn't even imagine? It felt a bit like having detention in summer school. We were forced to do nothing in a liminal state, but we could never quite relax. By the end of 2009, the U.S. unemployment rate hit 10 percent for the first time in twenty-five years. One in ten people in the USA was out of work. Home foreclosures reached 2.9 million in 2009 alone, with a total of nearly 7.5 million home foreclosures since 2007 when the Great Recession began.

The lingering effect that the Great Recession had on my generation—Millennials—is far-reaching and complex. Many, like me, graduated high school or college into a nonexistent job market, meaning we failed to gain the work experience that so many generations who came before us did. Our growth in our careers and professions was forever stunted by this lack of entry-level work in jobs with a long-term growth trajectory. Many people found themselves relegated to decades of low-paying service industry work, simply because those were the jobs hiring at the time, and from that point on, the only jobs in which they had experience.

By 2010, there were roughly 9 million fewer jobs on the market than there had been before the recession. For people in my age range at the time, 16–24, the unemployment rate hit a high of 19 percent, meaning roughly one in five people in my age group struggled to find work. The rest found low-paid work that didn't meet their qualifications or degrees. Millennials are the first generation who even into their thirties failed to earn as much as people who were born a decade earlier had at the same age.

In a response to the oversaturation of service workers and the instability of the labor market in general, something new took shape: the gig economy. In the years that followed the Great Recession, jobs at non-employer "establishments" within the gig economy dramatically outpaced traditional employers. Made up of self-employed freelance workers performing short-term tasks outside a traditional employment capacity, the gig economy is typically made possible by an app of some kind. We know them as Uber or Lyft or DoorDash or TaskRabbit, and it seems new app-based gig services pop up every day. The problem with these gig jobs, though, is that they allow for fewer worker protections, fewer benefits, and less ability for collective bargaining. In short, they're crappy, low-paying jobs with dubious legality.

Today, one in six Americans has a job outside of a traditional employment arrangement, and most of them are Millennials and Gen Z freelance workers within the gig economy. This is a problem because the gig economy is directly contributing to the increased labor exploitation of these two generations. Around one in seven gig workers earn less than the federal minimum wage on an hourly basis, and nearly one in three earn less than their state minimum wage. Studies have found that one in five gig workers went hungry in one year because they could not afford enough food to eat, while 30 percent participate in the Supplementary Nutrition Assistance Program, or SNAP, meaning that public tax dollars are subsidizing these gig companies' refusal to adequately compensate their workers. Meanwhile, the CEOs of these gig-based app companies are bringing in record-high salaries and compensation packages. The implication is astounding. The average taxpaying American is inadvertently paying the employees of billion-dollar corporations so they can buy things like food while their bosses hoard what should be their workers' earnings. These corporate CEOs are stealing from us all.

The housing market, too, has been forever marked by the effects of the Great Recession. While 2007–2009 saw millions of people losing their homes to foreclosures, it also saw an increase in real estate corporations purchasing single-family homes to use as investment properties. Many foreclosed-upon homes were sold in bulk at auctions, facilitating the easy mass purchasing of them as assets. In California alone, the number of owner-occupied homes plummeted by 320,000 from 2006 to 2012. Meanwhile, the number of renter-occupied single-family homes increased by more than twice that. Today, would-be first-time home buyers are forced to compete with major real estate corporations like Blackstone to purchase their first home, contributing to declining rates of home ownership across the United States.

In all, Millennials who lived through the Great Recession have had to contend with unprecedented economic instability, and those who graduated during the recession in particular have been linked to higher premature death rates, including from things like drug overdoses, sometimes called "deaths of despair." The Great Recession was a large-scale economic failure brought about by the ineffectiveness of capitalism, and people my age are still dealing with its aftermath.

We are more likely to be in debt, less likely to have good wages, less likely to have adequate savings, less likely to have career stability, and more likely to encounter severe mental health problems as a result of the experience.

At the punk house, we survived by sticking together—by sharing the last of our food stamps with our friends, or putting together basement show fundraisers to pay each other's rent. Elsewhere across the country, other Millennials packed into tiny houses, three or more to a room, to weather the economic storm. While our politicians bailed out their friends at major corporations and left us to fend for ourselves, we did our best to bail each other out, too. It's the lesson that we learn time and time again in moments of crisis: we're stronger together. We left the Great Recession with triumphant understandings of what communities can do when they work together, juxtaposed with the harsh realization that the people in power didn't care about us and never would. When left by the rich and powerful to fend for ourselves, many of us chose to fend together. Millennials might have been the first generation in U.S. history to collectively realize that capitalism was built on a house of cards, while the rich took bets on when and how it would fall.

Eventually, my unemployment benefits came to a close, but the fashion industry in San Francisco failed to rebound as quickly as other industries. I had survived the Great Recession with a little help from my friends, but my professional future working in San Francisco was a non-starter. I imagined an alternate reality, one where the Great Recession had never happened, and I was working full-time at Levi's with the stable, steady corporate design job of my dreams. In those fantasies, I had things that were so simple but felt unobtainable to me now: a studio apartment, health insurance, and a savings account. It was hard to accept the fact that something that had been so close was now so far out of reach. Exasperated, I called one of my friends in Los Angeles to commiserate.

"I just don't know what I'm going to do for work," I said, near tears. "There aren't jobs here anymore, not like there used to be."

"Why don't you just move to Los Angeles already," he said, sounding annoyed. "You know, the place with all of the jobs? And all of your friends? And all of the better parties, if I'm being honest. San Francisco does *not* have good night-life."

I laughed a little. "Our house parties are fun!" I said, intentionally missing the point. "I don't know. I guess I'm afraid."

"Life starts at the end of your comfort zone," he quoted. "Or whatever."

In that moment, it felt like no truer platitude had ever been spoken. I could stay in San Francisco and drown trying to piece together freelance and part-time work without a safety net, or I could move to Los Angeles and try my hand at getting a more stable job in a bigger market.

On January 1, 2010, I gave in. I packed my things into a U-Haul and drove it across the Bay Bridge, crying as I said goodbye to the city I loved.

Making It Out of a Recession Alive

Recessions are no joke. In periods of economic downturn, it may be more difficult to find or retain employment. You may find your wages stagnating, prices rising, and general financial panic all around you. Here are some tips for making it through a recession in one piece:

1. Find out which government assistance programs you are eligible for. Your state should have its own state social services agencies. Often, these will include programs that offer financial assistance and support, especially if you are in economic crisis. Visit usa.gov/state-social-services to see what's available in your state. Don't hesitate to apply for everything. You never know what you'll be eligible for. If you qualify for it, it's for you. Don't be shy about taking help when you need it—it's funded by your tax dollars and mine. I'm personally telling you right now that I want my tax dollars to help you out when you need it, and I'm sure there are millions more people who agree! Your city might also have a building called something like the Department of Social Services or Department of Human Services where someone is on staff to help you apply.

2. If you lose your job, apply for unemployment assistance immediately. If your hours get cut, remember that you can apply for partial unemployment assistance, too, to cover the loss of hours.

3. Keep up-to-date with current laws regarding things like evictions. In crisis situations, there tend to be emergency laws passed to protect people from things like eviction. Find out the federal, state, and city protections available to you and keep on top of them! They often are extended and altered, and you want to make sure you're taking advantage of every protection you're entitled to!

4. Experiment with growing your own food. Things like microgreens and herbs are easy to grow in small spaces like a kitchen counter and can help you save when times are tough. Some foods can easily be regrown from food scraps, too, like potatoes, onions, garlic, celery, carrots, lettuce, basil, mint, cilantro, parsnips, shallots, and sweet potatoes.

5. To scratch your shopping itch, set up clothing swaps with your friends. Trading your clothing with each other can feel like cleaning out your closet and shopping at the same time. It's a win-win.

6. Scour listings for free stuff on Craigslist when you need something for your house. I've gotten vacuum cleaners, refrigerators, couches, televisions, mattresses, and more from the free section of Craigslist. Sometimes people even give away food and plants. Be sure you're checking every free resource available to you before spending money on anything. If you've lost your job and you have more time available, you can get free furniture on Craigslist and fix it up with paint to make it feel like something new.

7. If you lose your job, view the time off as an opportunity. When we're stressed out, it's really easy for us to not take advantage of the time off many of us encounter when we're unable to work through a recession. We're too worried about making ends meet to enjoy the break, and for many of us, it's the only chance we have to ever take a break at all. Try to remember to carve out little amounts of time to enjoy yourself. Try learning a new skill in the time off work. A lot of skills you can teach yourself at home for free on YouTube. Alternatively, use it as an opportunity to work on art or a project you've never been able to get around to. You can also use this as a chance to do absolutely nothing. It might feel weird, but start by scheduling hours of your day where you're not allowed to do a single responsible or productive thing. When you schedule in time off, you usually feel better about relaxing because it's what you're supposed to be doing right now.

8. If you find yourself panicking, take this time to come up with a financial plan. Imagine the cheapest scenario for you to ever possibly live. Map it out. Where are you living? What is your income? What is your budget? Who do you live with? You don't have to act on it, but just knowing you have a "shit is hitting the fan" backup plan will go a long way to helping to ease your mind in times of uncertainty.

9. Trade skills with people in your community. If you're great at baking, for example, but have some clothes that need hemming, consider offering to make bread in exchange for alterations with someone you know who sews. Most of the time, just offering goes a long way and you'll find your friends and family and neighbors—with more time on their hands due to layoffs—will help you out for free.

10. If you have student loans or other debt, check to see if you can defer your payments due to economic hardship. You might end up paying more interest in the long run, but depending on how dire your financial situation is, the extra cash from not making those monthly payments could be worth it.

CHAPTER 7

We're "Comfortable"

"Do you like living in Los Angeles?"

I was at a house party. A friend of a friend—a hairstylist—was chatting with me about my recent move to L.A.

"Sure," I told him. "I loved San Francisco, but Los Angeles is so much more practical."

"What do you mean, 'practical'?" he asked.

"Well, you know," I said, "it's just an easier place to be. It feels a lot like Fresno to me."

"Fresno?" a girl nearby interrupted, shocked. "How does Los Angeles remind you of Fresno?" She seemed offended by the comparison.

"Well, it's kind of suburban," I said. "There's strip malls and parking lots and single-family houses and drive-thru restaurants. It kinda looks like Fresno, even . . . just more."

She balked. "Los Angeles looks nothing like Fresno."

"It does where I live, in Koreatown," I said, "and where most of my friends live—in Westlake."

"Westlake?" she gasped. "Westlake looks nothing like Fresno! Westlake Village is beautiful."

"Not Westlake Village," I said, confused. "Westlake, the neighborhood in between downtown and Koreatown. By the freeway."

If *A Tale of Two Cities* took place in the greater Los Angeles area, it might have been called *A Tale of Two Westlakes*. Westlake Village, on the west side of town, is an upper-crust white enclave of a little over 8,000 people where the average household income exceeds $160,000 per year. By contrast, the Westlake neighborhood on the east side of Los Angeles is home to over 100,000 people—mostly foreign-born immigrants from Mexico or El Salvador—who earn more like 10 percent of that.

"I've never even heard of another Westlake," the girl said with an air of contempt.

"What neighborhood do you live in?" I asked.

"Beverly Hills," she replied.

That explained it. Beverly Hills was so far away from the Los Angeles I knew and loved that it wasn't even a part of Los Angeles city. It was its own city, with its own laws and rules and police station, which seemed to be hell-bent on keeping the surrounding "riffraff" of the greater L.A. area from coming into the hills and disrupting their perfectly clean and curated way of life.

"What do you do for work?" I asked, probing. Maybe she was famous—an actress or something.

"Oh, I'm too young to work," she said with a laugh. "I go to FIDM."

FIDM, the Fashion Institute of Design & Merchandising, was one of the Los Angeles fashion schools I had researched as a teenager, a point in my own life when I already had years of work experience under my belt. If this twenty-something was too young to work, I wondered what that meant for fourteen-year-old Madeline carrying snacks in a giant box around her neck walking up and down stadium stairs in the summer sun. Tuition alone at FIDM was around $23,000 per year—nearly twice what I paid to attend school in San Francisco. I wasn't sure who could afford to go to a school like that.

"What do your parents do for work?" I asked, trying to make sense of her life.

"My dad owns a few businesses," she replied nonchalantly.

I cracked the code. If you're ever confused about how someone is pulling off a lifestyle that you can't quite make sense of, the answer is usually rich parents.

"Oh," I said, doing my best to smile politely. "You guys are rich. Yeah, I guess you're not coming to the parts of L.A. that look like Fresno too often."

"We're not rich," she said, defensively. "We're comfortable."

Comfortable. When I was growing up, the word "comfortable" meant that dinner was on the table and there was a roof over your head. In certain parts of Los Angeles, though, the word "comfortable" seemed to mean that your parents owned multiple businesses and lived in a mansion somewhere near the beach. The children of "comfort" in L.A. had an American Express platinum card in their dad's name—the kind of credit card that had no monthly spending limits. They swiped away all month long without thinking of the price of their drinks or clothes or meals or concert tickets, and most of them never even saw the bill that arrived at their parents' mega estates on the west side of town. There, a family money manager paid the bill off promptly each month without question. In some circles, I had come to learn, "comfort" was another word for "excess."

On the east side of town, though, far from the affluence of Beverly Hills and Malibu, Los Angeles did feel a lot like home to me. My grandmother grew up on the east side of Los Angeles herself before rising rents and diminishing work opportunities forced her family to relocate to Fresno in the first place. Those east side strip malls that felt so familiar had old Hondas and Nissans and Toyotas parked out front, sometimes held together with shiny silver duct tape at the bumper or side-view mirror—the telltale sign of uninsured drivers colliding with each other on the busy Los Angeles freeways during their daily commute. The further west you went, a different type of Los Angeles emerged—one with sun-soaked celebrities driving fancy sports cars downhill from their mansions to buy $20 smoothies and designer drugs. The west side is where the affluent live. The eastsiders are the ones who clean their houses.

While most of my Los Angeles friends spent years trying to convince me to give the city a chance, my friend Remy had also spent years trying to convince me to give him a chance. We'd met when I was just eighteen years old in the fall of 2004 when his band played my friend's art opening in Downtown L.A. We bonded over music and fashion, and I'd sometimes crash at whatever filthy party house he was living in when I came to L.A. to visit. The houses he lived in were always something to behold—with bare mattresses plopped in random places like hallways or the dining room, and with the kitchen appliances sometimes pulled out into the living room to make space for DIY band practices. Once, when I was around twenty years old, I opened his kitchen cabinets to find nothing in them but a single can of soup.

"What's going on here?" I asked, perplexed.

"Well, the can of soup is there because we don't have a spoon, so nobody could figure out how to eat it," he said.

"Why don't you have a spoon?" I asked, incredulous.

"Well, we just have the one fork," he replied, as though it were the most normal thing in the world.

Later that night, while out to eat at a cheap restaurant with Remy and his roommates, I brought up the cutlery situation in their house.

"Who has just one fork?" I asked. "What is up with you guys?"

His roommate Abraham looked off into the distance wistfully, as if remembering something painful.

"I haven't seen the fork in a while," he said. "Does anyone know where it is?"

Remy responded by getting up from the table and stealing a handful of forks from the restaurant's service cart.

"Here," he said, shoving them into his bag. "Now we have forks."

That night, I took him to the grocery store and bought him some groceries.

"You need to eat more," I told him.

"Yeah, yeah," he said. "Food is just so expensive."

I understood. At my most broke in San Francisco, I once ate a bag of expired microwave popcorn dipped in leftover chocolate frosting. It was all I had in the house. The popcorn was mushy and strange, but the chocolate frosting concealed the weird spongey texture. Most days, I just ate a combination of potatoes and rice—things that were affordable at the grocery store but lacked any real nutritional value. Whenever I had a little bit of extra money, I went overboard—spending it at dinner in a restaurant, ordering everything that sounded good on the menu. It was feast or famine—my inconsistent approach to finance reflected my youthful outlook on money in general: you'd usually be broke, so when you weren't, you'd really need to make it count by getting yourself all the special little treats you'd been denied for so long. This, I decided, was how you made life worth living.

When I finally moved to Los Angeles (roughly three years after the fork incident), Remy and I rented a studio apartment in Koreatown together for $1,100 per month. It was massive—one thousand square feet—and it was a corner unit on the top floor with views of the Downtown skyline out one set of windows and views of the hills out the other. If you angled your head just right, you could see the Hollywood sign from the toilet, which was the closest thing to luxury I'd ever experienced. We each paid just $550 per month, which felt like a bargain to me coming from the even more inflated rent prices of San Francisco. Still, I had other expenses to contend with: student loans and credit card bills. I was racking up massive amounts of debt, and I hoped I'd be able to find a job that would serve as the light at the end of the tunnel.

Unlike in the small and competitive market of San Francisco, Los Angeles was a huge place where there was always work to be found. Like San Francisco, though, the jobs in my field—apparel design—all paid around $10 per hour. It was barely enough to live on, let alone enough to handle the expense of my new student loan payments and a car. Los Angeles was a car-centric city, like most places in the United States, and the pressure to acquire a new vehicle could add $300 or more on to my monthly expenses. I broadened my job search, applying for administrative assistant positions where my degree wasn't even relevant or necessary. Those jobs paid more than ones in my field, starting at more like $15 per hour and paying up to $25. So much for my college degree, I thought with a sigh.

I interviewed for five different positions the first week I arrived in L.A., digging through moving boxes to scrounge up anything I could that remotely resembled appropriate office attire. I smiled and nodded my way through every interview, trying to craft a persona that screamed "I'm reliable and hard-working, but humble and eager to learn!" At twenty-three, with nearly a decade's worth of work experience under my belt, I'd learned a few things about what prospective employers were looking for: they wanted someone who went above and beyond, but never threatened their boss's power. I could be the perfect worker bee: mindless, buzzing, in constant motion without a thought of my own, if it meant collecting a paycheck. I took out my nose ring, kept my hair dyed a sensible natural color, and covered up all my tattoos. Getting employed was a matter of survival. There was no room for luxuries like fashion.

By my final interview of the week, though—applying to be the assistant to the director of sales and marketing at a high-end jewelry brand—my business casual was all in the wash. Frustrated, I put on a cardigan over my normal clothing—a vintage lingerie-style tank top and a pair of ripped jeans—and sent a text message asking them to forgive my appearance in advance since I'd just moved to town and my clothing was all packed away. It was an unprofessional message to send, and I assumed that it, coupled with my appearance, would cost me the job, but I figured it was better than nothing. When I arrived at the interview, the Director looked me up and down.

"I'm so sorry about . . . this," I said, gesturing to my outfit. It was a far cry from the trousers and collared shirt I usually tried to wear to office interviews, and I felt my face flush hot with embarrassment.

"Don't apologize," she said with a smile. "It's fashion, it's what we do."

The Director liked me, I could tell. She smiled when I spoke. I liked her, too, for what it was worth. She was eccentric and offbeat, speaking a bit like a character that I imagined would have been written into an episode of *Sex and the City*, had I ever seen it. She could speak fluent Spanish with a European accent, something I'd never heard before, and wore layers of jewelry piled high on top of a simple T-shirt. Looking at her was like looking into a world I'd only ever heard existed—something mythical and faraway and glamorous that seemed out of reach for someone like me.

At the end of the interview, I asked if she could clarify the starting wage for the position, since it hadn't been listed online.

"Oh," she responded happily, "it's ten dollars per hour!"

My face paled.

"I'm so sorry to have wasted your time," I said politely while standing up. "I unfortunately cannot afford to live on ten dollars per hour. I have student loans and rent to pay—I'm sure you understand. Apologies. Thank you for the interview, though. It really was lovely to meet you."

As I stood up to exit the room, the Director jumped up to her feet after me.

"Wait," she said. "I like you. You're fashionable. You get it. And you seem like a hard worker. I think this could be a good fit. What were you hoping the pay would be?"

I thought about Laura at the photo lab in Santa Cruz. What would I realistically need to live an all right life in Los Angeles?

"Well," I said, "I think it would have to be something more like twenty-five dollars per hour."

I expected the Director to apologize and wish me well on my job hunt. After all, it was over twice the wage they were offering. Instead, she looked me in the eyes and nodded her head once in understanding.

"I'll see what I can do," she said earnestly.

A few days later, the Director called me on the phone.

"I couldn't get twenty-five dollars," she said, "but I got eighteen. I want you to know I really fought for it. Is there any chance we can make this work?"

I thought about my other job offers. There was a corporate assistant job at a big building downtown. The pay was good, more like $20 per hour, but I'd have to wear a suit all day which meant added costs for a whole new wardrobe, and there was no opportunity for growth. The position was nowhere near my field, and I wouldn't be qualified to advance beyond the assistant role. There was a job offer to be a receptionist at an office in Koreatown. The office was staffed entirely by older men, none of whom seemed interested in my humanity—just my ability to type 102 words per minute. During the interview, they called me a "young woman" in a way that made my skin crawl. I could only imagine how much stranger the dynamic would be if I was in the office every day. I remembered something a teacher once told me about job hunting: it's better to be at the bottom rung of a ladder you want to climb than at the top of one you don't want to be on. I liked the Director, and the prospect of being in a position that at least provided some tangential training in my actual field seemed valuable on its own.

"Okay," I said. "I'll do it. But I want a salary and performance review after six months."

"Done," she said.

The Director owned a house in the neighborhood of Silver Lake on the east side of town. We worked out of a spare room in her home, loosely connected to a network of other employees across the globe via telephone and email. Her house was in a rapidly gentrifying neighborhood, one I specifically tried to avoid in my own house-hunting efforts due to ethical trepidation about my presence being a negative factor in the "change" happening there. I was low-income and working class, but still felt a bit like the Harbinger of Gentrification. Wherever I went, other people—ones with more money than me—saw my presence like a waving green flag on the shoreline proclaiming "Come on in, the water's fine!" If I moved into a neighborhood, it seemed it was just a matter of years before the taco shops and laundromats were replaced with fancy coffee shops and organic candle stores.

To the Director, though, buying a home in an "up-and-coming" neighborhood just made sense.

"It's going to give me a fantastic return on investment when I sell it come retirement," she said. "Did you know you're supposed to have two million dollars saved for your retirement? Who can muster up all of that? Buying a house is the best chance we have."

I struggled to position the Director in my mental framework of money. The six-figure salary and beautiful home in a gentrifying neighborhood was something that teenage punk rock Madeline would have associated with "the enemy." In reality, a six-figure salary didn't make a person rich in Los Angeles—even if it meant they were a lot richer than I was. In the year 2010, HUD set the "very low income limit" in L.A. at anything less than $63,000 per year, which means you'd have to make over $30 per hour to just not be considered broke. The Director was nowhere near the Beverly Hills and Westlake Village socialites with $100 million or more to their name. She was just a middle-class person doing her best to figure out a survival plan as a single childless woman in her forties.

Part of her survival meant answering to the owner of the jewelry brand—a horrific man with a short fuse who subjected her to psychological and verbal abuse nearly daily. She weathered it all for the chance at having a comfortable life with a nice place to call home and enough money to live off until she died. In addition to performing her regular job duties, she also took on the role of a protector at the company—shielding other employees from the very abuse she suffered at the hands of the Owner every day.

"I have to guard them," she told me once, pointedly, "from him."

In this role, the Director moved masterfully. She deftly scheduled meetings and appointments in complex maneuvers to minimize the most fragile or vulnerable employees' exposure to the Owner. She kept women away from him especially, lest he do something offensive or inappropriate. For my part, I was never allowed to be in the same room as him.

"He will sexually harass you," she said flatly.

If small businesses often thought of themselves like a family, the Owner of this one was the explosive neglectful father who came home from work in a bad mood ready to make everyone in the house feel uncomfortable and unsafe. The Director played the protective mother, closing doors around him and taking the brunt of the yelling lest anyone else be subjected to his outbursts. It wasn't a role she should have been expected to take on, and it felt gendered in a way that reeked of patriarchal expectation of emotional labor on the part of women in the workforce. I was supposed to hate bosses and people who wore expensive shoes, but truth be told, I *liked* the Director. Was she the Enemy? She certainly didn't seem like it.

The Director's life, instead, appeared to be one of constant paradox. She had a lot of power at the company, but also not very much. At any given moment, the Owner could decide to undermine her planning or organizing, to do whatever he wanted—even if that meant firing people she considered top staff, or berating her over the telephone for hours. She made a good amount of money, but not nearly as much as the Owner. She had a nice house and a few items of clothing I'd categorize as "expensive," but she seemed to acknowledge that planning for her retirement was an ongoing source of financial stress in her life that she was trying her best to navigate. She lived a humble and modest life in many ways.

One of the most confounding things about the Director in my mind was her car. The Director drove an old Jeep—new enough to not be considered vintage or classic, but old enough to be a perplexing choice to me given her income bracket and impressive work title. It was champagne gold from the 1990s—hardly the car I associated with "directors"—and it seemed like every few months, something on it broke.

"Why don't you get a new car?" I asked her one day. "Something nicer?"

"Why would I get a new car?" she asked, seeming genuinely confused. "This one is paid off and it works fine. Repairing it every few months is a lot cheaper than buying a whole new vehicle."

The answer surprised me. "Wouldn't a new car be just a couple hundred dollars extra each month?" I asked.

"Sure," she said, "but that would be a couple of hundred dollars less per month going into my retirement account, and cars are depreciating assets."

I didn't know what a retirement account or a depreciating asset was, but I nodded along anyway like I understood.

"Are you saving for your retirement?" she asked me.

"No," I said, shaking my head. "I'm just trying to pay off debt and survive."

"I think this is going to be a growth job for you," she said, smiling.

I didn't realize it at the time, but the Director was going to teach me things about how the world worked. A few weeks later, she came back from a work trip to Europe—where the Owner of the company lived—and plopped a phone bill down on my desk.

"Two hundred dollars," she said.

I looked at the bill. It was for nearly one thousand dollars.

"What do you mean, two hundred dollars?" I asked. "This is well over nine hundred."

"Two hundred dollars is all I'll pay," she said. "Make it happen."

I stared at the bill on my desk. I knew you could negotiate debt, but I had no idea how you went about changing the amount of money you owed on something like a phone bill. The idea of calling and asking a customer service person to bend or break the rules for me seemed both ridiculous and terrifying. Could they even do that? I sighed and picked up the bill, trying to figure out how I was going to make this happen. I called their customer service line pretending to be the Director and spoke with the person who answered.

"This bill," I said, slowly. "I think . . . maybe there's a mistake. I think . . . it's wrong?"

"No," they said, pulling up the account. "It's right. You went to Europe and used data roaming the whole time. You used a lot of it, too, it looks like."

"Okay, sorry, thank you—have a good day," I mumbled, and hung up the phone.

"They won't do it," I told the Director.

"Try again," she told me flatly, then turned to her computer to work.

I called the customer service line back. Someone new answered this time.

"I have a bill here," I said, more confidently. "I need to negotiate a lower price. I can't afford to pay this."

"Ma'am, we can't just change the bill," the man on the phone said, seeming to stifle a laugh. "You used the data, you have to pay for it."

"Can I . . . speak to your manager?" I asked, my voice raising up high at the end.

"You can try," the man said. He connected me to a supervisor.

"What seems to be the problem?" the supervisor asked coldly.

"I can't afford to pay this bill," I told him. "Can you . . . can we . . . like, uh, negotiate?"

"Negotiate what?" he asked.

"Like, a lower price," I said. "Like, say . . . two hundred dollars."

"We don't really do that, ma'am," the man replied. "You'll have to pay the bill in full, or we will send it to collections. Is there anything else I can help you with?"

"Oh," I said, sighing in defeat. "No, not really. That's all."

"Have a nice day, then," he said.

He hung up, and I listened to the dial tone for a second in my ear.

I turned back around to the Director.

"I think you have to pay the bill," I told her. "He told me they can't change it. I talked to a manager and everything."

"Try again," she said.

If this was an exercise, it was humiliating. I called the customer service line back again and this time, a woman answered.

"You're from Los Angeles?" she squealed while pulling up the Director's data. She had a sweet-sounding southern accent and I could hear the smile in her voice when she spoke. "Oh, that's so amazing. I would just love to get to go there one day! What do you do for work?"

"I work in fashion," I said half-heartedly.

"Wow," she gasped. "That must be so glamorous. Just like *The Devil Wears Prada*!"

I perked up.

"Kind of," I said. "Yes, actually, just like that. Have you seen the movie?"

"I have," she said. "I just love it! That Miranda Priestly, what a character!"

"Okay, well, I have a situation right now that's actually . . . a lot like *The Devil Wears Prada*," I told her. "Only I'm Andrea, the assistant, and my boss is a lot like Miranda

Priestly, the editor of the magazine, and I have to figure out a way to make her happy or I'm going to be in big trouble. I don't know what to do. Can you help me?"

"Ooooh," she replied happily. "How exciting! Yes, I've got you. What do we need to make happen?"

On the phone, I explained the bill. I told her all about how the Director plopped it down on my desk and yelled a number, how I'd spent the whole day calling and talking to people, and I wasn't sure exactly how on earth I was going to make this happen. As I explained, I looked over my shoulder at the Director, who was sitting within earshot of the call. She didn't flinch or react as I explained the story, even at the parts where I leaned into the absurdity of the request or implied that she was difficult and unreasonable for wanting this in the first place.

"Hold on a second," the girl on the phone said, clacking away on her keyboard loudly. Something was happening. I'd never made it this far before.

"Okay," I told her. "Thank you for even listening, honestly, nobody else let me get this far!"

"No problem," she said. "We girls have to stick together. Okay, I think I have an idea. Now, if your boss had purchased the international data plan before leaving the country, she could have had unlimited data on her trip for an extra hundred dollars for the month. Her regular phone plan looks like it's around fifty dollars per month, meaning her total monthly bill would come in at one hundred and fifty dollars, well below the two hundred dollars she told you she needs it at. I just checked and I can retroactively apply that purchase to her account with a manager override, and it just so happens that my manager here owes me a favor. Do you mind holding while I get her approval?"

"Of course not!" I gasped, shocked. "Thank you!"

A few minutes later, the override was entered and the Director's final phone bill had been amended: $152.12— much less than the $200 she'd demanded. I hung up the phone, speechless, and turned to her.

"I did it. I can't believe I did it," I said, shocked. "Did you know they'd be able to change it? Had you done that before or something?"

"No," she said. "But people usually have the power to do much more for you than they are willing to admit. The phone company doesn't actually need the extra eight hundred dollars. It's just about finding someone who is willing to listen to you and bend the rules a little in your favor. I told you, I think this is going to be a growth job for you."

The Director smiled, then held up a huge sparkling silver-and-gold ring. "Now, tell me," she said. "How much do you think this ring should cost?"

"A hundred dollars?" I said, pulling the number out of thin air. I'd never spent more than $15 on a piece of jewelry in my life.

"*A hundred dollars?*" she scoffed. "Noooooo, look at all of the detail on this! Making the mold alone must have taken hours—plus the sterling silver and eighteen-karat gold on here? The pricing works out to thirty-four hundred dollars on a conventional model, but I think that's a bit too high since there's so much silver on it."

She stared at the ring, gently moving it back and forth so that it glistened in the sunlight coming through the office window. "I think it needs to come in at more like thirty-one hundred dollars," she said. "I'll do that, we'll take a small loss but we'll make up for it in volume."

The Director spun back around to her computer, inputting the new price. Stunned, I stared at the back of her head, and then at the ring on her desk, which apparently cost more than my first two cars. There was a lot about the world I didn't know. In my desire to not ask for too much, it turns out I hadn't been asking nearly enough of the world around me. The trick, I realized, was in figuring out how much "enough" truly was. The Director was right—this would be a growth job for me, in more ways than one.

. . .

While I adjusted to my new job, Remy—a brilliant musician burnt out by years of near misses in the music industry—signed up for college, enrolling in a new field of art called motion graphics at a prestigious Los Angeles art school. From an outside perspective, Remy's financial background seemed to be a lot like mine. He was thrifty and frugal, wearing clothes from secondhand stores covered in holes from years of wear. He carefully rationed out his leftover food, making a $3 burrito from a truck down the street last for days. Like most talented musicians, he had always seemed to be on the verge of a big break that never quite came to fruition. He was the quintessential "starving artist"—committed to his music whatever the cost. He worked day jobs off and on, retail jobs at places like Ed Hardy and American Apparel around Los Angeles—the types of stores that hired hip well-dressed young people to act as billboards for the brand to lure in potential customers—but seldom worked more than a few shifts per week.

I was considered the more financially stable of the two of us. My income was more consistent, after all, and I often found myself treating us both to things like $40 dinners—fancy by my standards—or movie dates at the theater. One weekend, we drove to the Grand Canyon on a whim—driving straight through all the way in the middle of the night to make it there and back in time for me to go to work on Monday. On the trip, it was me who paid for things like gas and the strange little hotel room we stayed in next to a carnival in a small town a few miles away. I was used to helping out people in my life who had less than me, a holdover from my days in the Tower District when we all helped each other get by. Looking at Remy, it made sense that I would be the one to pick up his financial slack while he worked on figuring out a life plan that would pay the bills.

As my first year of living in Los Angeles came to a close, Remy invited me to his family's home in Portland, Oregon, for the holidays. I knew his parents were still married, and I expected that with a two-income household, they probably lived in a house rather than a small apartment like my mom or dad. I expected a modest house—a Craftsman-style construction (commonplace in Portland) somewhere on the outskirts of town. As we drove to his parents' house from the airport, though, I was surprised to see us turn in to a gated community on top of a huge hill. As we entered the community at the base of the hill, I saw giant two-story homes with expansive backyards and brand-new cars parked out front. The higher up the hill we drove, the more extravagant the houses became. I looked out the window, perplexed. Finally, we reached nearly the top of the hill and pulled the car into a driveway in front of a massive house decorated with pillars and a fountain out front. It overlooked all of Portland below, with gorgeous views either way you turned. The Director's house looked shabby by comparison. We walked in the front door and I dropped my bags on the marble floors, speechless.

"This is the nicest house I've ever seen," I sputtered, in a state of shock.

The ceilings were so high you could fit another floor on top of us. The back wall of the house was made entirely of windows and glass-paned doors leading out to a balcony. The furniture was brand-new and top of the line, some pieces still with tags on them from a store his parents owned in the city.

"My dad worked as an architect for a while," he said casually. "He designed it. Come on, I'll give you the tour."

Remy led me around the house, showing me the huge kitchen, formal dining room, breakfast nook, spacious living room, and two bedrooms and bathrooms.

"Do we stay in the spare room here?" I asked, peeking my head around the corner of one of the giant doorframes that seemed twice as tall as any door I'd ever seen before.

"Oh, we're not staying on this floor," he said.

I was puzzled. From the outside, the house appeared to be just one story—massive, yes, but all on one floor. Where were the other stories? I looked up, wondering what I'd missed, but Remy instead led me around a corner to a giant staircase, going downwards. I peered over the edge of the stairs and grew dizzy watching it descend multiple floors below us. I stood for a second, frozen, trying to take it all in.

"We could take the elevator if you'd rather do that?" he asked. "With the bags, I mean."

"There's an *elevator*?!" I shrieked.

The house had two additional floors below, built into the hillside. Each floor was enormous, like its own separate house, complete with its own wraparound balcony and view of the city below. The second floor down had four bedrooms, two bathrooms, and a giant living room with a fireplace, television, piano, and leather sectional couch. The third floor down was for entertaining, he explained. It had a sauna, home gym, wine cellar, and ballroom—among other things. By the time we reached the ballroom, I felt my blood beginning to boil.

"You let me buy you groceries!" I told him, exasperated. "Why didn't you tell me your parents were rich?"

"They're not rich," he said, annoyed. "They're . . . comfortable."

Back at home, confounded by the realization that Remy's parents were far wealthier than I could have imagined, I thought about the Director. I was learning more about money than I ever thought possible, and not just from her. As I left my apartment one day, I stopped to pick up a flyer that was shoved into my door handle. These flyers showed up from time to time, in Spanish, advertising job openings for sewers at the American Apparel factory downtown. The positions paid far better than average sewing jobs around town—$20 per hour. I'd never bothered to apply because I didn't speak Spanish that well, but the Director didn't know that. I took the flyer with me to work and put it on the Director's desk.

"What's this?" she asked. "Why is this on my desk?"

"It's a flyer for a job opening," I told her. "They dropped it at my house today. It's for a sewing supervisor at the American Apparel factory downtown. They make two dollars per hour more than I do. I know how to use the machines they advertise on the flyer. I learned in school. Just something to think about. My performance review is coming up, that's all."

The Director held the flyer in her hand and looked at me with a strange mix of shock and pride.

"Noted," she said, nodding.

Back at home, I prepared for my upcoming performance review with dedication and intention. I scoured the internet looking for comparable pay for my job in Los Angeles. I found a graph online showing the range of pay, from low to high, with the average outlined in the middle. My pay was below average for the industry. I printed the graph out and brought it with me to my performance review a few weeks later, folded up in my bag.

"Would you say my performance is below average, average, or above average?" I asked the Director the day of my review.

"Above average," she said confidently, nodding.

"I'm so glad you think so," I replied, pulling out the paper. "Here's a graph of average pay for this position here in Los Angeles. As you can see here, my current pay is in the below average range for this position. My desired pay of twenty-five dollars per hour works out to around fifty-two thousand dollars per year and is here in the average range. Since you think I'm an *above* average employee, according to this chart, I should be making above average wages, upwards of seventy-five thousand dollars per year. However, I know that this is a relatively small company and might not be able to afford a salary like that at this time. I like working here, and I would be thrilled to stay on at the discounted average pay rate of fifty-two thousand dollars."

The following week, I received a pay raise and shift to a salaried position of $52,000 per year, plus health insurance. It worked out to take-home pay of around $3,000 per month.

For the first time in a long time, it felt like I could finally breathe financially.

"This is the most anyone in this position has ever earned," the Director told me seriously. "I had to fight with the Owner for days on this, but I want you to know it's because I think you're worth it."

There was a whole lot of money out there in the world, more than I thought. I didn't need a lot of it, but I deserved more than I was getting, that's for sure. I was determined to get enough of it to scrape by.

When I think back to working for the Director and how hard I struggled to position her economically in my mind, I realize now that categorizing people with six-figure salaries as "rich" was a disservice to the average American worker, who would need nearly that just to have a shot at totally normal things like saving for retirement or owning a home. Pitting low-wage workers against middle-wage workers does little to alleviate the economic stress that low-wage workers experience, and does everything to remove the social pressure from the uber-wealthy who benefit the most. Realizing that "richer than me" did not necessarily mean "rich" was difficult for me, conceptually, and ignited a frustration that was hard to parse. When I was able to sort through it, though, I came to find that my frustration was more with the system on the whole than with any one person who managed to actually earn the six-figure salary we all needed if we wanted to comfortably achieve the American middle-class dream we were promised.

As I learned more about the way money flowed through the world around me, I developed a framework to understand how things "worked." What I realized is that the rich don't work a job for money, not like everybody else. The rich own companies and apartment buildings and make everyone else—people like me and people like the Director—do their work for them. There was no denying that the Director was better off than me financially, but as I saw her struggle to make imperfect decisions in an imperfect system just to ensure her own survival, I realized that we had more in common than I originally thought. We were both running the same race—me in my Dr. Martens and she in her Ferragamo pumps; she was just a little further ahead than I was. Neither of us were winning.

How to Negotiate Higher Pay

When it comes to finding a job, it's always better to be at the bottom rung of a ladder you want to climb than to be at the top of one you don't want to be on. Being on the bottom rung of the ladder doesn't mean you can't negotiate higher pay, though! Here are three ways to get higher pay out of your current job:

1. Consult the internet to see if you are being underpaid in your current position, and if so, share that data with your current employer. Look up your job online in your area to find average pay rates. You might need to enter your pay to access the data, but that's okay! It's crowd-collected, so entering your salary helps other people know what to expect. If your pay is in the lower rung, ask your employer if they think your performance is at least average. If they say yes, show them the graph and ask for average pay to match. If your pay is at the average level, ask if your performance is above average and if so, request the pay to match.

2. Leverage other job offers. Apply for a few other jobs in your field, following through to the interview stage. If you receive an offer higher than your current rate, show your offer letter to your current employer. Tell them you love the company and enjoy being a part of the team, but have just received an offer to go somewhere else. Ask if they can beat the offer. Oftentimes, at the very least, they will match it. If they cannot, you now have an offer for a better job in your field, which you can feel free to take. Switching jobs is also an excellent way to earn more pay! This practice is sometimes called "job hopping," and job hopping results in salary growth that is 12 percent greater compared to people who stay in the same position over time.

3. Utilize wage transparency and collective bargaining. You and your coworkers are stronger together. Remember that in the United States, your employer cannot legally prohibit you from sharing your salary information with your coworkers, even if they try to discourage it. The more you and your coworkers know about each other's wages, the better idea you have about what is fair pay and what your company can afford. If your individual attempts to negotiate a raise fail, it's probably time to unionize at your company! On average, union workers earn 11.2 percent more than non-union workers do. Search the internet for union organizers in your field to get help.

CHAPTER 8

Rags to Rags

One day in 2011, I walked into the Director's house and found her sitting at her desk, in her chair, waiting for me.

"Uh-oh," I said grimly. "Is today the day I get fired?"

"Heavens, no," she said, shaking her head. "We do need to talk, though. I'm leaving the company in thirty days. I just . . . I just can't do this anymore, you know?"

I knew. In the past few months alone, I'd heard from coworkers that the Owner had sexually harassed a sales representative, hurled a racially charged comment at a client, and referred to an employee as a "big bitch" on a conference call, then fired them, only to hire them back a few days later.

"What happens to me?" I asked, confused. Surely, I couldn't be the assistant to the director of sales and marketing if there was no director of sales and marketing.

"You'll keep doing the tasks you've been doing," she said, "and realistically take over some of mine when I leave, I assume—things like photo shoots and line sheets. You'll be fine. You're too essential at this company now, they need you. No pay increase, of course. Sorry about that."

Of course. Still, I felt lucky to have a job at all. Over the next few weeks, I slowly moved my work supplies out of the Director's office and into my studio apartment to begin working from home. The Director and other employees felt confident that my work was valuable—essential even—but I knew too much about the Owner to trust that my position would be protected for long. I started scouring Craigslist looking for gig work to transition into what would surely be another stint of prolonged unstable freelancing. I took side jobs doing styling and design work on nights and weekends. I woke up in the middle of the night most nights with a panic attack, terrified of losing my job.

One day, I was talking with a friend, Brit, whose life paralleled mine in many ways. Although I didn't know her back home, she also moved from Fresno to Los Angeles and had a degree in apparel design.

"What if we started a business together," she said one day. "Just so we had something stable we could work on. Get us out of this bad situation we're both in."

"What would the business be?" I asked her. "I don't have any money. Maybe two hundred dollars I could pitch in?"

Even with my raise up to $52,000 per year—which I had thought was a dream salary that would be more than enough to pay for my every whim—I was having a hard time getting by. It seemed like as fast as the money came in, it went out. I felt like a failure. I had what I considered at the time to be a good salary. Why wasn't I able to make it work? The answer was my debt, which due to the high interest rates seemed to increase every month rather than go down. I was contending with a seemingly insurmountable pile of it, which grew so slowly around me every day that I hardly noticed it happening. There was a car loan for a seemingly reliable Volvo that turned out to be a lemon, credit card debt from medical emergencies and countless repairs to the lemon of a car, and a personal loan from struggling to balance the credit card bills. Combined with my student loans, I owed more than my annual salary in debt: $52,200. If debt was a club and my monthly payments were the fee for entry like I'd told my mom when I was a kid, I was beginning to wonder if the membership was even worth it.

On top of having absolutely no idea how money functioned, I was stressed out all the time and constantly looking for "special treats" to dull the pain—call it the "chaotic spending" category in my monthly expenses. I didn't realize it then, but I was also struggling with ADHD, which made impulsive spending an issue in my life that was hard to control. Still, I could muster $200 to put into starting something new.

"I could put in two hundred dollars, too," Brit said. Like me, Brit was bogged down with debt from years of trying to exist in a system of relatively low pay and high costs. "We could start simple, with what we know—vintage clothing. We could rework or modify the vintage stuff, and then maybe even start to sell our own designs, too, made to order—not a lot of money up front. We could sell it all online so we don't have to pay rent somewhere."

It was a compelling argument. We were two broke Millennials, in debt at shaky unstable jobs with no future. Maybe we could make our own future.

"Okay," I said. "I'm in. Let's do it. Let's set a goal—we'll have a website up and running by January of next year."

It was September, which gave us months to prepare for launch. To start, we needed to pick a name. On a piece of blank printer paper, I scribbled out what seemed like hundreds of options. Brit read the list over and grimaced.

"I don't know," she said. "It's so much pressure. How do you choose one?"

"I think maybe the name doesn't matter so much," I said. "Maybe just pick one you hate the least."

"Ugh," she moaned.

Brit was a perfectionist. I viewed perfection as the enemy of done. Together, we balanced each other out. Eventually, she settled on "Tunnel Vision." We went to the county clerk's office and, four hours later, left with a registered business and a certificate authorizing us to legally "do business as" the name Tunnel Vision, which cost around $25 to file. Our California seller's permit was free. We had $375 left from our combined start-up fund of $400.

Back at home, I plugged numbers into a spreadsheet, trying to figure out exactly how much product we would need to launch with to repay our start-up expenses. Since everything was one of a kind, we'd need to put in a ton of work for each piece—sourcing it, repairing it, photographing it, and listing it—to only be able to sell it once. The labor costs were high, so every piece would have to be worthwhile. Vintage was easy to find but hard to make profitable for exactly that reason. The next day, I presented my numbers to Brit.

"I think we need to launch with a hundred pieces," I said, showing her my data.

"Sounds great!" she replied. "What's our budget?"

I tightened my lips and lowered my eyes. "Uh . . . three dollars per garment."

"Three dollars?" she said, eyes wide. "That's, like, impossible!"

It was disheartening. Most vintage clothing is "picked" from rag houses—giant warehouses full of clothes that thrift stores and charities rejected. It's why vintage sellers are called "pickers"—they're sometimes allowed to "pick" through the discarded items and select pieces to save. It's dangerous work given the industrial nature of the warehouses; here in Los Angeles, a picker once died when a pile of clothing collapsed on them. Pickers have to sign on to high minimum purchase amounts and have a valid reseller's permit to even be let into the building. Prices tend to be between $8 and $200 per piece, and you're lucky if you can get out spending less than $1,000 per visit.

Rag houses are something of a spectacle to marvel at. They are the final dumping ground for secondhand clothes, like a giant cemetery where clothes go to die. Piles of clothing reach up the equivalent of two stories or more. They're packed together sometimes in bales like hay and moved from place to place on a forklift, sorted based on the quality and fiber composition of the item. Sometimes, items reach a rag house after being rejected from a thrift shop or charity for being in poor shape, with holes and stains that need repairing and cleaning. Other times, items simply weren't fashionable enough for the customers at thrift stores to buy or practical enough for people going to charities to use.

Once garments arrive at a rag house, there are a few different places they end up. Some garments, usually newer products that were made with recyclable textile compositions but haven't yet started to biodegrade, are converted into industrial rags. Others, usually garments made from longer-lasting synthetic fibers, which have a lifespan ten times longer than natural fibers, are sent to poorer countries, where they decimate regional garment markets much to the chagrin of the locals. Others—clothes that are old enough to be novel and in good enough shape to still be wearable—are "picked" by vintage sellers who think they have a specialty customer who won't reject the product like a traditional thrift store customer might.

Finding rag houses to pick from is something of an insider secret. Shrouded in mystery, rag houses are often passed along by word-of-mouth referral from one picker to another. Very often, you have to know a guy who knows a guy just to find one. Even if we did find a rag house, spending just $3 per item would be a stretch.

"Maybe we can modify things to get more bang out of them," I volunteered. "We can buy dresses and turn them into two separate pieces—a skirt and a top. We both know how to sew."

"Yeah," she said, nodding along. "We can cut up double-sided T-shirts and turn each print into a separate item—a tube top or halter top or something like that. We can dye things, too, to make them more special . . . or add patches."

With a little creativity and ingenuity, we might be able to pull this off. First, though, we'd need to find a rag house that would take us on as a new client, and ideally with no minimum appointment buy. In the meantime, we spent nights and weekends after work raiding our own closets looking for pieces to donate to the cause and started a stockpile in the living room of Brit's six-hundred-square-foot apartment.

. . .

One day, Brit and I attended the opening of a vintage store in town. It was run by two women we knew a bit from the internet. We figured that at the very least it couldn't hurt to network. That's what fancy men who wear business suits do, right? As it turned out, there was something to that whole "networking" thing. At the launch party, we met a man who worked for a local rag house; he was in charge of finding new vintage clients. The minimums were higher than we were looking to spend—$500—but he made an exception for our first visit, waiving the minimums and allowing us to check it out and buy what felt right. We faxed his office a copy of our seller's permit and set up an appointment for the upcoming week.

At the rag house, they presorted vintage goods into giant cardboard boxes, big enough to stand in. Garments were separated out into categories and eras: 1980s dresses or 1990s jackets. We dug through the boxes making giant piles on the floor, trying to grab as many 1970s dresses as we could find. In the end, we maxed out our $300 budget and left with giant trash bags full of stinky old clothes, which we took back to Brit's living room and dumped out on the floor. We sorted the garments into piles, picking out things that could be altered or dyed to become more special and unique pieces, or things that could be turned into more than one item. One by one, we mixed dye baths in old buckets and sewed garments with our dinky little Singer discount home sewing machines on the floor, hunched over from 6:00 p.m. when work ended all the way until two or three in the morning the next day. Over the next few months, we built an arsenal of garments, some hanging on a rod in Brit's living room in a makeshift closet, others piled high on the floor. By December, we'd reached one hundred garments total—our goal and enough to launch the website. We scheduled a photo shoot, hiring a friend of Brit's to model, and set up a makeshift studio against a sheet of white fabric in Brit's living room, pushing the couch as far back against the wall as it could go to make room to take photos.

The lighting was atrocious, but fortunately, I'd taught myself Photoshop on that pawn-shop laptop years before. I spent hours in Photoshop and Lightroom struggling to make the photos look somewhat presentable, grappling with weird shadows and strange crops. We chose January 13 as our launch day—an unlucky number. I signed up for a free trial website and made a makeshift logo for the top of it with a moon in the middle of the "o" in Tunnel Vision. Then we spent two weeks uploading every single product to the store. The website was private with a countdown timer on the landing page that linked to an email sign-up list. Anyone who signed up for our email list received a discount code for 50 percent off their entire order on launch day. In my head, the sooner we could get people shopping with us, the more likely they would be to shop again in the future. I wanted to build *momentum*. We started an Instagram account and took to the internet to market our new website every way possible.

At 9:00 a.m. on launch day, we made the website public and sent out the discount code to our email list subscribers. We sat with bated breath, bracing ourselves for nothing. Then, at 9:13 a.m., our first order came in. It was for a pair of jeans covered in floral patches. We sold them for $32.50— a price far too low for our labor and time spent finding them and repairing them. However, we got a customer, and that meant the world. Thirteen minutes later, another order came in—this time for four pieces, two of which we'd reworked ourselves on the living room floor, totaling $90. One minute after that, another order came in—this time for three pieces totaling $57.50. By the end of the day, we'd managed to sell $3,078.45—spread out over fifty orders. It was more than either of us earned in a month at our normal jobs. Our website, though, was down to just four items left available to buy. We were nearly sold out, and PayPal froze our account for thirty days due to "suspicious activity" as a result of our sudden "boom" in sales. We had no product available on our website to sell for the rest of the month, fifty orders we needed to ship, and no access to money for the next thirty days to buy more product or pay for shipping fees. We bought shipping labels by maxing out my personal credit card. The business, I figured, would just have to repay me when the funds were released. In the meantime, we needed to figure out how to get more product.

Tunnel Vision quickly became a roller coaster we couldn't escape, not that we necessarily wanted to. We weren't making money from it yet, and I wouldn't take a paycheck home from it for years to come, but it showed us that we were capable of generating some form of money directly from our own labor, which was motivating. We fell into a routine, working our day jobs for forty hours per week, then meeting up nearly nightly to ship out orders and strategize. Eventually, our funds were released from PayPal and we made another trip to the rag house, this time spending money on more expensive and higher-quality items that we thought our customers would better appreciate. We purchased leather jackets and fancy gowns and old tooled leather belts and worn-in vintage denim. We booked photo shoots on weekends and tried to increase the number of items we had available to sell. More product meant more money. Months went by in an endless cycle of unpaid labor. What little profit we had after our expenses were paid was set aside with the goal of developing our own made-to-order clothing designs. Finally, we had enough money saved and we took to Craigslist to find a professional patternmaker to start work on our own clothing line. We both had patternmaking experience of our own— paid for by tens of thousands of dollars in student loans—and were able to get through the basics. However, with full-time jobs still on our plates, the intricacies of patternmaking and pattern grading to adjust each pattern for different sizes weren't exactly something we had time to take on.

We found our first patternmaker for our house brand, which we called Bad Vibes, on Craigslist right away. He was an older gay man who specialized in making kink and fetish clothes for leather daddies but wanted to expand into women's wear. We showed him our designs—short shorts with grommets and lace-ups, plus items made from faux leather. It was a perfect match. At our first fitting, though, we all burst out into laughter when we realized he'd made the patterns with extra space in the crotch to accommodate a leather codpiece.

"I'm still new to women's wear!" He laughed, putting his hands up by his face as if to say "Don't shoot!"

"Well, all clothing is technically gender neutral," I said. "I just don't know how many of our customers are wearing leather codpieces on the day-to-day, regardless of the equipment they're packing."

He persevered, though, and after a few months' time and several fittings, we eventually had a collection of shorts to photograph and list on the website—made to order, with a three-week turnaround time. It wasn't much, but it was something, and it felt like we were making progress towards our goal.

Back at my day job, things were a never-ending source of anxiety. Every time I received a phone call from the main U.S. office in Milwaukee, I answered with a pit in my stomach.

"Hi," I'd say. "Is today the day I get fired?"

Usually, the man on the other end of the phone—a supervisor named Keith—would laugh and say, "No, just checking in." One day, though, Keith simply sighed deeply and said, "Yes."

I felt the breath leave my body. It felt like I'd been punched in the gut. I knew it was coming, but that didn't make it any better. "Okay," I said, nodding my head in acceptance. "What now?"

"I'm so sorry, Madeline," Keith said, sounding sad. "We all tried to fight for you. You do good work. You didn't do anything wrong."

"It's okay," I said, trying not to cry. "I knew it was coming when the Director left. It was just a matter of time."

The job always felt too good to be true. It was the first time since graduating college that I'd earned consistent, reliable income. After the years I'd spent in and after college piecing together gig work to make ends meet, finding a steady job felt like winning the lottery. Losing the job felt like losing the winning ticket. It hurt to think of what could have been, but I never expected to win in the first place. Now, I'd just have to find a way to make ends meet again.

"I'll send over a list of the inventory we have on record in your possession," Keith said. "If you can check it off and get it back to us in the mail, that would be great. I'll have the office process your last check too."

Later that day, the inventory list popped up in my email. It was a list of all the jewelry items the main office recorded that I had in my possession—things from marketing projects over the years. When I opened the list, though, I was shocked to find it was short roughly $1 million of product. I called Remy over to my computer to look with me.

"Look," I told him. "They only think I have around two hundred and fifty thousand dollars' worth of jewelry here. But I have so much more. Bags more. I have more like one point five million dollars' worth of jewelry here."

We stared at each other, eyes wide. Neither of us said it, but we both understood. I could keep over $1 million worth of jewelry, and nobody would ever know. I wouldn't be able to sell it for $1 million, but after years of selling and pawning random odds and ends to make rent, I was friendly enough with the guys at the local pawnshop that they'd surely buy it off me for a quarter of the value at least.

"What do I do?" I whispered.

Remy paused for a minute. "I don't know," he said. "I mean, you keep it, right? They fired you. The Owner is a creep. Nobody even knows you have this. They're not going to miss it."

"I know," I said. "We could pawn it. We could sell it. This could change my life."

We stared at each other in silence.

"When do you have to get everything back to them?" Remy asked.

"Tomorrow," I said.

"Sleep on it," Remy told me. "Think on it for a bit."

That night, I lay awake in bed wondering what exactly I would do with $1 million of jewelry. If I tried to sell it all at once, it might raise suspicion. I'd have to keep it, I figured, and sell it over time. Or maybe I could drive across the country, selling one piece in a different town every day. If I didn't go to a pawnshop, there's a chance I could get even more for it. My stomach twisted into knots.

The next morning, a coworker called to check in. She'd heard I'd been let go, and just wanted to let me know she'd miss me.

"You heard why, right?" she said over the telephone. "That douchebag."

"Why what?" I asked.

"Why he decided to let you go?" she said. "He was bragging about it on a conference call. He wants to buy a new sports car. I asked who was going to do your work with you gone. He said it wasn't his problem and we'd figure it out."

After the phone call, I sat down with the jewelry at my desk in the apartment. I carefully separated out the pieces on the inventory list, checking them off as I went. When I was done, I made a separate spreadsheet on my computer, inventorying the unaccounted-for items, putting their price down next to them. Just like I'd guessed, it was an extra $1.25 million of product. I stared at the screen, wondering exactly what kind of person I was. The Owner of the company was an asshole, that much was certain.

I thought about the conversation while staring at the jewelry. The Owner didn't care about me, I figured. Why should I care about him? Then, though, I thought about the people working in the central office in Milwaukee. What if, somehow, this came back to hurt them? What if at the end of the year they took inventory and realized they'd somehow come up over a million dollars short on product? What would the Owner do to them? I imagined the receptionist, Cathy, with her two pit bull rescues, who had once spent an entire month scouring the jewelry archives trying to find a sample of my favorite ring to send me as my company holiday gift. I imagined her needing to find a new job after something like a decade working at the jewelry company, all because I decided to be selfish and spiteful now, here, in this moment. I felt nauseous. Then I thought about Keith taking the heat from the Owner firsthand—Keith, who'd once hand-made me a dragon ring in sterling silver with ruby eyes, just because he was practicing jewelry making and thought I might like it. My coworkers were good people. They didn't deserve any trouble.

I packed up the jewelry and emailed Keith. "Hey there," I said. "I have everything on the inventory list ready to go. I also have this other whole batch of inventory, too—spreadsheet attached. It was from marketing in the spring. I'll send that over, too."

I put the jewelry bags in a box and slapped a priority shipping label on it, insured for $2 million, then walked the box down to my busted Volvo and drove it personally to the FedEx processing depot. As I handed the box over to the FedEx worker at the counter, I wondered what type of car the Owner was going to get. It would probably be a Maserati, I figured. He was obnoxious and tasteless like that.

That night, I ran some numbers. Tunnel Vision was averaging around $4,000 per month in sales. Our expenses were around the same. There was no way I could make the business my full-time job. I applied for unemployment on the state website and sat down to watch a movie with Remy on the couch, trying not to throw up from the stress. My mind was racing. Rent was due in two weeks. I had no savings. Most of my bills were due on the fifteenth. How was I going to pull this off?

"I don't know what I'm going to do," I said out loud, half to Remy and half to myself.

"Well, you kinda spend a lot of money on food," he said. "You could easily cut that down."

I glared at him sharply. It wasn't the input I needed at the moment, and besides, I had a big picture problem that $400 a month in food and $250 a month in entertainment wasn't going to solve.

"Sure," I told him flatly. "I can cut out around five hundred dollars in monthly expenses. I still need another one thousand to pay my bills, though."

"You applied for unemployment, right?" he asked.

"Yeah, but who knows when that will come through, if it even does," I said.

"Were you laid off or fired?" he asked.

"I didn't do anything wrong," I reasoned. "So, I guess I was laid off."

"So, you're good, right?" he asked.

I thought back to what Toni said about unemployment. Someone would have to be a real asshole to deny a former employee's unemployment claim. The Owner was, indeed, a real asshole. If the claim went to him for approval, there's no chance I was getting it. If it went to Keith, though, he would probably approve it, as long as the Owner didn't know.

"We'll see," I said, rocking back and forth on the couch, biting my nails.

Instead of sleeping that night, I spent hours scouring Craigslist for jobs. I applied for dozens of positions— receptionist jobs, administrative jobs, even entry-level design jobs that somehow still only paid $10 per hour despite years of cost-of-living increases since I'd last looked. My cover letters were frantic, panicked messes that reeked of the terror of the recently unemployed. Maybe, I thought, I could get back into styling. It was inconsistent work, but it was something I was okay at.

Around midnight, Remy came up to me and placed his hand on my shoulder.

"You're not going to get another job at midnight on a

Friday," he said. "You should get some sleep. You need rest and a clear head."

He was right. I shut my laptop and went to bed, where I lay in the darkness staring at the ceiling. I'd given two and a half years of my life to the jewelry company, going above and beyond at every opportunity—caring about the business as though it were my own. It had gotten me absolutely nowhere. To the Owners of the world, the workers like me were always disposable. We were pawns to be maneuvered or people to be abused, nonhuman entities to be cast aside as soon as it was convenient to do so. I wondered how much money the Owner made, and thought about how hard the Director had to fight for me to even get the "low-income" wage—according to HUD—of $52,000 that felt like so much to me the last two or so years that I worked there. Was life really an endless string of being bounced around from company to company, from Owner to Owner, being seen as a line item on a balance sheet—a number to get as low as possible to maximize profits?

As I fell asleep that night, I thought about Tunnel Vision and Toni. There had to be a better way to do things. I was determined to figure it out.

How to Buy a Car

In the first half of my twenties, a lot of my financial stress and subsequent debt came from buying a car that was a total hunk of junk! I got myself into a cycle of debt and car trouble, all because I didn't know how to go about shopping for a car and I didn't know when to throw in the towel and cut my losses on the one I had. Now, if I were in a position where I needed to buy a car, I'd do absolutely everything differently. Here's what I learned about how to buy a car, the hard way, through trial and error:

1. Figure out your budget. Experts say the total price of the car you purchase should be between 10 and 20 percent of your total annual income. When I bought my 2002 Volvo, my annual income was $37,440. This means my car budget should have been $4,800—$9,600. My $10,000 car was out of my budget! Too often when buying a car, we think about how much we can afford per month rather than the total price of the vehicle. The best way to think about money isn't month to month, it's long-term. To know the long-term value of a car, switch your thinking to its total overall price as it compares to your annual income.

2. Shop for long-term reliability. Once you have your budget, do an online search for "best used cars under $_____"—filling in the blank with your maximum budget. You'll find a lot of lists. Read through all of them and make a note of cars you see pop up lots of places. If multiple people have clocked that

car as a reliable purchase, it's a great place for you to start to shop around.

3. Search online for the car you identified from your lists of reliable vehicles. Remember, don't just shop for the brand of the car. Toyotas might be well-known as reliable vehicles, for example, but the 2021 Toyota Supra is considered an unreliable vehicle, with three recalls issued in one year. When it comes to reliability in cars, it's the brand (or make) as well as the model (car type) and year that matters. Some years of cars are more reliable than others. When you search online, don't be afraid of private sellers. They can be just as reliable as a dealership, sometimes even more so.

4. When setting up a meeting with a private seller to view a car, do a quick online search for mechanics in your area who do "pre-purchase inspections." If you find one near the seller, call and ask what their availability is for a pre-purchase inspection. Then contact the seller and see if they'd be open to meeting at the mechanic shop you found. You'll be able to save time by checking the car out in person and getting the rundown from a mechanic on the spot. If the seller hears the mechanic outline what's going on with the car, you'll both have a good foundation to negotiate the price from there.

5. Don't be afraid to negotiate the price of a car! Come equipped with research—either screenshots on your phone or printed-out data—showing the market rate for the vehicle in question. Search "fair market price for [whatever car you're looking at]" online beforehand. You should find a range of pricing, based on the condition of the vehicle, whether or not it's been in any accidents, and how many miles are on it. Use that to decide what's a good or bad price on the car. If you're at a dealership, don't let them bully you into paying too much! Never be afraid to get up and walk away. You can always find another car somewhere else.

6. Ask the seller for the VIN of the car you're looking at. VIN stands for Vehicle Identification Number, and it can be used to locate a record of everything that's happened to the car. You can search the VIN number for free online to see a brief history of the car in public databases or use it with a paid service like Carfax or AutoCheck to purchase a fuller report of the car's history. This report will tell you if the vehicle has been in any accidents, which could lower the value of the car and give you a heads-up that there might be issues in the future.

7. When it comes to financing, cash is king with private sellers but financing is often preferred at dealerships. At a dealership, negotiate the price of the car before telling them how you'll be paying. They're more likely to give you a good deal on a financed car if the dealership offers their own in-house financing, since they'll be making money from you in the form of interest, too. When it comes to buying a car, compare financing offers in your price range ahead of time with multiple lenders. Try to get a quote in your price range from at least three different lenders. That way, you can go with the loan that has the best terms—which usually just means the lowest interest rate. You can still use financing with a private seller, but your lender might have certain requirements for the vehicle, like the year it was made.

8. If you're short on cash, you don't want to be caught underinsured. When you're broke, your instinct might be to get the cheapest insurance possible. However, it might actually be better for you to get the cheapest car possible and pay a little bit more every month for insurance. Liability insurance means that if you get into an accident in your vehicle and do damage, your insurance company will cover the damage you've done to anything besides your car. However, the last thing you want is to buy a car, crash it, and not be able to afford to replace it! Other types of insurance that might be

helpful include uninsured/underinsured motorist coverage—meaning your car gets covered if the person who hits you lacks liability insurance to cover the damage to your vehicle, as well as things like gap insurance, which means if your car gets damaged and you still owe money on it via a car loan, the insurance will cover the difference between the value of the car and what you still owe. Without gap insurance, if your car gets totaled while you have a loan out for it, there's a chance you could still be on the hook for making payments on it every month. If you can't afford to buy a car twice, it's always a good idea to thoroughly explore your insurance options.

9. Don't skimp on the oil changes. It might be tempting when you're broke to forgo regular maintenance on your car. However, this is only going to hurt you more in the long run. With regular maintenance, your car can last up to fifteen years. Consider buying a car code reader. They're usually cheap—around $20 to $25—and if your car's "check engine" light comes on, you can hook the car code reader up to the vehicle yourself to figure out what's going on with it. Often, if something pops up on your code reader, people at a car part supply store can help you figure out what's going on with it for a lot less than a mechanic can. The more information you have on your side when going in to see a mechanic, the less of a chance they'll sell you on non-essential services.

10. Know when you're in over your head. A good general rule is that if the cost of repairing your car in a year is more than half the total value of the car, you should probably consider selling it.

11. If your car is old enough and you want to get rid of it, look into car buy-back programs in your state. Many states offer programs where they will pay you money to get your old gas-guzzling fume-emitting clunker off the road. Sometimes, these programs will pay more than you could get just by selling your car outright.

12. If you already own a car you suspect may be out of your budget, don't feel stuck with it. Look online to see how much you could get by selling it. If you can get more by selling it than you currently owe on the car loan, it might be a good idea to turn it in and buy a cheaper car. If the car is worth less than you owe on it, this is called being "upside down" on the loan. Even if you're upside down, it might make sense to sell the car and take the loss to reduce your overall debt burden. For example: if you owe $7,000 on a car that's only worth $5,000, you might consider selling the car for $5,000 then paying that amount towards your existing car loan, leaving $2,000 that you owe. If you then purchased a $3,000 car on a loan, you'd only owe $5,000 in total. It might not feel great to take a loss, but if you're in a tight spot, owing $5,000 on vehicles instead of $7,000 is actually a better financial move long-term and will put more money in your pocket.

13. Remember that cars are the biggest waste of money most of us will encounter in our lifetimes! They go down in value over time and cost a lot. But for many Americans who don't live near public transportation, they're a necessary evil. Try to keep your spending on your car as low as possible—don't be tempted by shiny new things just because they are pretty!

CHAPTER 9

Capitalism Killed My Boyfriend

I fell in love with Drew on a Saturday. It was a hot day, ninety-nine degrees in Joshua Tree—a small desert community just a few hours outside of Los Angeles where adobe houses dot the otherwise desolate landscape of unforgiving heat and dust. The locals talk to you with missing teeth and sunburnt noses, putting their hands on their hips and scowling at the luxury cars in the parking lots.

"Where ya from?" one asked me, as I stopped for gas coming into town.

"L.A.," I said, "but don't worry! I'm going back!"

He chuckled a bit, and we both knew why. Joshua Tree was changing into a hipster haven for people who couldn't hack it in the big city. Ramshackle buildings were being converted into second homes and vacation rentals. The locals saw the writing on the wall.

"I'm just out here for work this weekend," I assured him.

"Ah," he said, nodding and smacking his cracked lips. "Whatcha do for work?"

"I guess I'm a stylist?" I replied. It was a few months before I was laid off from the jewelry company, but I'd already begun preparing for the inevitable—taking up odd jobs here and there. "Stylist" was close enough. It was what I was doing that weekend, anyway.

I drove my janky car off the freeway and onto a dirt road that seemed to go on forever. My little black Volvo could barely make it through the potholed streets of Koreatown back home; I wasn't sure it would survive something unpaved. The car jostled and rattled and scraped against big chunks of dirt that might have been rocks. Finally, I found the address on the call sheet for the photo shoot: a big, sprawling house on a few acres of land, surrounded by Joshua trees and teeming with activity. The rest of the crew was arriving, too, carrying in suitcases and tripods and lights and gear.

I got out of the car and looked around. The house was one story, like most houses are out in the desert. I assumed it was to not obstruct the view—a beautiful 360-degree landscape of mythical tree shapes and staggering rock structures and bright hot sand that bounced the sunlight right back into your eyes even as it blew across your shoes. There, in the distance, I saw the figure of a person crouched down on the desert floor, alone and fiddling with something on the ground. They must have been crew of some kind, I figured, working on the shoot. I watched for a second, intrigued, before walking over to see if I could help.

As I approached, the figure came into focus. It was a man, in his forties maybe, wiry and tan and covered in tattoos, with waist-length brown hair topped off with a hat to shield his face from the sun. He wore tight black jeans with rips at the knees, the kind of rips you can't buy at the store. I'd tried to engineer rips like those on denim before. Some things—the rips and tears and signs of wear—can't be replicated. It's a blessing and a curse, the gift of authenticity: you have to put in the time, the energy, to make it real. Some things you can only get by wearing your clothing for years, straight down to the bone, until it falls off your body. I like to wear my clothes like that. It feels like you're getting your money's worth.

The long-haired tattooed man with the falling-apart

clothes was fiddling with his shoe—a big black boot that looked like he'd had it since the 1980s. He had a giant roll of silver duct tape and was wrapping it around the sole of the boot, straight up and over the arch, whirling the tape around in big circles to wrap it tight. It was a bit of an absurd sight, this man crouched over in the desert, taping a shoe. I was charmed.

"Whatcha doing?" I asked, walking up to block the sun. I towered over him, casting a shadow as he worked.

"Fixing my shoe," he said, not bothering to look up. Instead, he kept spinning the duct tape around his foot, trying to affix what surely was a broken sole back onto the boot. It didn't look like it was going well. Dust and sand and dirt from the desert floor kept blowing against the tape, making it difficult to adhere.

"It broke," he offered flatly as an explanation.

"You don't have another pair of shoes?" I asked him.

"I don't want another pair of shoes," he said, still not averting his gaze from his foot on the desert floor. "I like these ones."

He was funny. I smiled, a grotesque smile that shows too much of my gums and puts all of my crooked teeth on display for the world to see—the kind of smile I spent years practicing how not to do as a kid. It didn't matter, though. He hadn't looked up once since I arrived.

I don't believe in love at first sight—or even love at first 2.5 minutes, or however long I'd been standing there watching the man tape his shoe together. Still, this man duct-taping his shoe together was the most perfect person I'd ever seen in my life and I felt like I might throw up. My relationship with Remy back home was complicated, marred by disagreements about everything from money to drug use to what we wanted for our future. We were ethically non-monogamous, which took some of the pressure off. Still, though, falling in love with anyone could spell trouble for my already rocky relationship. The last thing it needed was the test of "new relationship energy" entering the equation. I turned and walked back to the house without saying another word, trying to shake the whole encounter from my mind.

Back at the house, I wandered around trying to get my bearings. There were four or so bedrooms, one of which was full of cots and single beds lining the walls, with a Jacuzzi in the center of it. The dining room table had been converted to styling headquarters. I plugged in a steamer and started to pull clothing from suitcases, hanging things on racks. After a bit, Kennedy approached me. I'd met Kennedy around town. In a whirlwind night of drunkenness and debauchery a few months prior, she ended up married to a friend of a friend, a hairstylist with a vaguely European-sounding name whom I'd known for nearly a decade. From then on, she was part of Remy's extended friend group. Kennedy was producing the shoot, in addition to doing makeup, and it felt more like a house party than a typical job.

"Hey," she said, smiling. "You're getting all set up, cool, cool. Did you meet Drew yet?"

"No," I responded. "Who's that?"

"He owns the brand," she said. "He's cool, don't worry. I got this job after the Fourth of July because we all ended up together on molly in a hot tub. He's fun, it should be chill. Tall skinny guy, long hair, covered in tattoos. You'll know him when you see him."

Oh, great, I thought. I fell in love with the guy who signs the paychecks. How bourgeois of me.

A few months later, I had lost my job at the jewelry company. I spent the weekend panicking, but by Sunday, Kennedy had already set me up with a part-time freelance gig designing emails for some fashion brands in town. It wasn't much, but it was something and I was desperate.

"I think you met the owner once," she told me. "His name is Drew. Do you remember him?"

Fuck.

"I remember," I told her with a sigh.

The next day, I drove my dirty old Volvo downtown to the warehouse where Drew's businesses operated. Downstairs, on the ground level, was Lip Service—a business Drew started in 1985 inspired by death rock fashion and his love of the Cure. Upstairs, on suspended metal platforms in what felt like the sky, was Kill City—a denim-based brand built on rock and roll that sold more classic and everyday pieces. The other brands, smaller things, fit in the nooks and crannies all around us. The first floor was all corsets and vinyl and labret piercings. The second floor was all motorcycle jackets and worn-in vintage Ts and Dr. Martens. There was a rivalry in the office, between the old-school freaks downstairs and the newer, more fashionable freaks upstairs—freak-on-freak crime.

Around lunchtime, Drew popped over to our end of the design loft. His office was only a few paces away; it had bright red chairs in the shape of hands, and a huge whiteboard where he sketched out ideas. It was littered with relics from the late '70s and early '80s L.A. punk scene. There was a giant metal spike on a podium with a plaque that read "Drew Bernstein: I was there!" Rumor had it that Drew was friends with Henry Rollins before he had any tattoos. He once brought Darby Crash from the Germs home to meet his parents and have Sunday dinner.

"Hey!" Drew said, with a big smile, bouncing over to our desks. "Who's this?!"

Of course, he didn't remember me. Of course, that made me like him even more.

"This is Madeline," Kennedy said. "She's doing our email marketing designs."

"Oh, rad!" Drew stuck his hand out. "Nice to meet you!"

"We've actually met before." I smiled. "Out in the desert? When you broke your boot?"

"Oh yeah, I remember you!" he exclaimed. "I fixed my boot, look!" He pulled his foot up and plopped it on the desk.

"Drew, get your shoe off my desk!" Kennedy yelled.

"All right, all right," Drew said, taking his foot off the

table. "I'll let you guys get back to work." He pointed at me, with both of his hands. "Madeline," he said, as though he was making sure he wouldn't forget it. "We'll chat later."

I watched Drew bounce away.

"I love him," I blurted out to nobody in particular.

Kennedy laughed. "Yeah, he's actually pretty great—as great as a boss can be, anyway."

"No," I said. "I love him. Like I'm in love with him. I'm obsessed."

Jen, the Kill City assistant designer, popped her head around her computer. "Are you serious?" she asked.

"Yeah," I said, shaking my head up and down definitively. "He makes my skin feel tingly and my heart hurt and my stomach twist in knots like I might throw up. Is he dating anyone? Is he single?"

"He's single," Jen said, "but he is kind of your boss now, even if you are just freelancing, so that's weird."

Was he my boss now? Jen was right. I sighed a long steady sigh of defeat. Having a job was more important than having another boyfriend. A boyfriend couldn't pay your bills—not the kind of boyfriends I'd had, anyway. I'd have to learn to make peace with my Drew obsession in my own way.

I spent the next few months living out every scene from a bad movie about unrequited love. I drove to work listening to romantic songs with saxophone at full blast, crying along as each track hit its crescendo. I fell asleep imagining cheesy moments of heart-aching fulfillment where Drew spontaneously professed his love for me. I walked the long way upstairs to my office each day, passing by his office even though I didn't need to, sneaking a glance at him while he worked. I began talking about Drew endlessly to my friends, trying to make sense of it all. I'd never felt so instantly and strongly connected to another person before, and I wasn't sure what to do with it. I sent frustrated and forlorn text messages to my friends at all hours of the night and day.

"Still in love with Drew," I'd write. "Everything hurts!" I'd add an emoji to lighten the mood—a ghost or a pile of poop. I felt like I had to get it out of me somehow or the attraction would eat me alive.

I gave up entirely on the idea of trying to earn his affection. It seemed too improbable, too far-fetched, especially given our dynamic in the workplace. Instead, I tried to earn small seconds of time, here and there—mundane interactions through which I could better know and appreciate him. I savored each new thing I learned.

THINGS I LEARNED ABOUT DREW

1. Drew's favorite forks were the black plastic ones from a specific Mexican fast-casual restaurant in the Valley called Poquito Más. He liked that the plastic felt rubberier there, but the good forks—the rubbery ones— were only at a few locations.

2. Drew wore a can opener around his neck all the time, every day, because when his band was on tour in the '80s it was convenient to just pop open a can of soup to eat in the van. Sometimes still, when he was hungry, he'd buy a fifty-cent can of soup and crack into it in his car, just like he'd done in the van all those years ago.

3. Drew was vegan now. He loved animals—way too much to eat them. He used to have a dog, an Australian Blue Heeler named Rocket. Rocket was his best friend for years, but after Rocket died, Drew decided the heartbreak of losing a pet was too painful to ever try to have a dog again.

4. Drew used to have a poorly done grim reaper tattoo on his arm but then he covered it up with a really well done tattoo of a fish. Now, though, he wishes it was still the grim reaper because he's decided bad tattoos are better than good ones. Any asshole with money can get a good tattoo now, he thought. Good tattoos were for posers.

5. Drew liked his job and thought work was okay, but mostly he thought the job would be a lot better if we didn't have to sell anything at all and we could just make

things all day, like punk rock summer camp. He only liked owning the business because he could hire his friends when they were down and out. Besides that, he thought money was a scam.

6. Drew's first designs all had messages on the tags reading things like "Give money to poor people." Drew always carried cash in his pockets just in case he passed by someone on the street who was asking for money. The government wasn't going to redistribute resources any time soon, he reasoned, so we'd have to do it on our own.

7. Drew used to play in that punk band Crucifix, but always felt like the band was way cooler than him.

8. Drew had obsessive-compulsive disorder. His house was organized meticulously and kept tidy to help soothe his brain. Still, though, he kept one black rubbery Poquito Más fork in his cutlery drawer—mixed in with his regular silverware, even though it didn't belong. He called it "exposure therapy."

9. Sometimes, Drew wore his hair piled up high on his head in a plastic claw clip, the kind that teenage girls wear to the mall.

10. Drew loved to learn about physics and space. It made him feel small and insignificant, but in a way that eased some of the pressure he felt about needing to make it in today's dystopian soul-crushing world.

Drew didn't take notice of me, but he did start to take notice of my outfits.

"Your style," he said one day, "it's what we need to be doing more of. It's subculture, but it's current. Have you ever done design work before?"

"Yeah," I said. "I have my BFA in apparel design, and I have a little clothing line of my own."

He nodded, pleased.

"How would you feel about being a design consultant for our newest brand?" he asked. "It's targeting people like you."

I jumped at the opportunity to both make more money and spend more time working closely with Drew. Over the next couple of months, I worked with him on concept development, reviewing designs and making mood boards and sketches. I took on more responsibility with photography and styling for the company websites, and I found myself working late every single night. Drew was always the first person in and the last person out of the building, and as he made the rounds before locking up, he'd often find me upstairs, still staring into the blue light of my computer screen, plugging away at spreadsheets and market research.

"Hey, you wanna go get dinner?" he asked one night, hours after everyone else had left for home.

"Definitely." I beamed.

We drove to a nearby restaurant that was built to look like a tree house. The patio was surrounded by plants and everything was lit with candles. It was set back off the main street without a sign and there was a valet stand out front. It was the kind of place I'd driven by a hundred times but never would have been able to afford.

"I'm buying," he said after the host seated us.

"Good." I laughed. "Because you're rich and I'm broke."

"I'm not rich!" he said, taken aback. "I'm middle class! I hate rich people!"

I raised an eyebrow.

"Middle class?" I asked skeptically. "Do you mean *comfortable*? Where do you live?"

"Laurel Canyon," he said. It was an artistic neighborhood in the hills, where musicians like Frank Zappa and Joni Mitchell and Jim Morrison once lived. It was on the west side.

"Uh-huh," I said, rolling my eyes in an exaggerated show of incredulity. "And how much is your house worth?"

"I don't know," he said. "I bought it in the nineties. Maybe two million?"

"Exactly!" I shrieked. "Rich!" I yelled, pointing at him.

"I will have you know," he replied, "that is a middle-class

house in Los Angeles. It is just really expensive here! I only pay myself one hundred thousand dollars per year. I have employees who make more than me."

I thought about the Director, who made a little more than that. As a business owner, I figured, Drew must earn more than just his salary. He wasn't a wage worker like everyone else. Surely, he had access to other privileges—things like profit or company credit cards.

"I don't know," I said. "You are a business owner. You must be at least a little rich."

"You're a business owner, too," he said. "Tunnel Vision, right? Are you rich?"

"No," I said, taken aback. He was beating me at my own game. "But that's different! You have employees!"

"I had more money before I had employees," he said, laughing. "Now I'm like a parent. I've got all these kids I gotta take care of. Someone needs a new car, someone's kid is going to college. We've gotta make sure everyone gets fed and is doing all right. There's no extra money left for me to take even if I wanted to!"

"Sounds like something a rich person would say," I said, half joking.

"I've met actually rich people, you know," he said, more quietly this time, nearly a whisper—like he thought someone might overhear. "And they are not like me. The amount of money they have, it's ridiculous. Evil. I have a good life. It's nice. But those people have more than they'll ever use or need. And they use it to fuck with other people. Everyone should get a house they like and drive a good car and be able to go to nice dinners sometimes. That's what I try to do at the company, anyway—give everyone who works there a nice life. You'd know if you worked there actually, more than just freelancing, I mean. We do profit-sharing programs. We buy people company cars."

"Maybe," I told him. I still didn't know much about how money worked, but it seemed improbable that a $2 million house was middle class anywhere, even L.A. "You still seem rich to me, though, so I'm gonna order drinks if you're paying!"

"That's fine," he said. "I don't usually drink, but I'll have what you're having."

Three drinks and two hours later, we were sitting in his car by the restaurant, completely drunk, in a world before Uber.

"I don't think you're supposed to get drunk with your employees," I told him, laughing.

"You're not an employee," he said. "You're a freelancer, it's different."

"I don't think you're supposed to get drunk with your freelancers," I whispered.

"You were supposed to stay sober!" he exclaimed. "I told you I don't usually drink. I'm a lightweight!"

"I forgot I'm on antibiotics right now for a tooth thing!" I squealed. "I didn't realize three drinks would do this to me!"

I left out the part about ordering the antibiotics myself from an online veterinary website in a foreign country. I was kind of in between health insurance at the moment. Freelance life was synonymous with struggle, it seemed.

"How do we get home?" I asked. "There are no taxis in L.A.!"

"In that case," he said, "I think we have to just wait here until one of us gets sober enough to drive. It could be hours. Are you okay with that?"

"More than okay," I said quietly.

We spent the next three hours in his car talking. We talked about which punk bands we liked, and which ones he played in back in the '80s. We talked about our childhoods. He told me his dad was a rocket scientist. I told him my dad was a sprinkler salesman, then laughed and told him I thought he might have been a drug dealer, too. We talked about how fast fashion was ruining the planet, and he told me about screaming matches he got into with companies like Forever 21 who were ruining not only the planet but also small businesses.

We talked about the profit-sharing program he ran at the business, and how he really did have employees who earned more money than him. He told me about his favorite clothing brands from the '90s, and I told him about my favorite contemporary clothing brands on the internet. He told me about how he always wanted to run an anti-sale—today only, 20 percent more! I laughed so hard I almost choked.

"That's funny!" I said, drunkenly pounding the seat of his car for emphasis. "We have to do that!"

"You really think so?" he asked. "Everyone always tells me it's a stupid idea."

"They don't get it," I told him. "I think we should do billboards. They should say 'Fill the void . . . with new jeans!' It can be a whole meta-marketing campaign, about how bullshit capitalism is!"

He looked at me and smiled, as if someone was really seeing him for the first time.

"Exactly," he said. "Yes, like . . . it's bullshit that we have to sell anything to be alive. Let's make fun of it a little. We all know it's bullshit! Can't we have a laugh at the absurdity of it all at least?"

Eventually, we sobered up, and he dropped me off at my apartment.

"Your apartment building seems nice," he said, before I got out of the car. "Do you have roommates?"

"I live here with my boyfriend," I said.

"Oh," he replied. "Cool! Yeah, I'll have to meet him sometime. Maybe we can go to a show or something." He waved goodbye as I closed the door. I walked inside feeling like I was floating on air.

At work the next week, we put our meta-marketing campaigns in motion. I designed billboards and ads that nobody else seemed to get, but that made Drew laugh until he fell out of his chair. We shared vegan snacks on our breaks and made jokes about punk rock.

"What's happening here?" Kennedy asked one day.

"I think we're just friends," I told her.

"But you still love him?" she asked.

"Oh yeah, definitely," I said. "More than I ever knew it was possible to love a person."

"What does your boyfriend think of this?" she asked. "Like does he know?"

I paused for a second. I remembered Remy side-eyeing me the night I came home from dinner with Drew. I was a little too happy for a normal work dinner. Remy could tell.

"He definitely knows I like Drew," I said. "But you know, we're open. We see other people. And anyway, Drew and I aren't like . . . dating. We're just friends. I don't think he's interested in me like that."

Inside, I hoped I was wrong.

As the months went on, it became apparent that I was in fact wrong—much to my delight. There was a magnetic chemistry between Drew and me, and eventually it became so palpable that it was impossible to ignore. If love is to understand someone and be understood by them, as I've always suspected, it's possible there were no two people more in love in the history of the world than Drew and me. We moved in sync with each other, creating a whole world between us with inside jokes and references that nobody else seemed to understand. Remy and I broke up, and within six months' time I had moved all my things out of my studio apartment in Koreatown and into Drew's Laurel Canyon house. He and his friends built me custom closets for my clothes, and we took weekend trips driving up the coast or out to the desert. We made our own hummus—skinning the chickpeas and everything—and ate fruit by the pool and went to gardening stores to look for Drew's favorite rare plants to put in the yard. He washed my hair for me and learned to make me coffee just the way I like it. We went out, we stayed in, we watched movies, we listened to music, we went to shows and sat right on the stage because he knew all of the bands. I left my things in piles around his house, oblivious, then felt sick with guilt over disrupting his home.

"It's okay," he'd say. "I like seeing your things around, it reminds me that you're here."

My friends told me, "You two, you make me believe that love is real."

I woke up every morning feeling something I had never felt before: happy. The happiness was twofold. I was in love, obviously, but I was also experiencing something I'd never experienced before: financial security. Drew, aware of my struggles to understand money and secure steady employment, begged for me not to worry about helping with the mortgage when I moved in. Instead, he offered, I could pay for utilities and groceries, then put more money towards paying off my debt. Freelancing, my income was still inconsistent and varied, and with our new relationship, he didn't think it would be appropriate to hire me as an actual employee. This way, though, he could help ease my financial pressure on the expense end. I spent twenty-four hours per week freelancing with Drew's businesses, then thirty hours per week working on Tunnel Vision with Brit for no pay at all, just hoping that one day it would all be worth it. I still scoured Craigslist looking for other freelance work to do on nights and weekends. I was drowning in debt, but Drew had managed to hand me an oxygen tank and a mask. At least now I could breathe a little.

Slowly but surely, I threw more money at my debt—a hundred extra dollars here and there wherever I could. It seemed fruitless in my mind, though. I'd long accepted the fact that my debt would never be paid off. Instead, I figured, it would be something I'd carry around with me until I died. The freedom of having limited financial obligations, though, released pressure I didn't even realize I'd been carrying around with me for years. My lifelong struggles with anxiety seemed diluted in the wake of my newfound financial comfort. I worked better, with a clearer head. My decision-making seemed less impulsive and fearful. Instead, it was measured and practical. Sometimes, it felt like an entirely new person was living in my body.

"Is this what it's like to be happy?" I asked Drew one

morning, lying in bed as the sun rose. "I didn't know life could feel like this."

"I think so," he told me, running his fingers through my hair. "I've never had this before. Not until now."

I was in love, more than I ever thought was possible. I didn't care what happened in the future, as long as Drew was there to experience life with me.

A year or so after we moved in together, I started to hear rumblings of Drew's financial problems at work. Drew assured me, though, that everything would be fine.

"It's been a bad few years," he said. "But it's not the first time. We've been in business twenty-five years. This has happened before. Something always comes through last minute."

But as the weeks and months went on, "last minute" was rapidly approaching, and there had been no Hail Mary. Drew began to lose the bounce in his step. Sometimes, he woke up in the middle of the night panicking, gasping for air.

"What's your break-even point?" I asked him one day. "How far off are you from it every month?"

"I don't know," he said, shocked. "It's too hard to calculate. There are too many moving parts."

"Let me take a look," I insisted. "I'm pretty good with numbers."

He sent me spreadsheets and bank records and payroll records and inventory projections.

I sifted through them, creating intricately detailed spreadsheets of expenses and assets.

"You're currently running ten million dollars per year of gross sales," I told him. "That's a lot, you can work with that. But your expenses, here, they're more like eighteen million dollars."

"Only ten million dollars in revenue?" He balked. "No, that's too low. That's too low to pay for everything. It needs to be like twice that."

"Well," I said, "maybe it's time to downsize? We can get

your eighteen million dollars of spending closer to ten million dollars with a few changes here."

"Downsize what?" he asked.

"Here," I said, handing over a list of expenses. "I've highlighted in red people you can probably stand to lose completely—these people are very high wage earners, they earn more than you do, and it doesn't seem like they're pulling their weight at the business. Hotshot salesman types, all talk, no action. They drive fancy sports cars and cost the business money without bringing anything in. Then, maybe we can consolidate from three buildings into one—that will cut down on some expenses. There are other things we can do, too, like leveling out pay for the second-tier highest wage earners. Explain to them the company's financial position and ask if they'd like to stay on at a reduced salary that's more similar to yours and everyone else's."

"Do you mean firing people?" Drew asked incredulously while looking over the expenses. "I can't fire anyone. These people count on me. We don't fire people unless they've done something really wrong. We take care of people."

"Well," I told him, "you can fire these few high-ticket employees—the top highest income earners who probably have enough savings to get by anyway—and rein in your company spending, or you can lose the whole business and everyone gets fired, including your lower-ticket employees who probably don't have as much savings as those hotshot big earners do and would have a harder time getting by. It's your choice."

"I can't do any of this," he said, shaking his head. "Maybe I can try to file bankruptcy and sell the business at the same time, like Betsey Johnson did. Maybe I can find a buyer for the brands. The sale price can pay back some of the company's debt at least, and people can keep their jobs. Then, maybe I can sell my house to pay back the rest of the debt we owe."

"You don't have to pay back the rest with your personal money, Drew," I told him, confused. "The business owes the money, not you personally. Why would you sell your house—which you love so much and put so much into—to pay back the business's liabilities?"

"The people we owe money to," he said, "they aren't huge corporations. They're other small businesses, run by families who work in them, too. I can't do that to them. It's not honorable."

"Well," I asked, "do you have anything saved for yourself? Like a retirement?"

"Not really," he said. "One hundred thousand dollars. It's not enough for me to retire on, especially if I don't keep anything from selling my house. I failed. This was all in my control, and I failed."

"You didn't fail," I told him, wrapping my arms around him.

"This business was the only way I could ever prove to anyone that I wasn't a total waste, a total fuck-up," he said. "And it turns out, I was fucking up all along."

"Because of money?" I asked, incredulous. "You are so much more special and amazing and important than your ability to generate money. Money isn't even real—we made it up. You are a brilliant shining light in a universe full of other brilliant shining lights. You are real and you are here and you are loved, and we will be okay, we will be happy, no matter what."

He nodded yes, but seemed skeptical.

"I would love you the same if you worked at Burger King," I said, kissing his forehead and hands. "Maybe more, because then I'd get free French fries."

In the months that followed, Drew put his business up for sale, filed for bankruptcy, and sold his house. On my birthday, we went to put a deposit down on an apartment downtown, to rent, together.

"A new chapter," I told him.

"I like downtown." He nodded. "This is going to be fun."

We rushed to make it to the rental office in time to drop off our paperwork that day, but when we arrived, we were just two minutes too late. The office was already closed. I texted the leasing agent.

"Tomorrow is fine," she said.

"Tomorrow," I told him.

"Okay," he said, smiling. "Tomorrow."

He looked at me for a moment like he was trying to memorize my face, or maybe like he had a secret, or maybe like a combination of both.

"You know the thing about you, Madeline?" he said calmly. "You're a fighter. You're the kind of person who is always going to be okay. You always have been."

I cocked an eyebrow. "Sure," I said, laughing a bit. "I guess I am a fighter."

He was right, but I wasn't sure why he said it. We went home that night and fell asleep in each other's arms.

"I love you," he told me before we went to bed, kissing me on the forehead.

The next morning, I woke up, and Drew was gone. In the canyon by our house, he'd shot himself in the heart.

A few hours after Drew committed suicide, I found a note in his phone that said "For M." It was short, like a half-finished thought that never came to fruition. I must have read it a thousand times, over and over, in one sitting—trying to make sense of it all.

> If I died today, I think that would be alright. I would
> be happy knowing that I did my best, to live my life,
> and that I loved you.

The pain of suddenly losing someone you love is hard to explain to anyone who hasn't experienced it. The grief hits you in waves because your own body knows you can't handle it all at once. You feel numb for hours, then you're overcome with the most intense feelings of despair and hopelessness you can imagine. You shake back and forth, or you fall to the ground, or you scream out in agony. I did all three, over and over again, for months and even years after Drew died.

"This would be terrible if it were any boyfriend," I told my friends, whispering. "To lose any partner like this. Why did it have to be Drew, though? Why Drew?"

I knew the answer.

In the United States today, suicide is the twelfth leading cause of death. The rate of suicide is highest in middle-aged men. In a system of capitalism—which falsely claims your financial stability is a reflection of your productivity, and furthermore says that your productivity is linked to your worth as a human being—it's no wonder that a leading contributor to suicide deaths is experiencing financial stress; financial stress makes people up to twenty times more likely to attempt suicide. Looking back now, I see that Drew perfectly fit the profile of a man at risk to end his life. I couldn't see it, though, because it never occurred to me that the most important thing about Drew—even in his own eyes—might be his ability to generate money.

Perhaps the greatest pain in my heart is knowing Drew himself could not separate who he was as a person from who he was as a business owner, as a financial provider for others around him, as the stereotype of a man in the patriarchal confines of capitalism. The second-greatest pain in my heart is knowing that if Drew were a more traditional business owner—one who was in business just to maximize profits for himself at the expense of caring for his employees—he'd probably still be here today, but he wouldn't be the kind of person I'd even want to know, let alone the kind of person I loved. As the crisis of capitalism grows around us, more and more of us experience financial strain, putting pressure on our mental health in the process. Capitalism leaves us with few options for survival. We can be wage workers and run the risk of starving to death in an unregulated system that allows corporations to pay their workers unlivable low wages while charging their customers unreasonably high costs, all to pad the CEO's and owners' pockets (43 percent of people experiencing hunger in the U.S. come from households with full-time workers). Or, we can become small-business owners ourselves, struggling through the financial uncertainty of business management while being told that if we just worked harder we could be Jeff Bezos, pulling up on our bootstraps until they break or we do (65 percent of small businesses in the USA fail within their first ten years). Either way, it seems most of us are doomed to a life of financial strain and struggle.

When I think about Drew, I don't think about Drew, the Business Owner. I think about Drew, the funniest person I've ever met, the creative whirlwind of frenetic energy, the love of my life. I think about Drew taping his boot back together in the middle of the desert, my shadow cast over him while he worked. I think about Drew and me walking through the canyon—the same canyon where he took his own life—while he played guitar and Mo-Dog ran beside him.

I liked listening to him talk. "Talking to you is half the fun," he told me once, his head on the pillow next to mine. I wanted to hear every story he had, even stories that did not yet know they were stories. Tell me about the smallest scar. Tell me about your most boring day. Tell me about the thread count on your sheets. I wanted to know it all.

I liked watching him think. I liked the way he'd overthink—"I have a ruse!" he'd sometimes say. I liked the way he'd oversimplify—"we're all just stardust, man." I liked looking at him. I liked the crease of his eyelid. I liked his cheekbones and mouth. I liked his nose—I just liked that it was part of him, I guess. I just liked Drew, but most people did. He was charming like that, enigmatic, offbeat. He brought light to everything he touched, shooting through our stratosphere, crashing into our world. All we could do is grab hold and hang on for the ride. Drew was the most special person I'd ever met, and capitalism reduced the value of his life to a bottom line on a profit and loss statement.

Drew's death was a harrowing reminder to everyone who knew him that there is danger in assigning our value as human beings to our capacity to labor. Everything can change for us financially in an instant. Capitalism is throwing punches at us every way we turn. The way to roll with the punches is to remember you didn't ask to be put in the ring to begin with. Drew was right when he told me that I was a fighter. Maybe, though, everything shouldn't have to feel like such a fight all the time.

How to Manage Financial Stress

Statistically, most of us will reach a point in our lives where we experience significant financial stress. Here is what I've learned about money matters and mental health:

1. As long as there has been money, there has been debt. In a perfect world, we wouldn't have either, but we don't live in a perfect world. We live here, now. If you find yourself struggling with debt, just remember that all you can do is your best. You didn't create this system. You're just trying to survive it.

2. Nothing is permanent. You might find yourself in the worst financial position of your life, only to bounce back a few years later. Just try to ride it out. That's how life goes, and your ability to imagine a future that's better than now will be the most important skill you have. It's a form of revolutionary optimism, and you need that not only for your own mental health, but also if you want to work towards building a better future for everyone!

3. Financial failure is unfortunately a part of this system. Accepting the fact that you might financially fail at some point (or even at multiple points) in your life and that's okay will go a long way in preserving your mental health when it happens. The goal is not perfection. The goal is survival.

CHAPTER 10

From Each According to Their Ability, to Each According to Their Need

The day Drew died, I lost nearly everything in my life. I lost my partner and my future, of course, but also my primary source of freelance work and my home. Drew, for his part, left an envelope with $3,000 in cash in it on my side of the bed. One of his family members, however, promptly took the money from the house. A few days later, when the dust had settled a bit, one of his family members reached out to me to talk. I answered the phone, expecting to have a heart-to-heart over our shared monumental loss. Instead, I answered the phone to the following question:

"How much was he giving you?"

The question confused me. "Do you mean, what was my rate when I freelanced at his business?"

"No," he replied awkwardly. "How much . . . did he . . . uh . . . pay you?"

"For what?" I asked.

"To live?" he said, his voice going up at the end like a question.

"Oh," I said, understanding.

"Just, uh . . . let me know what you need," he said awkwardly into the phone.

Later, I called my dad. "His family thought I was a sex worker," I told him. "Because of the age difference, I think."

I was in my late twenties when Drew and I met. He was in his late forties. Drew had always felt uncomfortable with the age difference. I'd done my best to assure him these things sometimes just happen.

"Huh," my dad said. "Well, are they going to give you money?"

"I don't know," I said. "That's why they were asking me, right? To make sure I have money to move out of his house before the close of sale or whatever?"

"Probably," my dad said. "Do you have money to move?"

"No," I admitted. "I was going to pay for the deposit on an apartment the same way I always do—by taking out a cash advance from my credit card."

"Would Drew want you to have to do that?" my dad asked. "Or would he want you to have some of his money to move?"

I thought about the $3,000 in cash by my side of the bed. Surely, he'd meant that for me, right?

"He'd want me to be able to comfortably afford to move," I said.

"So," my dad said, "if the family has a little bit of his money, and you need money, and Drew would want you to have the money, why don't you just take some of the money to move?"

"I don't know." I sighed. "It feels like . . . like maybe it undervalues the relationship? I get why someone would think I was with him for money. And Drew did help me sometimes, but the same way any partner would help someone they love who was struggling to find steady work. I just don't want to underrate how important the relationship is . . . was. I wasn't with Drew for money; I was with him because I was in love with him. I don't want people to think he was like a creep or a scumbag or something."

"Look," my dad said, "his family—they're not gonna get

it. Most people won't get it, not unless they know you and saw how happy you guys were together. But fuck 'em, you know? Other people, they're gonna think what they're gonna think. If his family thinks of you as a sex worker now, they'll probably always think of you as a sex worker—whether you take money to move or not. And who cares if people think of you as a sex worker in the first place? There's no shame in that. People do what they need to do to survive."

I thought about my friends, many of whom had done sex work over the course of their lives just to survive. I thought about Anna Nicole Smith and trophy wives in the media. Then, I thought about my grandmother, who wasn't able to open a bank account without a father or husband signed on to it until her thirties and how women for decades needed to marry a man to have any legal rights to money at all. The relationship between women and men and money in a system of patriarchal capitalism has always been fraught. Drew paid the mortgage. I lived there for free because he liked me. Did that make me a sugar baby? Did even wondering do a massive disservice to the very real and different experience of sex work that my friends had? Did it even matter what anyone thought, really?

"Some of my favorite people are sex workers," I agreed with my dad over the phone. "I guess you're right, they're going to think what they're going to think—why do I care?"

"Exactly," my dad said. "So, you can feel weird about how these people view you and stay broke. Or you can feel weird about how these people view you and have enough money to at least move into your own apartment. Either way, let me know. I'll come down with a truck and help you move."

I texted Drew's relative later that day.

"I need three thousand dollars," I said. "To move. Deposit and first month's rent."

It felt like a fortune to me, and I wasn't sure if the family would go for it. A few minutes later, though, I received a reply.

"Done," it said.

Two weeks later, I was standing in an overpriced three-hundred-square-foot apartment trying to figure out how I was going to earn $1,500 per month for rent, not to mention another $1,200 or more each month for living expenses and bills. With no work lined up in the foreseeable future, I turned my sights on the one thing in my life that seemed to have the potential to be a viable income source: Tunnel Vision.

Since starting Tunnel Vision two years before, I'd put in enough effort to keep it operating at a consistent pace. After a year or so, Brit left to pursue a new business with a group of friends. This meant that for the last year, Tunnel Vision had been just me working as a sole proprietorship out of my house, with the occasional odd job for a friend who showed up in a bad place looking to earn some extra cash. Most months, Tunnel Vision did around $4,000 in sales, which is how I'd managed to qualify to rent an apartment in the first place. However, once I accounted for things like shipping costs, website fees, office supplies like mailers and printer ink, and the cost of the product, I wasn't taking much of a paycheck myself, if anything—usually, I kept around $500.

The day after settling into my new apartment, I sat on the couch with my laptop and set to work trying to turn Tunnel Vision into a real business—one that could actually pay my bills. I crunched numbers into a spreadsheet to figure out how the heck I could make the $2,720 per month I calculated I needed to survive. At the rate I was going, my take-home pay was just 12.5 percent of the business's gross monthly sales. That meant I'd need to sell nearly $22,000 per month just to keep $2,720. It hardly seemed feasible.

The most obvious driving factor for sales was availability of inventory. The more inventory I had, the more I could sell. However, unlike with a traditional retail business, my inventory was directly linked to the time I had available to find and post product. At that point I was carrying two different types of product on the website: Made-to-Order New and Vintage.

The made-to-order new items were sold in a slow, cumbersome process. I had samples of each of my designs, which I photographed on myself and posted to the website. Customers could place orders for which pieces they wanted, either choosing their size from our standard size chart or providing their own measurements for a truly custom fit. They paid in advance, and each week, I took their orders to my sewer downtown.

The sewer, a woman named Sofia, was the mother of my friend Gabriela, and she'd worked for years being exploited in a factory in downtown L.A. Los Angeles is the United States' garment production capital, with 45,000 garment workers in the city, the majority of whom are Latine or Asian immigrants. Sofia was a Latina immigrant herself and was unfamiliar with labor laws. For years, she didn't realize that she was earning less than the legally mandated minimum wage in the area, which isn't uncommon—garment manufacturing in Los Angeles is rife with human trafficking and labor violations, and preys on immigrants of color. In 2016, the U.S. Department of Labor found pay violations in 85 percent of garment manufacturing facilities in Los Angeles. In the city of L.A., minimum wage as of 2021 was $15 per hour. However, garment workers in the city limits that same year earned an average of just $5.85 per hour—with some earning as little as $2.68. A "Made in USA" tag on an article of clothing often means "Made in a Sweatshop in Downtown L.A."

By the time my friend Gabriela reached high school, she was fed up with her mother's exploitation in the garment industry.

"We're going to start our own clothing company," she told her mother one day, and by the end of the year, she'd delivered on her promise.

Not only had Gabriela started her own clothing company to help transition her mother out of the exploitative factories of downtown Los Angeles, she'd also put the word out to other local designers that her mother was available to sew clothing. I jumped at the opportunity, and soon I was purchasing finished pieces from Sofia, who sewed everything to order and set her own prices for fair labor, well above $20 per hour. Within a few months, Sofia was able to quit her job in the factory completely. Within a few years, Gabriela was able to hire her aunt and a family friend to sew for her business, too.

Sofia was a highly skilled patternmaker and sewer, and her work was more than worth the wait. The benefit to a made-to-order system was twofold: the company received the money first, then paid for the garments to be made, helping with cash flow because the only up-front production cost was having garment samples made and doing the patternmaking. And customers had the opportunity to input custom measurements if they wanted, ensuring the right fit.

The downside to the made-to-order system was the timing. Orders took anywhere from two weeks to four months to produce, depending on the workload at the time. It was difficult to ensure a certain delivery date, and for customers who'd never shopped with the company before, it was nearly impossible to maintain their confidence that the product they paid for was indeed coming, we just couldn't say exactly when. Often, I'd find the company bank account balance far lower than expected because customers filed fraud claims with their banks, who always sided with the customer. Sometimes, Sofia would make a product for a customer who had filed a claim just days before, meaning we were stuck with the product—often in custom measurements—and no payment for having made it. It was a complex, messy system in an Amazon-loving twenty-four-hour delivery world. More than once, I had a complete breakdown dealing with a hostile email from a customer who'd grown tired of waiting for their product to arrive.

The other product category I offered was vintage clothing, still typically sourced from a rag house. Within vintage, the largest challenge was just how much time and energy went into selling an item only one time. With a factory-made product, I could photograph the item once and sell it one hundred times. If I wanted to sell 100 vintage products, though, that meant 100 different photo sets. The labor costs associated with selling a vintage garment—sourcing, repairs, photography, editing, listing, packing, shipping—were astronomical, because the time that went into each piece was astronomical. I figured that if I wanted to take home $2,720 per month in Los Angeles, I needed to be paying myself something like $22 per hour before taxes. The cost of the actual goods sourced at the rag house ranged dramatically, but averaged around $12 per unit. Before even taking into account overhead, which was tricky to calculate—things like the monthly cost of maintaining the website, buying shipping labels and packaging supplies, paying for advertising, paying myself to create promotional emails or social media posts, buying printer ink, etc.—the bare minimum price that any piece of vintage could sell for needed to be $34.34. I set a mental note to never price a garment below $35, but struggled to explain the pricing to customers, who sometimes saw what they perceived to be an unwanted item from the trash.

Fortunately, we didn't have to pay additional rent on a commercial unit to house the product; instead, I rolled garments up tightly and crammed them into closets in my tiny apartment, covering the bulging closet space with tapestries to obscure the mess. I stored shipping supplies in my oven and kept a folded-up card table behind my refrigerator that I pulled out to pack orders.

Running a business was expensive—there were no two ways about it. The thing I learned fast, though, was that time was money. The faster I could work, the more items I could post to our website, which meant the more pieces I could potentially sell and the easier it would be to get my bills paid. Unable to truly allocate overhead, I figured it into the prices of the more heavyweight garments we sold. I might not be able to sell a simple shirt for more than $35, but I could sell a jacket or a pair of pants for $60 and hope it was enough to make up the difference.

The first month I worked on Tunnel Vision full-time, sales increased from $4,000 to $11,000 per month. I managed to earn my $2,720 of take-home pay, but it came with long hours. I was working 80–100 hours per week, amounting to a take-home pay of just $8.50 per hour—well below minimum wage in Los Angeles. As the months went on, the grueling work schedule became increasingly untenable. I was exhausted constantly and my body ached from carrying hundreds of pounds of clothing around between rag houses, the photo studio, and my apartment. Fortunately, I had lots of friends who were eager to help take some of the workload off my hands. Unfortunately, hiring people created financial instability within the business nearly immediately.

The thing about hiring people to help you is that you usually don't set off thinking "Ah, yes—how can I exploit the labor of others to turn a profit?" Or at least I didn't—I'm not sure about people like Jeff Bezos or Elon Musk. You usually set out trying to help your friends pay their rent, and when you run a small business, people you know come out of the woodwork looking for a job. Money was tight, but I figured I could set aside around $1,000 each month to pay friends for help here and there.

In the beginning, it was easy to administer: friends would approach me looking for a little extra cash, and I'd give them a couple hundred bucks to ship out some orders. Usually, they earned what I earned for their time—or maybe even a little more. My finances were easy to maintain, and the little extra here and there helped out the people in my life. However, as the business grew, more and more people I knew came to me, telling me about their desperate financial situations and asking if I had any work—and they meant *any* work—I could throw their way. My instinct had always been to help out my community in any way possible, so I met with an acquaintance who also ran a business to ask if she had any advice for how to grow my brand so that I could hire more of my friends. With a serious tone, she advised me to max out my credit cards on inventory.

"You've got to spend money to make money," she said, nodding her head like she knew something I didn't.

It sounded reasonable enough—like something rich people told each other while slapping one another on the back in a crowded oak-paneled room where they smoked cigars and laughed about their stock portfolios. To grow the business to the size it needed to be to support the people I cared about who were struggling to find work, I'd have to be comfortable investing money into it. What followed, though, was a period of three or so years that I call "The Doomed Periods: Part I and Part II."

THE DOOMED PERIOD, PART I: THE "MARKETPLACE" IDEA

As I started considering bringing friends on to help me at work, I became fixated on creating a system wherein people had ownership and agency over their roles. I wanted the workers to own the means of production, but I wasn't exactly sure how to make that happen in a capitalist system. The first idea I came across was that of a cooperative-style marketplace, wherein each member (including me) worked a certain number of hours for the business—working on photo shoots or shipping orders or posting to social media—in exchange for being able to sell a certain corresponding number of items on the website (usually vintage garments we each sourced ourselves, or our own garment and accessory designs sewed together on a dinky Singer sewing machine at home). From there, we all earned a 100 percent commission on our sales, and we used just the sales income from made-to-order products to fund the company's overhead.

It sounded great in theory. However, I was beginning to find that what seemed fair in theory wasn't actually fair in

practice. Instead, I at times felt like I'd re-created the capitalist "hustle" culture I'd come to loathe. Now, everyone who
worked at Tunnel Vision was the owner of their own tiny little
clothing business, and along with that came the stress of business ownership. Workers now had to manage their own purchasing budgets and sourcing times, as well as stay up-to-date
on consumer trends if they wanted to earn enough money to
live comfortably. Not everyone was good at it, either. Some
people struggled to understand trend cycles; they worked just
as hard as someone else but earned less money because their
product didn't sell as well. Frustrations mounted, and I learned
quickly that not everyone wanted to manage their own miniature business. Some people just wanted to get a paycheck and
go home. In trying to thwart capitalism, I accidentally created
something akin to *ultra* capitalism. I went back to the drawing
board to try to come up with a more equitable system, which
brings us to the Doomed Period, Part II.

THE DOOMED PERIOD, PART II: FROM EACH ACCORDING TO THEIR ABILITY, TO EACH ACCORDING TO THEIR NEED

The second system of worker payment we tried at the business was less precise. It was more based on what everyone
needed to survive, coupled with what people felt they brought
to the table at work as an asset. We had candid conversations
about workers' incomes and budgets and expenses, and tried
to come up with a system that paid everyone fairly based on
their needs. Having student loans, for example, would neces-
sitate slightly higher pay. Having less of a family safety net
would come with higher wages, as well. Confusion quickly
reigned. People from higher-income backgrounds had higher
expectations of what a "livable wage" was compared to people
from lower-income backgrounds. Those same people also had
different ideas of what their "needs" were compared to others.
     Without the standardizing force of a shared cultural or
social value system, manifesting ideas of "need" and "ability"
in our little workplace became virtually impossible. Suddenly,

we were late paying bills and the business became difficult to maneuver. Some people spent their days doing tasks that did not result in bringing money directly into the company—things like alphabetizing or senseless folding—and failed to see how that work was not beneficial to the bottom line. By this time, we were averaging between $200,000 and $250,000 in total gross annual sales but trying to support multiple people on that income. All of our incomes dropped to below the $20 per hour mark, creating massive financial strain on everyone. I began putting my personal bills on credit cards some months to make sure everyone else got paid what they needed to survive. Pay discrepancy was technically negligible—thirty cents here and there per hour—but the differences in income seemed to pit workers against each other; morale plummeted and I often found myself not earning enough to live. The second system was even worse than the first, and I went back to the drawing board, trying to consider how best to operate a business fairly.

Six months later, the lease on my tiny $1,500 apartment was up and I found myself moving into a three-bedroom house in Eagle Rock with lots of roommates and cheap rent. I split a room with my new boyfriend, Chris, and paid just $350 per month for my half. Tunnel Vision set up shop out in the garage. My personal budget suddenly had a lot more wiggle room, and I was able to stop relying on credit cards to make ends meet. Now, though, I found myself at the bottom of a financial pit I'd dug for myself, and struggling to climb my way out of it.

It turns out that I had picked a good time to cut down on expenses. The first six months of 2017 were catastrophic for business. Sales declined 30 percent, which took a massive toll on our already strapped cash flow. By June, the business was selling just $12,000 per month but carrying the burden of multiple employees. My personal income was averaging a little over $1,500 per month—or $19,000 per year. I took out personal loans again to help pay down my high-interest debt, but still struggled to make even my minimum monthly payments. I started taking scheduled "cry breaks" in my backyard. I had never wanted to own a business or be responsible for the incomes of other people. I just wanted a good job that paid my bills, and for all my friends to be okay. Where had all the good jobs gone? I scoured job listings online, applying for minimum-wage jobs only to be ignored for months on end. Graduating into the recession had thrown my career trajectory so far off course that I was somehow simultaneously overqualified or underqualified for every job on the market.

"If you get another job, what happens to Tunnel Vision?" a friend who worked at the business asked in a quiet tone one day.

"What do you mean?" I asked.

"Well, what about us? The business can't exist without you," she pointed out. "We don't know how to do everything you do, and frankly I don't think some of it can be taught. So, we all just lose our jobs?"

I realized then that I had re-created Drew's fatal mistake: in the great airplane crash of small-business management, I'd neglected to put on my own mask before helping others. The problem is that I was the pilot. Now the plane was going down and all of us would die in a fiery crash. I came to understand a hard truth about survival, which was that the business wouldn't exist to pay anyone's bills come next year unless I made some harsh changes to how things worked.

I decided that I had to do the very thing I'd told Drew to do three years prior: cut costs to save the business. I walked into the garage where Tunnel Vision headquarters was and laid everyone off except for two people. For the remaining two workers, I tightened the belt on job duties. The change in direction was too much for one employee to handle. She resigned a few months later. By the end of summer 2017, as the Doomed Periods were coming to a close, I had $63,012.50 of personal debt, $29,986.08 of business debt, an overdrawn checking account, one remaining employee, and no fucking clue how I was going to make it through the end of the year.

How to Feel Happy When Everything Around You Feels Sad

In a world where everything seems terrible and doomed to fail, how do you stay happy? I haven't figured out a foolproof way to be happy all the time, but here's what I have managed to figure out:

1. Don't move goalposts. Too often, we think we'll be happy when or happy if. Rather than waiting for something major to change in your life, try to force yourself to appreciate where you are right now. What do you have in your life today that ten years ago you could have only dreamed of having? Maybe it's something little, like your own room or a pet. Whatever the case, remember that Present You is living at least some of Past You's dreams. Take time to savor that.

2. Focus on the things you can control. So much of our lives is out of our control—at the hands of bosses or landlords or politicians or CEOs. Think about the things that you have some say over in your day-to-day life: what color you paint the walls of your home, what clothes you wear today, what music you listen to, what books you read. Savor those opportunities for control and use them to help build a life that brings you joy, even if that joy seems relatively small.

3. Remember to dream. Sometimes life feels like an endless futile circle of struggle and hardship. In these times especially, it's important to remember that there are a million different ways to live a life. Imagine what things in your life you could change if you decided you wanted to. Maybe you'd move to another state. Maybe you'd change your name. Maybe you'd start a band. Whatever your situation, imagining different potential futures helps you remember that things don't have to be all bad. You can always choose to live a slightly different life tomorrow.

4. Feel joy as an act of resistance. Be happy despite all the bullshit. Remember that you deserve it, no matter how much the world around you tries to convince you otherwise.

CHAPTER 11

If You've Ever Read
Rich Dad Poor Dad,
You May Be Entitled to
Financial Compensation

The employee who remained at the company was Camila, a UCLA dropout turned stripper who was looking to turn her interest in fashion into a humble job that paid the bills. Together, the two of us were able to run Tunnel Vision completely on our own, and my panic began to subside. Bills were getting paid on time again. I was earning less than I had in years past and still struggling with mountains of debt, but was feeling optimistic about the business for the first time in years. We moved from the garage into an air-conditioned spare room of the house, away from the horrendous heat of the Los Angeles summers. Tunnel Vision was even able to pay its share of rent for the room. The business had secured its oxygen mask in the midst of a freefall into certain tragedy, and now I had the chance to help secure mine and Camila's, too.

Soon, I implemented a new rule for how we got paid at Tunnel Vision: everyone, including me, earned the same day rate. I worked five days per week and Camila worked four, so my monthly pay worked out to be more than hers. However, the rate for hours worked was exactly the same. Conventional business writing would have me mark this moment with an "a-ha" of some kind—as though I came to a sudden realization about why everyone who worked at the business deserved to earn the same amount I did. However, the truth is a lot more mundane. It was easier to keep track of for accounting, and it just felt the fairest, especially coming off the chaotic money management attempts of the Doomed Periods.

Now, though, when I tell people everyone at our business earns the same pay, they often assume it was more conscious than it was.

"You struggled," a man told me once. "You decided that you don't want to see other people struggle like you did."

"You grew up thinking about your community and not just yourself," a woman told me once. "You were determined to think in terms of 'us' rather than 'me.'"

"You're angry at the government for failing so many people," a friend of a friend told me once. "You want to prove that it's not hard to take care of people if you try."

For any of this to be true, though, it means viewing labor exploitation as the norm and anything else as a benevolent gift of some kind. Paying Camila the same wage as me wasn't an act of generosity. She worked just as hard as I did, and the business couldn't run without her. It was just fair.

Still, Camila and I weren't earning a lot of money, and found ourselves still barely scraping by.

"We've gotta learn more about how money works," I told Camila one day, as we stood around a table packing orders. "People are always saying 'financial literacy,' but what does that mean? It seems like the answer is just that we need more money. But then you hear about those people who come into money and then blow it all making bad financial decisions, so it can't just be that we need more money, right?"

I thought about a girl from my hometown, Amanda. She grew up with a single mom who was struggling with addiction; the two were estranged from the rest of their family as a result. One day, out of the blue, a lawyer contacted Amanda. She must have been around twenty years old at the time. Apparently, Amanda's estranged aunt had died and left her $30,000 in her will. To people like us—broke kids from

Fresno—$30,000 was a life-changing amount of money. Amanda had big dreams for what she'd do with it. She'd start a business, she decided. Something she always wanted to do. In the end, though, she spent a year partying and blew through it all. She felt awful about it; it seemed shameful to mess up what was surely a once-in-a-lifetime opportunity. She just had been so confused and overwhelmed that the money sat in her bank account, slowly getting chipped away every single day until there was nothing left. Then, a few years later, another lawyer reached out. It turned out *another* estranged family member had died, leaving Amanda roughly the same amount of money yet again. She got a *do-over*. And what did she do? The exact same thing. The money sat in her bank account, slowly getting used up until there was nothing left to use. It didn't change her life. It just funded it for a bit. It's easy for that to happen when you're broke, though. You're not earning enough to comfortably fund your life in the first place.

"We need more money, obviously, sure," I told Camila. "But we also need to know, like, how money works. So we know what to do with money if we ever get more of it."

"Who knows how money works?" Camila asked.

I thought about it for a minute.

"Rich conservative old men," I said, decisively. "They're the ones who are always talking about financial literacy. We've gotta find an old rich Republican man to teach us about money."

"I probably could find a few," she said, laughing. She was still working at the strip club at night—a place surely full of rich men looking to spend money on a pretty girl.

"No, not them," I told her. "Someone we won't have to talk to. We've got to find, like, an audiobook or a podcast or something."

I finished packing up an order, then sat down at my computer and opened a web browser tab. I gazed intently into my computer screen as the familiar Google logo stared back at me. What should I even search?

How does money work, I typed into the search engine.

I hit Enter, and with that, Camila and I began a five-year journey into the world of financial literacy. From what I could tell, financial literacy seemed to be separated into three main pillars of thinking, which I nicknamed Consumer Minimalism, Working-Class Realism, and Exploitative Entrepreneurship. Each of them boasted a different approach to surviving capitalism, each with its own value system and moral code, with which Camila and I became quickly familiar.

CONSUMER MINIMALISM

The first financial literacy approach I came across was the ideology I called Consumer Minimalism, which seemed to place high value on people, the planet, and sustainability—at least at first glance.

"I found something," I told Camila after scrolling through the search results on my computer.

I pulled up an audiobook and hit Play. A velvety smooth feminine voice came through the speaker in our office, promising to transform our relationship with money, as well as our relationship to our community and the planet. We looked at each other and nodded. This was what we were looking for.

The message seemed to be that the more you could reduce your consumption, the better it would be not only for your own personal finances, but also for the planet. The consumer minimalist mindset eschewed thoughtless spending and sought to remind people that even something as simple as a pen still came from the earth, relying on natural resources to create. Mindless consumption, this outlook argued, was bad for the planet, while locking people into an endless cycle of work and misery to fulfill the constant desire to purchase more. Instead of earning an income just to spend it all each paycheck and start over again, one should focus on minimizing their expenses and maximizing their income, then investing as much as possible into a retirement account. The less you spend, this approach said, the more you can invest, and the more you invest, the sooner you can retire and finally get out of the rat race of the 9-to-5 job.

Consumer minimalists proclaimed that retirement wasn't something you just did at sixty-five after your whole life had already passed you by. Retirement was something you could do whenever you were financially ready, especially if your expenses were relatively small, and both your health and your quality of life would improve radically the second you jumped out of the traditional work and money relationship. I didn't even know retirement was a realistic option for someone like me. I always figured I'd work until I died, and this nihilistic macabre sentiment was echoed throughout the consumer minimalist's approach to money management.

"We aren't making a living," one book called *Your Money or Your Life* proclaimed. "We're making a dying."

They weren't wrong. Seventy-seven percent of Americans experience stress to the extent that it adversely affects their physical health. Nearly half of all Americans lose sleep over it. I should know; I was one of them. I thought about the nights I woke up in a panicked state, gasping for air and grabbing my telephone so I could check my bank account balance. We *were* all making a dying.

For the next few days, Camila and I played consumer minimalist audiobooks and media while we worked. It was enthralling, painting a picture of a better life made possible through strict regulation of your own personal finances and an acute awareness of the toll capitalist-encouraged overconsumption took on the world. One woman imagined a world where instead of paying someone to fix your car, you took the time to learn how to repair your own car because you weren't burdened by the obligation of a forty-hour-per-week job. Your job, she claimed, could instead be doing what you loved and learning how to take care of yourself. She pictured a community where neighbors with different skills helped each other get by. The secret to all of this was simple, she said: budget religiously, cut your spending as much as possible, and prioritize your retirement saving. Money could buy happiness in small doses, she agreed. However, you'd have to look inward and do some serious self-reflection to learn what things you purchased *actually* contributed to your overall happiness.

If I spent $6 on an ice cream, the books asked, how many hours of work did it take me to earn that $6—including things like commute times and getting ready for work? Was that amount of life worth the experience of eating the ice cream? What would my life look like instead if I bought a used ice cream maker from the thrift store and had the spare time to make all the ice cream I wanted for myself and my friends? I felt myself wrestling with ideas of value, consumption, and labor in ways I hadn't since my teenage years reading punk rock zines about syndicalism and worker councils. I understood instinctively the ideas of wasting your life working for somebody else and the appeal of purchasing things just to feel alive because the day-to-day existence of work was soul-crushing and stress-inducing. I understood less how to find the balance between "deserving" a special treat now and then, and mindless consumption.

Then there was the toll capitalism took on natural resources. The system relies on constant expansion to increase profits. However, constant expansion in a finite world hardly seems possible unless the resources are constantly regenerating. We already know things like oil and coal are non-renewable—they are finite and once they are depleted, they are gone forever. We also know things like lithium are facing increasing scarcity, too. From an ecological perspective, rejecting the constant consumption of non-essential new goods seems like the only way to curb the inevitability of total environmental destruction at the hands of capitalism. However, denying ourselves small conveniences or instances of joy while trying to exist in a system that we did not set up seems to punish the people who are already being punished by the system to begin with—low-income wage workers just doing their best to get by.

I myself was a business owner, but there wasn't enough profit in the business for me to even extract. I earned a wage for my work just like Camila did, and we both were struggling. Most of the product we sold was secondhand, too, which meant we weren't mindlessly producing new items just for the sake of it. We made new things, sure, but in small batches only to fulfill demand, minimizing waste and overproduction.

The consumer minimalist mindset asked the right questions for someone like me or Camila struggling to figure out how to derive pleasure from a consumption-based world while living on wages that didn't facilitate a comfortable level of consumption. However, the solution that it came up with was tricky. Investing in your retirement so that you can opt out of the senseless drudgery of a 9-to-5 job and instead utilize your skills in a community setting to help support other people who have also opted out sounds delightful—except for the fundamental logistical hiccup of how the U.S. retirement system is structured.

The U.S. retirement system relies heavily on IRAs and 401(k)s, which are both investment accounts utilizing the U.S. stock market. This is an exchange where everyday people can buy and sell stock—pieces of ownership of publicly traded companies. So, if you buy a share of Apple stock, for example, you then own a teeny tiny portion of Apple, and you can sell it to someone else if you want. The value of that Apple stock is speculative based on the projected future of the company. If the company goes out of business, a share of ownership of it is meaningless. However, if the company stays in business, the value of the stock might go up. If you buy a share of stock at a low price, like $5, then hold on to it for twenty years, it might be worth a lot more—something like $33. If you sell it at that point, you would have profited $28, and you might have earned dividends—cash payments from the company—along the way. IRAs and 401(k)s are really just stock portfolios—a diversified collection of stocks that American retirees are banking on increasing in value over time, which they can then draw on to live. In the greater scheme of investment, retirement investing is generally considered to be pretty low risk. Sure, there are bad years for the U.S. stock market, where every stock seems to go down dramatically in value. However, over long periods of time, the S&P 500 (an index tracking the performance of the 500 largest companies listed on the stock exchange in the United States) goes up an average of 10 percent per year.

The safest bet, according to experts, tends to be buying shares in a mutual fund containing a little bit of stock from each of those huge companies that make up the S&P 500. However, those are also the same companies wreaking havoc on the environment and exploiting their workers. Chevron, for example, is the fifteenth-largest company in the S&P 500. They're also the number 2 top polluting company in the world by carbon dioxide measurements since 1965. Halliburton is number 222 on the S&P 500. They were recently found to have illegally withheld $18.7 million in wages from over 1,050 employees. While most stock market investing is done on a secondhand market—meaning you're buying and selling stock to other regular people like you, not giving Halliburton your money directly, the stock still has value based on the work of those exploited laborers. HP (number 266 on the S&P 500) was reportedly caught using sweatshop labor in 2009.

Herein lies the contradiction of the consumer minimalism approach: *you* can opt out of contributing to environmental harm and having to submit yourself to the dull drudgery of a regular job, but only as long as the company whose stock you're holding contributes to environmental harm, and other people keep showing up to work the dull drudgery of their regular jobs at those companies. It doesn't offer a more ethical way to exist in the world. It instead offers regular people an imperfect solution for just trying to survive in the imperfect system that already exists.

It was exciting to consider a life where I cracked the code and got to quit working forever; however, it would be intrinsically impossible for everyone to do this. In some ways, it was just another form of individualism or escapism. Intrigued but disappointed, I turned my attention to the next school of financial literacy thinking—the one I nicknamed Working-Class Realism.

WORKING-CLASS REALISM

If Consumer Minimalism was a proxy form of hippie environmentalism, Working-Class Realism was the opposite. Steadfast, practical, and unrelentingly conservative, Working-Class Realism said yes, life is hard and you have problems, but if you're disciplined enough you can make out okay—not great, but okay—despite that. It was austere and steeped heavily in religious rhetoric of dignity and prudence, but it felt approachable and easy to understand, so Camila and I dove in.

I had originally set out to find a rich Republican guy to teach us about money, and Working-Class Realism delivered. On paper, the proponents of this type of thinking were everything I wasn't: evangelical Christians—men of family and God with a capital "G." They were also usually staunch proponents of the political right, consistently lambasting the very things I wanted more of: social safety nets and government assistance programs and gay-only grocery stores for transgender puppeteers (or whatever made-up thing the right-wing television media was trying to whip its viewers into a frenzy about that day). However, I quickly learned that it was men like them who created the system I was trying to exist in, so it would probably be men like them who were best equipped to teach me how to deal with it. If capitalism was a horrific board game, rich conservative men seemed to know the rules.

The most famous personality in the realm of Working-Class Realism stood out in his approach to debt. This guy hated debt—I mean really hated it—and had a strict zero debt policy, which he doled out in harsh truths. Shockingly, those harsh truths also seemed to revolve around an idea that the bank was your enemy—something I would not have expected from a businessman who seemed to love deregulation and whose right-wing values favored big business. He constantly reminded the everyday people in his audience that banks were there to make money from us, not the other way around.

I thought about my own life as I listened to his words. At my most broke, nearly all of my money was tied up in repaying debt—making just minimum monthly payments because I couldn't afford to pay more, all while interest rates continued to make that debt balloon out of control. I had always considered myself responsible with debt, using my credit cards only for emergencies like car repairs and medical bills. However, I wondered: What would my monthly budgets look like if I didn't have debt at all?

Some Working-Class Realism financial advisors also railed against the predatory check-cashing institutions found predominantly in low-income neighborhoods and neighborhoods of color, where financial literacy was less likely to be taught. Perhaps most shockingly, they cited structural institutional failings in explaining why people end up in debt, rather than blaming it on personal shortcomings like so many right-wing pundits on television did. Instead, these financial advisors seemed to say "Look, you didn't create this system— some rich guy did and now he wants to take everything you have from you. Be angry, don't let him take your money from you—fight back."

While the working-class realist top personalities hypocritically danced around their own roles as rich guys in the system (most of them were multimillionaires who owned businesses built on financial literacy empires), their lessons on money actually felt relatively commonsense and clear. Camila and I played audiobooks and call-in shows while we packed orders in the office. They talked about retirement planning and how even small portions of savings on a tight income—if done consistently over time—could create the healthy retirement fund we all needed. We heard of people like teachers and janitors earning $30,000 per year who still ended up retiring with a net worth of over $1 million just from steadily investing something like $200 per month over a period of forty years in their retirement accounts. These advisors criticized materialism and consumerism in southern accents, often while quoting the Bible. They advocated for side hustles as a means to survive—often telling even well-off people to not feel above getting a second job delivering pizzas if they'd been financially irresponsible in the past. They extolled the importance of never feeling too special to roll up your sleeves and do the dirty work. At the same time, they were surprisingly compassionate with people who struggled with mental health issues or physical disabilities and were just trying to get by on a small salary.

Listening to the mostly conservative audience base call in to these money-management shows, I couldn't help but think about how much I had in common with them financially. On the one hand, I was ethically and morally everything they would not like: a blue-haired bisexual leftist atheist who lived out of wedlock and in sin with her boyfriend and didn't even really believe in marriage, let alone think I'd ever have kids (and if they didn't like me, they certainly wouldn't like Camila given her night job). On the other hand, despite our political and social differences, our financial realities were often the same: we were all just regular people who weren't afraid of putting in hard work as long as it meant we could actually afford to live, and we were all frustrated with the system that seemed to make survival difficult no matter how hard we worked. We both needed someone to explain the rules to us.

Still, the crux of the financial advice was the same for working-class realists as for the consumer minimalists: invest in your retirement account. I wondered if there was an option for financial stability that didn't involve the stock market. Fortunately, there did seem to be one other approach. Unfortunately, it seemed to be even *less* ethical than buying stock: real estate investing. This brought us to the third type of financial outlook we found, the one I nicknamed Exploitative Entrepreneurship.

EXPLOITATIVE ENTREPRENEURSHIP

Camila and I started our journey into the third school of financial thinking by reading some of the most popular financial literacy books on the market, as well as listening to podcasts about investing. Advisors in this school of thought regularly conflated "intelligence" with money, creating a narrative that seemed to say "only the stupid are poor." Rich people own things: houses, apartments, buildings, and businesses. They then make money by having someone else pay their mortgage or do their work for them. The general message of the exploitative entrepreneurs was this: poor people are poor because they aren't *smart* enough to be part of the owning class.

It was the opposite of my belief system entirely, and it seemed hypocritical to me to acknowledge that in capitalism, some people are destined to be taken advantage of but that only the "stupid" find themselves in that position. How would a society work if everyone in it was "intelligent enough" to own assets and never labor? It was an unsustainable solution that prioritized individual exceptionalism to the detriment of common sense. To put it succinctly, if everyone owns a burger shop but refuses to work in it, who will flip the burgers?

The Exploitative Entrepreneurship path would have me cut Camila's pay down to minimum wage and use the extra money I earned from underpaying her to buy an apartment building. Then, I'd pay the mortgage on the apartment building by making sure the monthly rent I charged each tenant was way more than the mortgage fees and cost of maintaining it. In a few years' time, the apartment building would be so lucrative that I could take out a new loan based on its increased value and use that money to buy another, bigger apartment building. Meanwhile, if my business continued to increase profit by doing things like underpaying Camila, eventually I could stop working altogether and just live off the profit my business generates. In ten years' time, following the plans set forth by these advisors, I could own ten apartment buildings and work an hour per week if I wanted to, all while clearing a six-figure annual salary.

It was hard listening to the Exploitative Entrepreneurship crowd, mostly because I knew they were technically, mathematically, right. In a system of capitalism, this is how the rich made money: buying appreciating assets, taking out loans on the perceived appreciation, then using that money to buy another appreciating asset and do the same thing all over again. The appreciating assets were usually businesses— where profit was extracted by paying workers as little as possible—or buildings, where profit was made by charging tenants as much in rent as possible. It felt callous and cruel to me in a way that made my blood run cold. Exploitative Entrepreneurship reduced everyday people to line items on a profit and loss statement. As voices on our office speaker droned on about working smarter not harder, I'd shoot sideways glances at Camila packing orders at the table next to me. How could a business owner look someone like Camila in the eye, I wondered, and tell her she deserved to suffer so they didn't have to?

Over the weeks that we listened to financial literacy gurus tell us their perspectives on the world all day while we worked, Camila and I started to develop our own consensus about what was probably true and useful for us. What we decided is as follows:

1. Being debt-free was probably good. (Camila had a head start on this compared to me—she had no debt whatsoever.)

2. Buying a house seemed smart. (Otherwise you'd just end up giving some jerk your hard-earned money because he decided the place you lived in was an "income-generating asset" he wanted to own.)

3. Being mindful with your consumption of new goods was probably a good thing for both you and the planet. (We both had a leg up on this one—we were used to shopping for nearly everything we could find secondhand from the thrift store.)

4. Saving for retirement was doable even on a small income, and the elderly version of yourself who was most likely unable to work would thank you later.

5. There were no perfect or truly moral solutions in a system of capitalism, only survival skills—still, though, we should do our best to minimize our harm to others while trying to survive.

6. Investing in the stock market was imperfect, but the companies on the S&P 500 did make use of the public utilities we all paid taxes for—things like roads and power grids—so maybe we should all be entitled to get some value back from those businesses, even if the system doled it out in a clumsy, inelegant, and flawed way that required you to "buy in." Surely it was still a little better than just one rich guy owning it all himself.

7. We'd have to get comfortable making flawed and clumsy decisions ourselves if we wanted to have access to things like food and shelter in our old age.

8. Whatever attempts we'd made at keeping track of our finances in the past were probably inadequate; if we wanted to truly maximize our small incomes, we'd need to get a lot more detailed and a lot more disciplined.

With this in mind, I set to work developing a financial plan for myself. I opened a spreadsheet on my computer and plopped my debts into it, with the date—July 21, 2017—at the top. The list read:

DEBT	AMOUNT	INTEREST RATE
Credit card	$19,228.50	21.36%
Student loans	$16,557.75	6.84%
Car loan	$18,000.00	5.5%
Personal loan (debt consolidation)	$4,291.62	11.04%
IRS (tax debt from filing my taxes wrong, whoops)	$4,934.62	0%
TOTAL	**$63,012.49**	

In three years, I'd paid off less than $2,000 of debt—or roughly $666.67 per year, despite paying far more than that towards my accounts each month. At this rate, it would take me 94 years to pay off my debt in total. Something in my life needed to change.

I opened a new spreadsheet and started creating a budget. I'd made budgets before, but this time I felt inspired like never before. Not only would I make a budget, I'd make the most accurate budget of all time—one that showed my true spending down to the dollar, without forgetting a single thing. I opened my bank account records and went through all my expenses for the past month, plopping them into my spreadsheet.

INCOME	$1,800
Taxes	-$225
Rent	-$350
Credit card	-$200
Student loans	-$250
Car payment	-$250
Personal loan	-$300
Phone	-$150
Internet	-$50
Power bill	-$50
Gas company	-$10
Groceries	-$200
Pet insurance	-$50
Dog food	-$20
Car insurance	-$90
Tax debt	-$50
Netflix	-$10
Spotify	-$5
Hulu	-$7
TOTAL	**-$467**

No wonder I was so stressed out all the time, I thought to myself. Without even including gas for my car or a non-subscription-based entertainment budget, I was still overspending each month. I needed to find a way to cut $467 from my budget immediately. I rearranged the line items on my expenses, putting the things that would be hardest to change—like rent and my minimum monthly payments on bills—at the top and the things that would be easiest to change at the bottom. Slowly, I looked at each line item, working my way up from the bottom. My subscription services would be the easiest to change, but they were also the most insignificant—amounting to just $22 per month. I skipped them and moved up the list, plugging in a number for each item until it reached something I thought I could live with. If I wanted to get to a break-even point and then some, I'd have to defer my student loans, then find a way to cut my spending on my phone, internet, power, pet insurance, groceries, car, and car insurance. If I could pull it off, not only would I break even, but I'd also have an extra $40 or so per month—or $10 per week to use as my "allowance" so I didn't positively lose my mind. From there, I reasoned, I could find other ways to drum up extra cash to throw at my debt.

The first thing I tackled was my student loan debt. I called my provider and asked for an economic hardship deferral. With my income, it was an easy sell. Next, I moved on to my phone bill. Phone plans are notoriously confusing. I wasn't even sure what I was paying for. I knew $50 per month was to pay off my phone. When my last phone finally died, I'd gone into the Sprint store hoping to get the cheapest thing I could find. However, for someone like me without anything in savings and no cash on hand, the cheapest thing ended up being the monthly payments on a brand-new phone with no money down thanks to a promotion they had going on at the time. Being broke was more expensive than being rich sometimes. If I got a different phone, though, I could get rid of that monthly charge. I texted friends asking if anyone had an old phone lying around that they weren't using anymore, and dutifully Kennedy responded. She brought me her old phone that night. The next day, I went to the Sprint store desperate for help. I walked up to the first salesperson I found, channeling everything I'd learned from working with the Director.

"Hi," I told him. "Turns out I'm poor. And I don't even know if I can afford a phone. But if I can afford a phone, I can only spend like forty-five dollars per month. And I have this old phone I could transfer everything to, so I'm not paying to, like, own a brand-new phone. Can you help me?"

"Forty-five dollars per month, huh?" he said, scrunching his face up like he was thinking. "It's pretty low, but I think we can do that. Let's see what we can make happen."

We sat at his computer for what seemed like hours removing everything we could from my phone plan—things like hotspots and unlimited data and the old phone payment. We switched my phone out for Kennedy's old one. In the end, he smiled brightly.

"We did it," he said. "Look, forty-five dollars. It will start on your next billing cycle."

I felt invigorated.

Next, I called my internet company. I'd been paying for the fastest internet on the market. The cheapest they offered, though, was $50—which I could split with my boyfriend, making my share $25. Next up was the power bill. That would come down to my personal power consumption, I figured, meaning I'd have to be a lot more mindful of things like air-conditioning and heat. It wouldn't be instant and it would take behavioral changes, but if I was aware, it seemed within the realm of possibility. Then there was my pet insurance. I could have forgone it completely, but it had saved me in a pinch before. The last thing I wanted to do was be in a pet emergency where I needed to put a $3,000 vet bill on my credit card. I reduced my dog's plan to the cheapest one they offered, coming in at just $29.99 per month.

Next on my list was groceries. I thought about how I typically shopped for food. It was chaotic and unplanned, with seemingly random acquisitions of snacks and packaged items, mixed in with vegetables here and there. Things tended to expire or sit unused in my pantry for months. To make every dollar count, I'd need to be efficient with my food planning. I sat down with a cookbook and made a detailed two-week food schedule for myself, counting every onion and clove of garlic out for each recipe, with the goal of spending just $75 per trip to the grocery store every two weeks. I googled *cheapest foods to eat* and found lists recommending diets rich in lentils and rice and beans and pasta. Since every meal made two servings, I figured I'd eat the leftovers from dinner as lunch the next day. I filled in my two-week food plan down to the salt and pepper and it came in at $74.62. I saved meal prep checklists in my kitchen like a bible. I listened to the "experts" and vowed to never go grocery shopping while hungry, lest I impulse-buy.

Last up was my car. If I got a cheaper car, I decided, I could probably drop the price of my car insurance along with it. I'd recently opted for a newer and more reliable car after years of running into repeated bad luck with older and more beat-up cars that appeared at first glance to be in my budget, but ended up being money pits in need of constant major repairs. While the consistency of the car payment and reliability of the newer car was nice, all the comfort in the world didn't change the fact that I simply couldn't afford it like I'd hoped. I reasoned that there had to be a middle ground—maybe what they called a "nused" car, a portmanteau of "new" and "used" that was usually a three-year-old lease turn-in with minimal wear and tear. I took my car to the dealership and traded it in for a nused Kia. Weirdly, the nused Kia I left with was a little bit nicer, but with my trade-in and new lower interest rates, my monthly payments worked out to be less: $200 instead of $250. I called my car insurance company and told them my budget for car insurance: just $50 per month.

In the end, I managed to change my spending to allow for $10 of "fun money" per week. Now, I'd just have to figure out how to not go off budget. I had never lived a financially reck-less lifestyle, but my small treats to myself certainly added up each month. If I wanted to stick to my budget, I'd have to make it easier to stay on track than to veer off course. I wondered if it might be easier to set up a separate account for my fun money and make that the only debit card I took with me out into the world. I signed up for a new $0 fee checking account online with a bank separate from my own, then set up an auto-transfer of $10 per week to go into my new account. The new bank account had no overdraft possibility, and that $10 per week would be the only money I had regular access to. I nicknamed it my "allowance" account. As long as it was at a separate bank, I'd also have no way to impulsively transfer money in and out of it for other things. It wasn't much, but it was enough to take a weekend walk to get a cup of coffee or purchase one article of clothing at a thrift store if I wanted.

Last, I needed a place that the money earmarked for my bills could go. I set up a separate account nicknamed "Bills" and calculated out the total amount that would need to go into it each pay period to ensure bills got paid. I created an auto-transfer for the day after payday, taking the required amount and moving it into the bill payment account. I set up each bill to automatically be paid from the "Bills" account, ensuring I'd never forget about a payment or come up short. This meant that my regular checking account would only have $3 or so in it every week after I got paid from Tunnel Vision, which meant I'd never again make the mistake of looking at my account and thinking I had more money than I did.

With my new banking system in place, it would be nearly impossible for me to make rash decisions. Everything was fully automated, and I never had to wonder what was going on with my finances. I was still broke, sure, but the constant pressure and stress of checking my accounts and feeling out of control seemed to vanish completely. In one week, without an increase in pay, I went from panicking over money every day to seldom thinking about it at all. The peace of mind my new system awarded me was unmatched. For the first time in my life, I felt in control of my finances.

With my day-to-day cash flow automated, I tackled my big-picture financial goals next. I knew I needed to find an extra source of income to throw at my debt. I walked around my house collecting odds and ends to sell, like I had so many times before. This time, though, every single piece would be sold for dirt cheap on the internet—$5 or so—just to make sure it really moved, and the money would instantly go into my PayPal account. Separate from my other bank accounts, it was clearly identified as "extra money" so I could transfer it directly as a payment towards my smallest source of debt each week: the personal loan. Every month, I was able to drum up an extra $100 or $200 from my low-priced online sales to chuck at my personal loan. Slowly, the amount I owed got lower and lower. I was making progress like I never had before.

By the end of 2017, Camila and I both had a new outlook on money. For the first time in our lives, we talked about things like owning a home or saving for retirement—things I never thought would be in the realm of possibility for someone like me, living on what HUD designated an "extremely low income" in my city. The system was still horrifically flawed—leaving us all to fend for ourselves in a world where the exploitative entrepreneurs eagerly waited in the wings for a chance to take advantage of us whenever possible. This way, though, I felt more prepared to fight back. I couldn't change my income, but I could change what I did with it, and with enough work I could claw my way out of debt and free up more money in my monthly budget to go towards things I actually enjoyed and that mattered for my life. Once my debt was paid off, I'd have an extra $1,000 per month of my income freed up to put in savings for a down payment on a house.

We weren't on the Consumer Minimalism plan or the Working-Class Realism plan, and we certainly weren't on the Exploitative Entrepreneur plan. We were on our own, smooshing together the things we believed in a way that best suited our values and goals: minimizing excessive consumer spending that just served to make the über-rich even richer, but still allowing ourselves simple pleasures that made life worth living, while making every single cent we earned count as much as possible towards building the life we wanted. It seemed unreasonable that we should have to spend this much time meticulously deconstructing our finances just to survive, but in a society with no safety net, failure wasn't an option. We would do what we needed to do to get by, and in the meantime, we would take small steps to make a better life for ourselves. In a world where CEOs and billionaires never seemed satisfied, we were building the foundation for a life that answered the question "What is enough?" We didn't have enough quite yet, but we were on track to get there.

How to Budget

The most important part of a budget is making sure you can stick to it! Putting a plan on paper means nothing if you're not able to follow it. With that in mind, here's how you build a budget that you'll actually follow:

1. Don't approximate your expenses. Make it exact or don't bother making it at all. Open your bank records and comb through your transactions from the past sixty days, making sure you don't miss a single thing. Add things in to the cent, not just the dollar. Build the most accurate snapshot of your income and expenses that you can.

2. If your income fluctuates, use the lowest amount of money you can reasonably expect to earn in a month for your budget. All of your required expenses should fall under that threshold. Any extra money you earn on top of that lowest expected amount should be considered savings.

3. Make sure to give yourself an allowance, just for things you don't need but you want. This should be your irresponsible spending, and it is the most important part of your budget. If you don't give yourself an allowance, you won't stick to the budget! Put your allowance in a separate account with a separate debit card so you always know exactly how much you're allowed to spend.

4. For variable bills like power and household gas, use the highest amount you can expect to spend.

5. For variable expenses that aren't regularly occurring bills—like groceries or gas for your car—pick a system that makes sense to you. For me, keeping groceries separate and treating them like a bill made sense. Since I worked from home and didn't drive too often, I treated driving like "going places" and lumped it in with my allowance, since it felt like a "fun" thing most of the time. For work-related travel, my job was able to pay for gas. Everybody's budget looks a little bit different because everyone's life is different. Remember that the most important thing is building something you'll stick to.

6. Don't expect budgeting to end with just making a spreadsheet. You're making the budget to see what changes you can make in your life. Be prepared to follow your budget up by renegotiating bills or changing services. Your budget is a snapshot of your monthly cash flow. There's always room to change things around.

7. Automate as much as humanly possible. The more you can automate, the less you'll stress and the fewer opportunities you'll have for things like human error and impulse spending. Try creating a separate account just for your bills. That way, when you look at it, you'll clearly know that money is spoken for and you cannot spend it.

CHAPTER 12

It's Worse Than You Thought

Roughly one year into my financial literacy journey, I got a phone call from my dad.

"Grandma fell," he said into the phone, his voice raspy and scratchy like always. "She's okay. I just thought you should know. Her face is pretty banged up and she's got some bruises. Now that she's in the wheelchair, she's having trouble getting around her apartment. Your aunt and uncle and I are talking about trying to move her into a home, so at least she's not alone so much."

My grandmother had lived alone in her little apartment for a decade or so now, ever since my grandfather died of a stroke. My grandmother was a powerhouse—a strong, loud woman with no shortage of ambition and spirit. My grandfather was always her balance—a quiet, kind man who smiled when he spoke. Some mornings, when I'd had nowhere to go as a teenager, he'd call me to ask where I'd stayed the night before and if I needed a ride to work that day. He and my grandma lived in an apartment too far out of town for me to reliably take the bus to school or work if I'd slept there. Instead, he met me where I was those days and dropped me off at work whenever I needed. He never asked too many questions—just picked me up and smiled. Some days, he told me about his childhood working on a farm on the outskirts of town. He went to the same high school I did, only back then he had to ride his bike miles to get there, cutting through the farmlands and the orchards just to learn basic arithmetic in the big old building where my guidance counselor and principal now had their offices.

The day he had his stroke, I rushed down to Fresno from San Francisco, speeding as fast as my shitty 1997 Saturn would go down the 5 freeway, just so I could see him one last time. He was in a hospital bed in a cold, sterile room, with my grandma, aunt, uncle, dad, and cousin standing around him in a circle. This was before my grandmother lost her leg, back when she could still stand and walk without a wheelchair. When I walked in the room, he made eye contact with me and I think I saw him smile. He seemed to nod and close his eyes, as if to say that he knew everyone was there—everyone had made it—and it was all right now for him to say goodbye. He didn't last too much longer after that; he died later that day.

My grandmother—like me, I'm told—was a fighter. She was tough, and she held herself with a strength and confidence that seemed to pick everyone around her up off the floor and plop them upright in a standing position, ready to march on to whatever thing came next. The day my grandpa died, she kept her head up high and boldly proclaimed that he was a good man and she would miss him, but it was all right because she would see him again one day soon. After his death, she kept herself busy with projects, dutifully documenting our family history in large binders filled with family trees and photos. A picture of him hung on the wall by her front door for the next decade, wrapped in an ornate picture frame painted gold.

After a few years, one health issue turned into another, and before we knew it, my grandmother was in the wheelchair, one leg short, but in good spirits. When you came to visit her, she'd wave the stub of her missing leg up high in the air while laughing and shouting "Hello!," as though her stub was a hand greeting you. She found ways to maneuver around her apartment, clearing out tables and chairs to make it wheelchair accessible. She turned her oven door into a makeshift countertop so that she could still chop vegetables and cook. She learned to keep the beer on the lowest shelf of the fridge for easier access. The only trouble was getting from the living room onto her small porch, where she liked to keep a cactus garden to pass the time. It was there on the patio that she often fell, and it was getting harder for my dad and his siblings to keep watch on her.

"We've gotta figure out how to pay for wherever she goes," my dad said on the other end of the phone. "Dad— your grandpa—had some VA benefits. I think they'll cover something. We're just waiting to see."

It was the kind of conversation adults had with each other. I was nearly thirty, but in so many ways still felt like a child. Had I really been in grade school when my dad was this age? How did people do it? So many Millennials, like me, found our development stunted by economic tragedy in our formative years. We were slower to find steady employment (if we found it at all), slower to home ownership (if we were able to purchase at all), and as a result slower to have marriages and children (who could afford either?). Eager to rise to my new position as trusted adult, I thought about my grandparents' financial situation and considered ways to have useful input.

"Did Grandma have money set aside for retirement?" I asked.

"No," my dad said. "She got some Social Security benefits. But it's not enough."

"What about the house?" I asked. "Before they moved into the apartment, I mean. They lived in that house, the one that got torn down for the freeway to be built? Didn't they get money from the city for that? Eminent domain or whatever?"

"They didn't own that house," my dad answered, a bit confused. "They just rented it, for a long time, but just renting. Your grandpa—he was a good man—but he wasn't exactly . . . good with money."

I remembered the house we'd spent so many nights sleeping in when I was a child, with its brown shag carpet and the pull-out couch in the living room and the sidewalk out front that cracked and rose up high while the tall trees that lined the street reached their gnarled roots beneath it. It had always felt like a second home to me, or maybe even a first home. In my mind, it was always "Grandma and Grandpa's House" and it felt shocking to realize it had never been theirs at all. Instead, it belonged to some anonymous face who just cashed their rent checks every month.

"Not to mention," my dad was saying on the other end of the telephone, "the whole Rivera thing."

"What Rivera thing?" I asked. The Riveras were friends of my grandparents, maybe from church. They owned a store in town that sold hardware supplies and odds and ends. When I was a kid, we always shopped there for whatever we could.

"We have to support the Riveras!" my grandma would say in the car, smiling as we drove there to do our shopping.

"Well, you know," my dad said. "How they just gave all that stuff to us for free?"

"No," I said, confused. "What stuff?"

"Well," he said, "like . . . everything. They gave Grandma and Grandpa pretty much whatever they wanted for free. They knew your grandpa was bad with money. They wanted to help out, I guess. But now, the Riveras are dead and their kids took over the store and I guess they found a ledger keeping track of the value of everything they ever gave Mom and Dad. It's something like twenty thousand dollars' worth of stuff, and they want us to pay it back. They said we took advantage of their parents' kindness or something, I don't know. But I told them, look, we don't have twenty thousand dollars to pay it back. Those were gifts, from their parents, out of the kindness of their heart. It's a mess. So, we've gotta figure that out, now, too."

As my dad spoke, I replayed childhood memories in my mind—Laura Rivera's smiling face, our aimless shopping trips gathering whatever we could from the store. I'd always known that my dad and I were financially unstable, but my grandparents were a safe stable place to weather the money storms each time they came. It never occurred to me that they, too, were weathering a storm of their own.

"Oh," I said, softly, my voice faltering. "Okay. Well, I guess . . . let me know if there's anything I can do. I mean, I don't have money, but I could come down and help . . . move Grandma's stuff or something. I don't really know."

"It's all right, kiddo," my dad said into the phone, his rough, gravelly voice sweet in the protective paternal way it had always been. "Don't you worry about a thing, we'll get it all figured out. I just wanted to let you know what was going on. I love you, I'll keep you updated."

I hung up the phone with my head in a daze. There are some moments in adulthood where everything seems to snap sharply into focus for the first time. It's like walking into your house after being away on a trip—you smell it the way other people smell it, and it feels both foreign and like home all at once. As I stood in my backyard, thinking about Grandpa and the Riveras, it felt like I was seeing my own childhood for the first time, and everything I thought I knew was a lie. I felt both stupid and vindicated at the same time. No wonder life had seemed so much harder for me than for so many other people I knew. Where other people had generational wealth, passed down from grandparents to parents and from parents to kids, my family had generational debt—passed down the same way, with my grandparents and father doing their best to insulate me and protect me from the stress of it all. I'd always known my father was a good parent. Now, though, I understood how hard the task really had been and could appreciate even more how well he'd managed to pull it off.

A part of me had always assumed that my unconventional upbringing was the result of my father's unconventional values. He grew up invested in punk rock, showing me bands that sang about things like inequality and class struggle. I assumed we lived the way we did—vagabonds at times—because he consciously chose to reject the system. In reality, though, it was the opposite way around: punk rock had appealed to him because the system had already failed our family. He didn't play the game because he was never even offered a place at the board.

As I thought about my grandparents' financial reality, three questions came to mind:

1. How much better off would my grandmother be if she and my grandpa had been able to buy a house all those years ago rather than becoming lifelong renters, or if at the very least she'd managed to save the sizable sum recommended for her retirement?

2. What could I do to make sure I could afford my own end-of-life care when I reached my grandmother's age?

3. How did my family's relationship with money relate to my seeming inability to acquire financial stability in my own life?

The more I learned about my family's relationship with money, the more it felt like my destiny was predetermined from birth. It didn't matter that I got straight A's or graduated from high school early as valedictorian and got nearly a perfect score on my SAT. Kids from more comfortable economic backgrounds would always have more resources, from better-quality schools to more support and better networking connections. One study from Georgetown University found that 70 percent of rich kids with low test scores had become affluent by the age of twenty-five, while only 30 percent of poor kids with high test scores could say the same. I was seemingly destined to a life of high debt, unfulfilled academic potential, low professional attainment, and unstable finances just because of the family I was born into. My family's financial situation was far worse than I'd ever imagined. In some ways, it was a relief—as though I finally had an explanation for why life always seemed so much harder for me than for other people I knew. In other ways, learning the truth about my family's financial background felt like a nail in the coffin of my own financial dreams. Here lie Madeline's attempts to just have an okay life where she isn't stressed about money all the time. RIP.

The American Dream tells us that we can change our economic reality if only we work hard enough, but time and time again, we see that class mobility is a myth. Seeing my grandmother helpless in her old age was painful and difficult to swallow. She was always so strong. It felt like this, too, should be something that she could just stand up and fight. But she was old, and she was growing frail, and she couldn't stand anymore, and she was tired. It was a bit like seeing into my own future, and what I saw was heartbreaking. I wished so badly I had the money to make it all right—to buy her a nice little house to spend her final days in, with a hospice nurse with kind eyes and a warm smile, right there in the neighborhood of Eagle Rock where she had spent her childhood, in the place she loved so much and always wished she'd be able to afford to return to one day. I couldn't, though. I was making progress paying off my debt, but I was still $52,000 in the hole. I had no assets, no resources, and no clue how to help make anything better.

As I hung up the phone that day, Drew's voice echoed in my ears.

"You know the thing about you, Madeline? You're a fighter."

He was right. I was a fighter, just like my grandmother

before me. However, if being strong-willed and determined wasn't enough to help my grandmother in her old age, it wouldn't be enough to help me either. Fighting wasn't enough. I needed a plan.

Just like I'd done so many times before in my youth, I sat down with a notebook and wrote down my plan for the future:

1. pay off my debt

2. save a down payment for a house

3. plan for my retirement

4. help everyone I care about do the same

How to Get Out of Debt

Debt is like an empty well: easy to fall into, and nearly impossible to escape. Getting out of debt, though, can be the first step on a journey towards building relative financial stability for yourself by freeing up income to put towards things that will help build financial stability into your future. With that in mind, here are all of my tips to get out of debt:

1. Make a promise to yourself to not—under any circumstances—take on new debt! Be sure you budget precisely to make sure your cash flow is in a place where this is possible. If you find yourself in a financial bind, resort to selling things or taking on new work before using a credit card again. You're in pay-off mode, not add-on mode!

2. Download a credit monitoring app and familiarize yourself with your credit report.

3. List all of your active debt down to the penny. This would be anything that hasn't been sent to collections. Be sure to include your interest rate next to it. You can usually find this on your credit card or loan statements.

4. Rank your debt based on how extreme the interest rates are. High interest rates will make it even harder for you to pay off debt! Anything over 20 percent should be considered a red alert—get out of that as fast as possible! Anything between 10 and 19 percent should be considered orange alert—not great.

Anything at 9 percent or lower can be yellow alert—not a top priority right now.

5. Contact your lenders to see if they will reduce your interest rates based on your history of repayment.

6. See if you qualify for a balance transfer credit card. This is a credit card product marketed towards people who have existing high-interest debt that they'd like to move over to a lower interest rate. You can shop around for different options online; always try to find at least three offers before choosing which one you'll go with. The one you want is the one with the lowest interest and lowest or nonexistent fees. Sometimes, balance transfer credit cards will have introductory periods of 0 percent interest, which is ideal. However, if you find any card that has a lower interest rate than any of your existing debt, prepare to transfer the balance onto it. This will help you pay that debt off faster! Be sure to ask the new lender what steps you need to take to use the card for balance transfer purposes—there is often a specific procedure to follow.

7. See if you qualify for a personal loan to use for debt consolidation. Just like a balance transfer credit card, shop around online—looking for at least three options. If you find an offer that has a lower interest rate than any of your existing debt, prepare to move existing debt onto it. Your goal is—especially—to convert any "red" debt into "orange" or even "yellow" debt to help speed up your repayment plan!

8. Once you've switched out high-interest debt for low-interest debt wherever possible, it's time to come up with your repayment strategy. Avoid using debt relief/elimination and credit repair services—it's too easy to get scammed! You're going to handle this all on your own. There are two popular strategies: debt snowball or debt avalanche. Debt snowball focuses on paying off the debt with the lowest balance first. Debt avalanche focuses on paying off the debt with the highest interest rate first. The debt avalanche method saves you the most money in the end, but the debt snowball method taps into the psychology of your brain and might be better at keeping you goal-oriented and on track! If you start with the smallest amount first, you're going to pay it off more quickly, meaning you get the "yessss!" feeling sooner, making you more committed to your journey. Only you can decide which method is right for you! I used the debt avalanche, but I'd recommend the debt snowball to a stranger. Whatever the case, once you choose a method, identify your highest-priority source of debt—we'll call that your "targeted debt"—and put all of your attention on it.

9. While paying off debt, continue to make your minimum monthly payments of all outstanding debt. However, do everything in your power to find extra money to throw at your targeted debt. This could mean trying to free up extra money in your budget, or finding extra work or odds and ends to sell. Ideally, it's some mixture of both. Remember that all extra money in your budget goes towards paying off that debt! Well, almost all of it anyway. Make sure you still leave a little allowance in your budget so you don't get so discouraged that you give up on the whole thing completely. Remember: a plan is only effective if it's realistic.

10. Tell people you're paying off your debt! Don't be weird about it, but if friends want you to go do something with them that costs money or someone is pressuring you to go in on a pricey gift for someone else, be vocal about your financial restrictions. Say "I really wish I could, but I'm focusing on paying off debt right now so I have no extra money. Hopefully next year, I'll be in a better financial position!" Telling other people about your debt repayment efforts has three positive effects:

   a. It encourages financial transparency in your community, which is good for building healthy relationships with money.

b. It prevents you from feeling pressured to over-spend and go off-plan.

c. It holds you accountable to the people around you, adding extra incentive for you to stick with it! Nobody wants to be a liar.

11. Once you finally manage to pay off a debt in full, choose your next targeted debt source. Take the amount of money you were paying towards your previous debt source and add it onto your monthly payments for the new one. Example: You were paying $100 on Debt A every month. It's paid off now, so you've moved on to Debt B. Your minimum monthly payment on Debt B has been $50. You'll now pay $150 towards it instead, since that extra $100 in your monthly budget is now freed up.

12. Repeat step 11 until all debt is paid off.

13. If debt has already been sent to collections and you find yourself with a little bit of cash in savings, consider contacting the collections agency to attempt to negotiate a one-time lump payment for part of what you owe in exchange for them settling the debt and removing it from your credit report. Know, though, that collections agencies are notoriously unscrupulous. They may lie to you. Never give them any access to your checking account or information about your banking. Do not make payments online. If you reach an agreement, get it in writing before making a payment on it. Debt collection agencies may be willing to negotiate with you because typically they've purchased your debt for pennies on the dollar hoping to make a profit. They will play hardball and make you think they won't budge on how much you owe them, but most of the time, they are willing to make a deal. To negotiate, tell them that you owe many people money and have a limited amount of money available to attempt to settle old debts. First, offer to pay one-fifth of what you owe. If

they say no, tell them you're going to hang up and call the next person you owe money to and offer them the same deal, and you'll call back if you get no offers. If nobody accepts your offer for one-fifth of the debt, start your second round of calls. Now, offer to repay half of what you owe. Repeat the process. If there are no takers, start again offering to pay 75 percent of what you owe—if you have the money in the bank, that is. If you find no takers, it's okay to give up and wait to try again at a later date.

14. Remember that it's okay to fail. You're only human and you're doing the best you can. Many sources of debt stop adversely affecting your credit score after seven years if you stop making payments on it and cease contact with the creditor completely, meaning if you find yourself in a position where you cannot pay debt back, you might be all right with waiting seven years until your credit repairs itself—but this will depend on your financial situation and what type of debt you have. Your creditors may also sue you to collect on what they are owed. If they sue you, they will probably win. However, if you don't have assets—meaning savings in the bank, a car you own outright, or a home you own—you might be what they consider "judgment-proof," meaning they can't take anything from you even if they win because you don't have anything to take. It's a weird perk of being broke. They could, however, garnish your wages, which means they take a little bit out of your paycheck automatically until the debt you owe is paid off. There is a statute of limitations that varies from state to state that determines how long a creditor has to take legal action. Research this for your state. In most states, you will still technically owe the money to the creditor, but it will no longer affect your credit report.

CHAPTER 13

Home Is Where ~~the Heart Is~~
You Can Afford the Monthly Payments

In September 2019, I looked at my savings account balance and saw that it was $15,000.

"Holy shit," I gasped.

"What's wrong?" my boyfriend, Chris, asked, concerned.

"Nothing," I said, laughing a bit. "I have fifteen thousand dollars saved."

"Oh, yeah," he said nonchalantly. "Me, too."

"Really?!" I asked, my eyes opened wide.

"Well, yeah," he said. "When you and Camila started doing that money stuff, I was like, yeah, that's smart. I'll just do that, too."

Like me, Chris came from a modest financial background. However, unlike me, he grew up in a two-parent household where his parents owned their home and prioritized investing in their retirement accounts. Chris started his financial path in life with limited debt, which admittedly made saving money easier for him than it had been for me.

For me, clawing myself out of debt had been the first challenge. After implementing my automated budgeting plan, I was able to tackle paying off debt like never before. By December 2018, I still owed $14,007.20 on my student loans and $16,660.84 on my car. However, my personal loans and credit cards were fully paid off. The car was, admittedly, a little out of my price range and something I realistically should have traded in for something even cheaper, but it wasn't extravagant, either: a used Kia Niro hybrid. I liked it, and besides the gas mileage was good and it was reliable.

While contemporary debt repayment wisdom would have had me pay off my student loans and car payment aggressively once my credit cards and personal loans were handled, I instead diverted from my debt repayment and began saving a down payment for a house. It wasn't what the money experts recommended, but I figured if I was already paying rent, it was probably smarter to convert that to a mortgage payment on a house I owned as soon as possible. The place we were renting didn't have rent control—rent control was only for multi-family properties where we lived, not single-family homes like the one we rented. It meant that at any moment, our landlords could decide to raise our rent as much as they wanted. I was terrified every month that we'd get a notice in the mail for a rent increase to the tune of hundreds of dollars. Besides, houses just got more and more expensive every year. Soon, I was putting the $550 that had gone towards my credit cards and personal loans each month into a savings account. I figured in three years' time, I'd have $20,000 to use as a down payment on a home.

Just one year later, though, I was already up to $15,000, thanks to my tax refund from the IRS, and freelance work I picked up on the side. As I looked at Chris that day, I realized our goal was closer than I thought. We were somehow— against all odds—ready to buy a house.

The day that Drew died, his best friend, Paul, came over. He brought his new girlfriend, a woman I'd never met before. She sat next to me and talked to me a little bit throughout the day. At one point, she told me a story.

"When I was in college," she said, "my best friend died. Her boyfriend was distraught. He was like you are today, horrified—in anguish. She was his whole world, they were going to get married, spend their lives together, everything. And the day she died, he just kind of got *stuck*. He became so overwhelmed in his grief that he felt like moving on would be betraying her memory. So, he didn't move on. He refused. He just stayed . . . stuck. For years and years, he just remained stuck in that grief. He never dated anyone else, he never lived his life to the fullest. His life became a living tribute to her."

As she told this story, I stared ahead numbly, hardly listening to a word. Still, she pushed on.

"You don't want to get stuck," she told me softly. "You can't get stuck in this. You won't understand this now, but one day, months from now or years from now, I hope you remember. Don't get stuck here."

A year or so after Drew's death, as I was putting shipping supplies away, back into the oven in the tiny little apartment that I was definitely paying too much money for, I found a small cigar box that had fallen between my refrigerator and the counter. I recognized it instantly. It was the box where Drew kept his notes, scribbled onto napkins and scraps of paper—sometimes affirmations or goals, sometimes just thoughts he had throughout the day. A few months before he died, he'd emptied out all of the notes into a drawer in his office and we went through them together. One read:

> If only I could sell three thousand dollars per day on our e-commerce sites, then I'd be happy.

I read it to him out loud.

"It really says that?!" he said, shocked and laughing.

"Yep," I said, spinning the piece of paper around so he could read it. "Right here. Why?"

"That's what we sell now!" he said, picking up the paper.

"Are you happy?" I asked.

"No!" he exclaimed, still laughing. "Now I just want to sell ten thousand dollars per day!"

"Ah," I said, nodding. "The ever-moving goal post. Such is life."

After Drew died, I found the cigar box in a spare room of his house. I packed it full to the brim with some of my favorite little things of his—the can opener he wore around his neck, his spare keys, Polaroids we'd taken of each other, and little notes he'd left for me around the house in the two years or so we were together. That day, I sat down on my kitchen floor and opened the cigar box, taking each thing out like a treasure. I cried out in anguish as though the grief were a monster inside me begging to be unleashed.

Suddenly, I remembered the woman Paul had brought to our house. I thought about the story of her best friend in college and the man who loved her, the man who became so stuck in his own grief he could never love another person again. I sat up straight and wiped the tears off my face. I understood what she meant about getting stuck. There, crying in the kitchen on the floor while I held my dead boyfriend's keys, I realized that if I didn't take the right steps, this could be my life forever. I could be looking forward to a future where ten, twenty, thirty years from now, I'd still be clutching the mundane artifacts of Drew's otherwise magical existence, wishing to god I could go back in time for just one more glimpse of his face, one more second with him sitting in the sun, one more day looking up at the old dying tree in his backyard wondering how one day we would replace it—all while life went on around me. I was on my way to getting stuck.

Carefully, I put Drew's things back into the little cigar box and set it on top of my refrigerator. I got out my phone and downloaded a dating app—Tinder. I wasn't ready for a relationship, but I'd have to start thinking about dating at the very least, or I, too, would end up "stuck." On Tinder, I figured I could at least get some practice talking to people like a normal human being again.

Over the next six months, I threw myself into trying to date—meeting up with random people at bars for the obligatory introductory drink and awkward small talk until I even-

tually left the bar inebriated, took a car home, and fell asleep
crying in my bed. My life was a vicious cycle of stress and
heartache, and each segment—the days of work and the
nights of dating—served as an escape from the other. One
day, though, I met Chris.

I met up with Chris at a neighborhood theme bar called
Bigfoot Lodge. It was dark and quiet inside, and seldom
crowded—an ideal place for first dates. I was on a first-name
basis with the door guy, Kurt, who'd always give me a knowing nod when I showed up with some random man from the
internet. This day was no different. I met up with Chris outside of the bar, and as we walked in, Kurt tipped his head
down in a little nod, greeting me by name at the door.

"You come here a lot?" Chris asked.

"Kind of," I said awkwardly.

Inside, we sat in a dark booth in a corner and made small
talk about our lives. Chris was quiet, maybe even shy, but he
was funny and when he looked at me, it felt like someone
was really seeing *me*—not just the horrific trauma of the loss
I'd endured. I hadn't felt like myself in a year. It was as if
Chris reached his hand inside of the gunk and muck of grief
inside me and pulled a Madeline out—battered and covered
in grime, but still me. As I made my way home from the bar
that night, I smiled for what felt like the first time in months.
Now, four years later, we were going to buy a house together.

I wasn't sure how buying a house worked exactly but I knew
you needed a loan to do it, so I called my bank to talk to a
mortgage lender. The man on the other end of the phone was
gruff and pushy, like a lumberjack with a sales pitch. He threw
out a lot of words and figures I didn't understand like "PMI"
and "closing costs." In the end, he emailed me a letter saying
we'd qualified for a loan all right, but only to buy an $80,000
house. My heart sank. In Los Angeles in 2019, median home
prices were $641,340, and you'd be hard-pressed to find any-
thing for sale under $500,000. I searched the internet for

clues on what to do now. Trudging through message boards, I found the story of someone who was in a position similar to mine. However, they had gone to a mortgage broker for a second opinion after their bank presented them with less than favorable options. I had never heard of a mortgage broker before, so I typed it into Google:

What is morgage briker

Autocorrect would figure it out. I shrugged and hit Enter. Sure enough, results popped up on the screen:

"Mortgage Broker: Definition, How They Work, and Responsibilities"

I clicked on the first link, an article on Investopedia:

A mortgage broker is an intermediary who brings mortgage borrowers and mortgage lenders together. . . . A mortgage broker helps borrowers connect with lenders and seeks out the best fit in terms of the borrower's financial situation and interest-rate needs. . . . The broker earns a commission from either the borrower, the lender, or both at closing.

I read and reread the description. Got it, I thought. The mortgage broker is like a personal shopper for home loans, and sometimes you as the borrower don't even have to pay them—the banks do. Content, I opened Yelp and searched for a mortgage broker near me. The first person who popped up called himself "the Friendly Lender." He had around 80 reviews and a five-star rating. His pictures showed a friendly smiling face, looking straight into the camera. A phone call wouldn't hurt, I reasoned. Nervous, I called the number on the screen.

"The Friendly Lender" chirped an upbeat male voice on the other end of the phone.

"Uh, hi," I said awkwardly. "I'm, uh, interested in buying a house but I don't think I'm quite ready yet. I was wondering if, um, you can tell me what I need to do to . . . get there? To get ready, I guess."

"Well, sure," the man on the other end of the phone said. "But can I ask why you think you're not ready now?"

"Well," I said, "my boyfriend and I don't have a lot of money. We're low income—very low income according to HUD for Los Angeles—and we don't have a ton saved up."

"Hmmm. Why don't you email me over some information and we'll see what we can do," he said. I could hear the smile in his voice as he spoke.

After I hung up, I emailed him everything he'd requested:

1. Pay stubs from the previous year for both me and Chris

2. A screenshot of our credit scores

3. A screenshot of our savings accounts

4. A summary of the monthly minimum payments I was making towards my remaining debt

A few minutes later, I received a phone call back.

"You're not in too bad of a position," he said. "If you'd like to purchase now, I think I can find you a loan together for up to five hundred thousand dollars. Interest rates are low, and that really helps your case."

My jaw fell open in shock. "HALF A MILLION DOLLARS?" I shrieked into the phone.

"Yep," the mortgage broker replied. "I know it's not a lot, especially in Los Angeles, but it should be enough to get you into something."

It was more money than I'd ever dreamed was possible. Still, we had to consider what that looked like in terms of monthly mortgage payments. A half-million-dollar loan would have put our monthly mortgage payments somewhere around $3,000 including insurance and taxes, which was far too much for our tight monthly budgets to comfortably accommodate. In the end, we set a firm budget of $420,000 for ourselves. With an FHA loan—a government-sponsored loan that allowed for down payments as low as 3.5 percent—our down payment would be just $14,700 total (or $7,350 each), meaning we had more than enough to cover that and our closing costs with our $15,000 each in savings. I set alerts on Redfin and Zillow for new listings in our price range and started hunting.

Just a month later, I was discouraged. The only listings popping up in Los Angeles in our price range were condominiums—like apartments but for sale, and unfortunately, the type of loan we were eligible for rarely worked with condominiums in Los Angeles. To work, it needed to be a free-standing house, and on top of that, the HOA fees for a condominium (homeowners association fees that cover common grounds and some utilities) were significant, adding sometimes $500 more to your monthly housing expenses. I'd gone from riding the high of the pre-approval to the low of realizing that there were simply no houses available to purchase in our budget, even with half a million dollars.

"Have you tried looking on the outskirts of town?" a friend asked me one day.

We had. The outskirts of Los Angeles are home to many suburban communities, mostly communities of color or communities of recent immigrants. Houses were in our budget there, but our presence felt violent in a way that was hard to communicate. Chris and I went to open houses for recently remodeled homes in otherwise traditional neighborhoods where business signs were in Spanish. We watched as throngs of other young white adults crowded the flipped homes, eager to get in somewhere, anywhere they could afford. Neighbors stood in their front yards and grimaced as if to say "There goes the neighborhood."

At one open house, Chris—whose grandmother had emigrated to the U.S. from Mexico years prior—looked at me, the corners of his mouth drawn down to his chin, with disappointment on his face.

"Maybe if I spoke better Spanish," he said. "But this doesn't feel right. We're not supposed to be here."

I agreed. We were, after all, the Harbingers of Gentrification. But where were we supposed to be? The obvious answer was somewhere with generational ties. However, my grandmother's old neighborhood of Eagle Rock was far too expensive now for our budget. Dejected, I called Kennedy to chat.

"I want to buy a house, too," she said.

"You totally should," I told her. After Drew's death, her career as a makeup artist took off. Now, she was working high-end fashion jobs all around the world.

"No," she said. "You don't understand. I want to buy a house *too*. But I don't want to spend a lot of money. You know me: I like to have money to have *fun* with. So, what if we bought a house together. Something like a duplex—one unit for you guys, one unit for me. Then we can be neighbors!"

I'd never heard of anyone buying a duplex together to live in. Mostly, I figured it was wannabe landlords who owned those. I wasn't even sure if it was possible to buy a duplex on an FHA loan. I opened my laptop and did two Google searches as she spoke:

Do FHA loans work on duplexes

Los Angeles multifamily homes for sale

The search results came back and my eyes opened wide. This might actually work. For starters, FHA loans do work with duplexes, and duplexes in Los Angeles were selling for not much more than a single house, meaning it was nearly like getting a house for half off—two houses for the price of one. There was nothing in Eagle Rock, but just one neighborhood over in any direction, there were a few. We could maybe pull this off.

By the end of the day, the Friendly Lender approved all three of us together on one loan: $1,000,000.

Kennedy called me, shrieking. "A MILLION DOL-LARS?" she yelled into the phone.

"We can't afford five hundred thousand dollars, though, not really—not me and Chris," I told her. "We've gotta look for something more like . . . eight hundred thousand dollars. Otherwise, the monthly payments are way too high for us."

At $800,000, the monthly payments would be around $2,500 per unit including mortgage, interest, this thing called private mortgage insurance (or PMI, required to get our low down payment), property taxes, and homeowner's insurance. It was a lot more than I was used to paying for housing, but it would mean that in thirty years I wouldn't have a house payment at all. On top of that, if I was never able to get my retirement savings together, at least in my old age I'd have a house I could reverse-mortgage—a process where you basically sell your house back to the bank in exchange for money to live comfortably on in your retirement. I wouldn't be able to pass my house down to any heirs in that case, so there wouldn't be "generational wealth," but I didn't even know if I'd want kids in the future and at the very least I wouldn't be a financial burden on family. This was an investment in my housing and my retirement all wrapped up in one.

We found a real estate agent in town and sent her the three houses that popped up in the radius around my grandmother's old neighborhood. Less than a month later, we'd put an offer in on the cheapest one—$830,000 for a "detached duplex," meaning one plot of land with two houses built on it and a garage in the middle between the two. The houses were around a hundred years old, still with their original hardwood floors (albeit in a botched state). They were rough around the edges, but beautiful. We wrote a heartfelt letter to the seller about how we weren't real estate developers or investors; instead, we were people who were priced out of the traditional real estate market and had come together to buy as a small community when rugged individualism had failed us. On our own, we were broke. Together, we had more power. We couldn't afford much, but we could afford this one property. The letter worked. Our offer was accepted over two others, and we officially entered a period called "escrow": thirty days wherein all of the loan details get firmed up, the home inspections are conducted, and any remaining negotiations take place. When we found leaking pipes and shaky foundations on our first inspection, the seller dropped the price $30,000 for us, bringing it down to an even $800,000.

When escrow closed, I had $5,000 left in my savings account.

The unit Chris and I moved into was one thousand square feet and had three bedrooms and two bathrooms. When we purchased the property in 2019, a similar home in central Los Angeles would have cost roughly the same price to rent—a little under $2,400 per month. However, by 2022, the rent for the same place would be a thousand dollars more than our mortgage payment. If we were to purchase the same home just three years later, we'd be paying $1.5 million for the property (nearly double). Not only had home prices gone up, but so had interest rates. I knew purchasing a home was a good financial investment, but it never would have occurred to me how much money we'd end up saving on housing by buying, especially when we did. By purchasing, we'd effectively locked in our own form of "rent control." Even as inflation occurs around us, our price for housing will remain relatively the same until our loan is paid off in thirty years.

I was seeing firsthand why home ownership is one of the greatest predictors of financial stability for most Americans. In ten years, the owner of a single-family home accumulates an average of $225,000 in wealth based on the equity the home develops alone, which helps to explain why the median homeowner has forty times the household wealth of the median renter. In just three years' time, my personal share of equity in the property was already $125,000. Since families already pay for housing, replacing rent with an asset that appreciates in value is one of the easiest ways for people on limited incomes to build wealth. They just have to figure out how to save the down payment and qualify for the loan, which is easier said than done. If you can find a way to pull it off, though, and keep making the mortgage payments on time, it might change your life for the better.

From a more commonsense perspective, it made sense to me that renting would be more expensive than owning. Landlords aren't performing a public service; they rent units out for more than the mortgage cost so they can make a profit. In 2021, it was cheaper to buy than to rent in around half of the metropolitan areas in the country; for the other half, it's just a matter of time before a home you purchased becomes cheaper in terms of monthly mortgage payments than rent in a similar neighborhood.

On average, rents increase 5.77 percent per year in the United States. If instead of purchasing our home in 2019, we paid the monthly cost in rent—$2,372 per month—and it increased at 5.77 percent per year, by the time our mortgage was paid off in 2049 we would be paying $12,764.09 in rent for the same home. Real estate investors want to create a nation of renters, and it's easy to see why: there's massive profit in price-gouging people for rent. The alternative to paying exorbitantly high rent prices is being unhoused, and most people are going to do everything in their power to keep a roof over their heads.

The commodification of housing is an evil that will never make sense to me. How have we let greed go so far that the very things we need to stay alive, things like shelter, have become reduced to commodities for the rich to profit from while the rest of us struggle? When corporations drive down real wages for workers, purchase as much housing as they can get their hands on, then raise rents to exorbitantly high rates, how is an average person supposed to break free from the cycle of corporate exploitation? The two seem inextricably linked.

Like most things in life, it's hard to fight on your own, but it's easier in numbers. On my own, purchasing a home seemed like an impossibility. With a little help from the people closest to me, though, it went from being impossible to being one of the best decisions of my life.

We moved into our house in February 2020. The house—our unit, which we refer to as "our house" anyway—is a back house set deep down the driveway behind the main house on the property. The neighborhood is one of the oldest in Los Angeles, next to equestrian clubs and city buildings, and it seems like every house in our neighborhood has a back house. There's something special about our neighborhood. It's a place to settle down and plant roots.

Back in the day, our neighborhood was a farming community. It was in an old river flood plain, which made the soil rich and fertile—prime for growing food. In the 1800s, it was part of a massive privately owned ranch, but in 1868, part of the ranch was sold to a private real estate developer. In 1902, the area we now call our neighborhood was subdivided into smaller plots to be sold to prospective home developers. Our plot of land was one of them; the front house was built in 1916, and our little back house was added in 1922. When we purchased the house, we received a copy of the original permits filed by the city to build, half typed and half handwritten: "Board of Public Works, Department of Buildings: Application for the Erection of Frame Buildings, Class D."

Some of the older people in my neighborhood remember the early days—back when half of the neighborhood or so was still farmland and their parents used streetcars to do their daily shopping. Sometimes, when I walk to the liquor store on the corner to grab a snack, the older men who stand on the corner show me pictures of what it was like when they were kids. One man showed me pictures of him as a kid sitting on a fence, nothing behind him but fields of horses. His dad, he tells me, was a cowboy—an actual cowboy—working for a big corporate farm right here where we stand. Now, though, the farm is long gone and it's just houses as far as the eye can see.

The men who stand on the corner are friendly. They

are older now, the age of fathers and grandfathers, but tell me when they were younger, they ran this neighborhood—drugs, guns, the whole nine yards. They laugh and relive their glory days. They point to fences they hopped over while running from the police, backyards they crouched in when drug deals went wrong, places where they saw their friends die. My eyes get wide and my lips pout.

"That sounds rough," I say softly. "I'm so sorry."

"It's business," they say, and shrug, as if shaking the trauma off their shoulders.

The men on the street look out for us now. They make sure the younger guys don't graffiti on our house. They keep watch when I go on late-night walks. When I forget my wallet, they buy me chips at the store. They tell me to never be afraid of them, that they're there to keep the neighborhood safe, and I believe them. I pay it back however I can. I call locksmiths when they lock their keys in their car. I buy them beer when I see them in the shop. I always have time to stop and chat about the old days, the way things were. Ron tells me he used to be an expert break-dancer back in the day. Charles tells me he loves beautiful women and hates bullies. They tell me jokes and smile when they see me walking towards them, welcoming me like a guest in their home. I am a bit of a guest here; this is their neighborhood, they don't have to say it out loud—we both know it.

In the summertime, on the Fourth of July, everyone in our neighborhood spills out of their houses onto the streets to watch the illegal neighborhood fireworks shows shut down the block. We all stand next to each other—me with my blue hair, Ron with Blue Streak Rockets, Charles with his big smile missing teeth—staring up into the sky, watching fireworks explode above us. We laugh and hug each other and smile while the kids play with sparklers in the middle of the informally closed road. This is what community looks like, I think. My house might be an appreciating asset—something I've done financially right. More than that, though, it's my home. I could live here forever.

Our house isn't much to look at. It's small compared to most houses in the U.S. Electrical wires and light switch boxes sit on the outside of the walls, protruding. The floorboards squeak when we walk over them. Some are missing gouges of wood; most are scratched up beyond recognition. They've been stained a deep rich dark brown color in an effort to conceal the imperfections. They're a century old, though, those wooden floors. They know things we can only imagine. They don't owe us perfection.

Nothing in the house needs to be perfect for me to love it. I painted the cheap siding on the living room walls dark blue and decorated the space with secondhand knickknacks from thrift stores and Craigslist. From my mother before me, I picked up techniques that make an inexpensive house feel like a home. Chris keeps the plants alive—nearly fifty of them scattered around the front porch and inside every room. I saved up the money to remodel our kitchen, covering the floors in discounted tiles and saving a half-broken oven range from the landfill. The light doesn't work right and we had to reapply the interior seal, but it cooks our food and looks nice doing it. One day, we'll remodel every room of the house. Every room will have proper walls, then, where the electrical cords run inside them instead of along the baseboards. Until that day comes, though, we make do with fresh coats of paint and thrifted artwork hung on the walls.

The house represents something to us. It's an investment in our financial future, but it's also our version of enough. It's not excessive or glamorous or a status symbol of any kind. It's something better than that. It's stability. It's comfort. It's peace. Sometimes, when I'm cooking dinner in my kitchen—still the same budget bowls of lentils and mush I've been cooking for years, the ones that allowed me to save enough money to put a down payment on a house like this in the first place—I look around and wonder who first decided to put a price on the idea of home anyway. It doesn't make sense to me. The price is too subjective to even be calculated. This place, it means $1.5 million now to some faraway investor looking at a screen. They call sometimes, asking me if I'm looking to sell. I just hang up the phone. You can't put a price on this feeling—the feeling of finally being somewhere safe, somewhere I can stay for the rest of my life if I'd like. That's what it means to be home.

How to Buy a House

Buying a house gets harder and harder every year. Here is everything I learned from purchasing and what I think you need to know to pull it off too.

1. Mortgage providers look for a few things to determine how much money they'll lend you to purchase a home:

   a. Credit Score: Ideally this will be 620 or higher (though some lenders have programs for lower credit scores).

   b. Debt-to-income ratio: If you add up all your monthly debt repayment obligations (i.e., minimum monthly payments on all debt) and divide it by your gross income (before taxes), it should be 36 percent or less in order for lenders to consider you a safe bet to receive a mortgage.

   c. Savings: For a "conventional" loan, lenders like to see that you have 20 percent of the price of the home saved as a down payment—however, some conventional loans can be granted with down payments as low as 10 percent or even 5 percent. If you have less than that, an FHA loan might be a good option; the house will have to meet certain requirements and you'll have to pay an extra amount monthly towards PMI (private mortgage insurance), but your down payment will only be 3.5 percent of the purchase price. If you live outside a major metropolitan area, look into the USDA rural development loan, which grants down payment assistance to the extent that you might not need a down payment at all. Whichever way you go, you'll still need money for "closing costs"—which are usually between 3 and 5 percent of your loan amount. On top of that, they'll want to make sure they're not clearing your savings out completely. It helps to save extra—something like an "emergency savings"—both for qualifying purposes and for your own peace of mind.

d. Income: Lenders will use your income as it's reported to the IRS every year to help determine how much you can afford to purchase. If you're self-employed, they will require more data than if you have a regular W-2 job. In the end, lenders will calculate how much extra money they think you have available in your monthly budget based on your income after paying things like debt and bills to realistically put towards your mortgage payment. This will all work together to help determine how much you'll qualify for.

2. Be aware of variable-rate or adjustable-rate mortgages (ARM). These mortgages will have interest rates that change over time. While some data show they are ultimately cheaper in the long run for many borrowers, for low-income borrowers they can create financial instability that is difficult to deal with.

3. Reach out to a mortgage broker, not just a regular bank or lender, to get a better idea of what mortgage products exist on the market to help with your individual situation. Don't lie to the mortgage broker about anything—they are on your side! Their job is to help you find a loan that works for your budget.

4. Once you talk to a mortgage broker or lender, they will provide you with a "pre-approval letter" or "pre-qualification letter" showing how much they think they can find you a loan for. You then take that letter to a real estate agent to help you find a home. Most real estate agents won't work with you until you have one of these letters.

5. If you find that you're priced out of your area, consider going in with friends or family to purchase a multi-family property together. There's no limit to how many people can be on a mortgage together, and in many places you can do a "condo conversion" after purchasing to legally separate each unit into its own property, making it like a housing co-op.

CHAPTER 14

Whoa, What Happened?

When we moved into our house, Tunnel Vision had a small home office in the front with three big windows that looked out onto the yard. It was a tiny space, the second-smallest one we'd ever had—second only to the apartment in Los Feliz where I stored shipping supplies in the oven. I measured everything meticulously—the room, of course, but also our desks and shelving units, plopping everything into a scale model on my computer to figure out where things would go. It was a tight squeeze, but it would have to do. I let Camila pick out the paint color for the walls—a rich plum purple. We hung up patchwork velvet curtains that I found at a thrift store, trying to make it look homey, and a $5 light shade from IKEA. I hung it too low, though, and it hit Camila's head every time she stood up from her desk.

The business was still just me and Camila earning the same day rate, something like $150 per day after taxes. I liked thinking in post-tax income; it felt the most real, like what we could expect to put in our pockets. It made budgeting easy and clear. Camila still worked four days per week and I worked five. She shipped orders and answered customer service emails. I sat on the couch in the living room updating our website with vintage listings, usually while watching cheesy horror movies. The movies helped me focus. I later learned this was typical for people with ADHD—apparently you need enough of a distraction that you're not looking for other ones.

One month after moving into the new house, we started to hear rumblings of a new virus popping up in the United States—a coronavirus that caused a severe illness called COVID-19. By March 19, less than two months after the move, the state of California was on lockdown. Camila and I worked from home with bated breath, wondering what exactly was going to happen. I expected a global market shutdown—something akin to the Great Recession or maybe worse. In a few months' time, I figured, I'd be on unemployment applying to work data entry jobs from home for minimum wage—competing with other workers over scraps. As the days turned into weeks, though, sales continued at a steady pace and even began an upward trajectory. Unable to leave their homes, people took to the internet for a distraction. E-commerce began to boom.

The primary challenge with running an e-commerce website during a lockdown is figuring out where you're going to get inventory. Businesses were doing their best to operate in a COVID-safe capacity, with varying degrees of success. Rag houses were closed, which meant we were unable to secure enough clothing to keep the vintage business in motion. Made-to-order clothing with our regular seamstress, Sofia, was off the table—she was now busy with her daughter's clothing line, which had grown massively over the pandemic as well. I could sew, of course, but where would I get the materials? The downtown fabric market was a ghost town and secondhand fabrics were nearly impossible to source even when there wasn't a global pandemic occurring. I found a rag house on the East Coast that did bulk orders by mail. It was run by one person who pulled from their existing inventory, piecing together bundles as best they could to fulfill your requests. I started placing monthly orders; it was always a surprise seeing what we got. After a few months, though, their inventory was depleted. The boxes became more and more sparse when they showed up in the mail, the clothes just a bit stranger.

By March 27, the U.S. government opened unemployment benefits for those laid off work due to the pandemic. However, many of my friends—especially those who had previously been self-employed—struggled to qualify. People were desperate for cash. I was desperate for inventory. Friends messaged me, eager to sell whatever they could from their closets. It was a win-win. I drove to their houses and picked up boxes left on their front porches—contactless— paying them digitally from inside my car while they waved, always from six feet away. We couldn't book models. Instead, we photographed the pieces on ourselves, pinning things that didn't fit quite right and adding it into our item descriptions as an apology: "This item was pinned on Madeline. It would better fit . . . someone who wasn't Madeline, sorry."

Eventually, even the supply of vintage clothing seemed to dry up. It was out there, of course, behind the giant industrial roll-up doors of the rag houses in South Los Angeles, packed tightly into bales or covered with tarps. Nobody was there to sell it to us, though. I think eventually they started calling problems like that "supply chain issues."

My friends called me, speaking in hushed panicked voices that reminded me of the Great Recession.

"What's going to happen to us?" they asked. "How are people supposed to pay their bills?"

"They'll send everyone back to work soon," I told them, more annoyed than reassured. "The government doesn't care about us. They'll send people to work to die, all for the economy."

I didn't want to be right, but in the months that followed, I'd be proven correct. The government introduced every measure imaginable to "stimulate the economy"; very few prioritized public safety. At my house, our little business seemed to float on—a ghost ship making its way through the wreckage of other ships who'd passed before us. Sales were steady, up even. We waited for the other shoe to drop.

When the other shoe did drop, it was not in the way we expected. Camila injured her wrist at home one day. The injury didn't heal like it should have. She struggled to do everyday things like drive her car, hold a plate to eat, or use the remote control on her television. She spoke to doctors and physical therapists who guessed at a diagnosis but weren't certain. What they were sure of, though, is that she needed rest.

"How much rest?" she asked, panicked. "I have to work to afford to live."

"As much as you can afford to take," they said awkwardly. It was a non-answer that illuminated just how deranged our for-profit healthcare system and lack of social safety net truly are. They might as well have said "Hope you don't die!" and left it at that.

"Look, sales are . . . good," I said, whispering lest I jinx it. "Why don't you stay home and rest for a month or two. Tunnel Vision will keep paying you your normal rate as long as we can afford it. We'll play it by ear."

She spent the next couple of months recuperating at home, using speak-to-text to send messages checking in. Nothing seemed to get better, though. I needed someone to fill in while she was away. I posted an alert on my social media: "Anyone looking for extra work? COVID-safe environment (I don't leave my house). $150 per day, 5 days per week, Central LA. HMU."

Within seconds, I received a text message from someone I knew from the vintage world—a woman named Kenna who ran her own vintage business selling at flea markets on weekends.

"Hey, just saw your post! I'm looking for work—flea markets are all shut down, I'm immunocompromised and stuck in my house losing my mind. Let me know what you think!"

I responded instantly. "Can you start tomorrow?"

In less than thirty seconds, the position had been filled. I removed the post from my Instagram, but was shocked to find that around ten other people had responded too.

"That fast?" I thought. People must really be struggling. I counted myself lucky.

KENNA

I first met Kenna at a place vintage pickers call "the bins." It's a public store owned by a big-brand secondhand clothing mega corporation, where items that weren't sold in their stores are tossed into giant blue bins for people to pick through. Pieces are weighed in most locations and sold by the pound, for prices as low as a dollar or two per piece most of the time. The bins are full of vintage sellers who can't afford things like a resale license or the minimum-buy amount at major rag houses. They're competitive and cutthroat, and if you stay all day you're bound to see a fistfight or two break out over who grabbed a T-shirt first.

In the chaos of the bins, Kenna was something of an enigma. She had long blonde hair and wore tie-dyed jeans; she hardly ever took her headphones off. Sometimes, I stood by her as she went through her picks—catching her rejected items mid-air as she threw them back.

"I know this is bad form," I told her with a laugh. "Your taste is just so good."

"You could just buy wholesale from me instead," she said, raising her eyebrow as if to say "Not cool, man."

So I bought wholesale from Kenna for a while, until COVID lockdowns made it impossible for her to work. Since Kenna was immunocompromised, getting COVID could mean a death sentence. She sat locked in her studio apartment all day, slowly going mad during lockdown. The government didn't care what happened to people like Kenna, and she knew it. When protesters in conservative towns like Huntington Beach took to the streets to fight against things like mask mandates, Kenna just shook her head.

"I can't blame regular people," she said, "even if they are endangering my life. Most people aren't bad, they're just not equipped to handle something like this. This was a massive government failure. Individual people shouldn't be tasked with keeping me safe. I pay a government to do that. Instead, the government used my money to let a million people die from COVID and increase the military budget to kill more people in different parts of the world."

Kenna was an anomaly: a hopeful cynic. She saw the world as it was, but never stopped thinking we could do better. Kenna couldn't go to the bins during lockdown, or risk working a regular job, but she could come to my tiny home office and help ship orders. It was something.

Training Kenna was easy. She knew what she was doing—she'd worked in vintage as long as I had, and even had experience owning a vintage store of her own, in addition to doing flea markets on weekends. She was hardworking and savvy like Camila. We fell into a groove.

"Things seem like they're going well still online," she said.

"Kind of," I replied. "Sales are good, but trying to find inventory has been a nightmare. Everything is closed."

"Have you thought about making more of your new designs?" she asked. "Not made-to-order, I mean, like production runs. Some factories are still in business with COVID-safe protocols."

I'd thought about it before. Once, I'd made a small production run of our best-selling shorts with a sweatshop-free factory. It was expensive and required a lot of up-front cash to produce—money that you wouldn't make back for months. You can get anything made cheap in a sweatshop, of course—shirts made for as little as $2 sometimes, terrifyingly low prices with harrowing implications from a human rights perspective. For sweatshop-free facilities, though, the cost is premium—anywhere from $10 to $100 depending on the piece. When you pay people fairly for their labor, things cost more money, and I wanted to pay fairly.

"It's expensive," I told Kenna. "But not out of the question, I guess . . . especially if the production runs are small enough that there's no excess or waste, and the facilities are good enough that people are being paid well, especially with COVID safety protocols."

"Why don't you apply for a small business loan?" she asked. "The SBA is doing a lot of financing now to help businesses stay afloat. I know a lot of people who've gotten them."

It didn't hurt to apply. I went to the Small Business Administration website and filled out a form. "Desired Loan Amount" blinked in front of me on the screen. How much did we need? I pulled a number out of thin air: $65,000. A few seconds later, I received an email response. We were approved. They deposited the funds two days later.

I stared at our business bank account in awe. Sixty-five thousand dollars? It was more money than I'd ever seen in my life, even if it was just a number on a screen.

"What are you going to do with it?" Kenna asked.

"Make it count, I guess," I replied, not sure myself.

I drafted up a small collection to produce with the funds:

Two rib knit tank tops with embroidered artwork
Two pairs of faux fur pants
One faux fur reversible coat

Next, I set to work vetting manufacturers—spending hours on virtual tours and FaceTime calls, scouring through third-party certifications for things like workplace safety regulations and pay structures. Within three months, we started to receive our new designs. Kenna and I crammed inventory into every corner of the tiny office possible, shoving tank tops into the narrow gaps between our shelving units and the walls. Things sold nearly as fast as we stocked them. Chris lost his job working at a surf shop in January 2020. By July, his unemployment benefits had expired. We hired him to help us ship orders, making the same rate as Kenna and me—$150 per day; the three of us danced around each other in the tiny room we called an office while Mo-Dog slept inconveniently underfoot. We dodged each other's elbows as we hunted for items to ship out and pieces to photograph. By the time the coats arrived in September, the office was packed to the brim and in utter chaos. Kenna looked at me with exasperation.

"Where are the coats going to go?" she asked meekly. They were bulky huge things, packed as tightly as possible into giant boxes, but impossible to contain.

"I guess we can keep them in the garage?" I volunteered.

We piled inventory everywhere imaginable—the hallways and living room, the front porch and garage. By October, both Chris and Kenna were skeptical of the tiny home office's ability to sustain the business.

"What's going to happen for Black Friday?" they asked, looking at each other out of the corners of their eyes.

"I think it's time to consider renting an office," Chris said decisively.

"What if sales dry up?" I asked, frightened.

"What if they don't?" Kenna asked.

I looked around the room. Jackets spilled over the edge of every surface. Shipping supplies teetered on top of the printer. Every five seconds, Kenna or Chris hit their head on the IKEA light dangling from the ceiling. At this point, I realized, it was an issue of safety. They were right. We'd have to rent an office.

That week, I signed a lease for a one-thousand-square-foot office across the street from my house. It was an old, strange building. The owner wanted something inside that didn't draw too much attention. The front windows were covered over in boards. The space seemed huge at the time— something we would surely struggle to fill. The rent was terrifying, too: $2,000 per month.

Come October, the first round of COVID-related unemployment benefits were starting to expire. They came in six-month increments, and people were getting antsy. Friends and old Tunnel Vision employees texted me nearly daily—variations of the same text messages: "Hey, just thinking about you! New stuff looks great. If you need any help for Black Friday, let me know!"

By November, we'd added two more people to the team: Kelsey and Story.

KELSEY

I met Kelsey when I worked at Lip Service. She was a punk chick from the San Fernando Valley with bleached hair and homemade clothes covered in patches and pins. She ran the sample store on the ground floor at Lip Service and viewed Drew as something of a mentor. The day Drew died, Kelsey came to our house. We cried while staring blankly at a wall. Kelsey had helped me with Tunnel Vision work in the past—nothing consistent, just here and there as needed. She was a true believer in the power of goodness, and she had an energy that was infectious. The first day I met Kelsey, she told me she just wanted to have a nice life. At the time, I wasn't sure what she meant. The older I got, though, the more I came to understand. She didn't want anything fancy or special. She just wanted to be happy. She just wanted to have enough. On my own journey to understanding exactly what "enough" meant, Kelsey's words echoed in my mind like a compass marking the path.

After Drew died, Kelsey got a job working at a popular buy-sell-trade vintage store in Los Angeles that marketed itself as being progressive and worker-oriented. When COVID hit, though, the company proved itself less concerned with the safety and well-being of its employees and more concerned with maintaining profit whatever the cost. Management urged employees not to disclose their positive COVID tests to coworkers. Kelsey lived with her mother, an elderly woman with a potentially compromised immune system. She worried about her mother's safety, and wondered how in good conscience she could endanger her mother's life for something like $16 per hour.

As Black Friday approached, Kelsey sent me a text:

"If you need any help for Black Friday, I'm here ☺"

Kenna and Chris agreed that we definitely would, so I gave Kelsey a call.

"We might need some help," I told her. "Sales have been . . . wild. But I don't know how long it will last. So just for Black Friday, if you want. Pay is one hundred and fifty dollars per day——take-home pay, plus COVID testing and we'll buy lunch. It's just temporary, though."

"Sure it is," she said, laughing.

"What's so funny?" I asked.

"I don't think it's going to be temporary," she said.

Kelsey believed in Tunnel Vision. More than that, she believed in me.

"We'll see," I said. I hoped she was right, though. Kelsey, Kenna, and Chris all needed the work. I needed to be someone they could count on.

STORY

As Black Friday grew nearer, sales showed no sign of slowing down. We'd managed to pay back our initial small business loan in just a couple of months, and were bringing in our second batch of made-to-order designs: four baby Ts and four slip dresses. I looked at Kenna, worried.

"We might need even more help for Black Friday," I said. "I can see how Camila's feeling, maybe she can help a little. Her plus Kelsey, that's a start. But we might need someone else, too."

"I think I have a friend," Kenna said. "She's a workhorse—tough. She used to help me at the flea markets. She comes from a rough background and she had a bad year. She'd probably appreciate the work."

A few days later, Story showed up at the office. Story was doe-eyed and petite, covered in tattoos from her neck down to her hands. She had a quiet intensity and a willingness to do whatever it took to get the job done.

"This job is really saving me," she said. "You have no idea."

She'd been in trouble at other jobs she'd had in the past—vague complaints about her "attitude" or her "intensity," things we both agreed wouldn't have even been an issue were she a man. When I looked at Story, I saw elements of myself. She was a "fighter," but wished she'd never had to be. We both trudged on in the face of adversity, not because we delighted in a challenge but simply because we had no choice.

Black Friday came and went. Camila came back to work part-time, easing her wrist back into the idea of working. The job she came back to, though, just a few months later, was very different from the one she'd left. We had a proper office, and she had coworkers for the first time in years. The paid lunches continued and the sales kept coming in. Day by day, I grew comfortable with the idea that this thing we'd created might last, at least for a little while longer. The jobs became permanent; Kelsey had been right.

"What if we got everyone bringing home three thousand dollars a month after taxes, for four days per week of work?" I asked one day. It was January 2021.

"I know it's not a lot," I said. "Not really, anyway. One day, I'd like it if we all could be middle class in Los Angeles. That feels like it would be *enough*. To do that, though, we need to earn at least sixty-five thousand dollars per year based on HUD data. But this—it's a little over fifty K each, and it's a start."

"I mean, that would be amazing," Story said. "I've never made that much anywhere in my life."

"Okay," I said. "Let's just do it then. Let's just see how it goes."

That's how both our universal wage and four-day work-week for all full-time workers became official. People ask sometimes how we ended up deciding on a four-day work-week. The answer isn't cut-and-dried. For a while, it's all the business could afford to pay for. I worked five days per week, everyone else worked four. Eventually, the universal wage was enough that I didn't need to work five anymore. By the time the business was big enough that it could afford to pay people more, it simply made more sense to give them raises than to increase their hours to match mine. Everyone was productive in the time they were there. The work got done. It hardly seemed like each person working an extra eight hours per week would make a significant difference to the volume we were able to produce. If anything, it might make people more burnt out and less productive.

What I knew intuitively to be true, other companies quantified with data. In 2019, Microsoft Japan implemented a four-day workweek without reducing pay for its workers. The result? Productivity increased 40 percent. The year prior, a New Zealand trust management company tried a four-day workweek and found similar results: a 20 percent increase in productivity. In 1974, the UK government limited work hours to just three days per week and only saw a 6 percent dip in productivity overall. The most productive countries in the world—like Norway, Denmark, Germany, and the Netherlands—only work 27 hours per week on average.

It might seem counterintuitive, but the reasoning is sound. The more you work, the less accurate you are. When your workload is so significant that it cuts into your ability to sleep well, this trend is exacerbated. Someone who has been awake for 17 hours straight, for example, has the performance ability of someone with a 0.05 percent blood alcohol level—which is legally drunk in most places in the United States. Overwork-ing has negative health effects across the board, in fact. In one study, University College London found that employees working a 55-hour week faced a 33 percent increased risk of stroke compared to people working just 35–40 hours. In another study, the U.S. Centers for Disease Control and Prevention found working 61–70 hours per week increased the risk of heart disease by 42 percent, and working 71–80 hours per week increased it by 63 percent.

Indeed, the origins of the 40-hour workweek have little to do with science, and everything to do with precedent. Following the Industrial Revolution, workers worked on average 70–100 hours per week, which probably explains why—when coupled with unsafe work conditions—35,000 people per year were dying in factories by the year 1900. The standard workweek in American factories during this time was six days per week, with 10–16 hours of work per day. In 1818, the factory owner and social reformer Robert Owen began advocating for an 8-hour workday—a 50 percent reduction in the standard workweek. The capitalist owning class of the 1800s thought this sounded ridiculous. It wasn't until May 1, 1926, when Henry Ford mandated an 8-hour workday for factory workers at the Ford Motor Company, that the idea of the 8-hour workday started to take root in the private sector, and companies saw that not only was it possible, it actually led to more productivity.

Now, over a hundred years later, the idea of the eight-hour workday seems set in stone, but that precedent might actually be making workers less productive than we ultimately could be. Today, 52 percent of workers report being burnt out and 60 percent say their work-life balance is "poor." Scientists agree that the ideal workweek should probably be far less than 40 hours but disagree at what exactly the ideal productivity point is. What we do know is that the average human brain can only focus on a task for between 20 and 90 minutes per sitting, and only 4–5 hours over the course of a day—meaning the average worker is probably only focusing on their work for between 20 and 25 hours per week anyway.

By 2021, our standard full-time workweek at Tunnel Vision was 32 hours, Monday through Thursday, 10:00 a.m.

to 6:00 p.m., with a paid lunch break and fully paid lunch meals, too. By 2022, we had dropped the hours even further: 28 hours, Monday through Thursday, 10:00 a.m. to 5:00 p.m. with a paid lunch break. The first quarter we dropped to a 28-hour workweek from 32, our sales increased 52 percent from the previous year. We added fully paid top-tier health insurance for the team with our newfound increase in revenue.

By September 2021, pandemic relief in the form of unemployment benefits was coming to a close. All around us, people began to panic once again. Many businesses closed down entirely. At our business, sales were up 774 percent over the previous year; we were officially a multimillion-dollar business. Our wages increased to a take-home pay of $4,000 per month, or something like $72,000 per year in gross income. Raises were doled out equally, all of us earning the same amount together. We'd officially become middle class in the city of Los Angeles, something up to this point I would have thought was impossible—we were all earning the most money we'd ever earned before in our lives. Sales grew, and the business's needs grew along with them. Soon, we needed a dedicated customer service person (Marcella), a dedicated image retoucher (Lizzie), a dedicated photographer (Leeanna), a dedicated videographer (Babylungs), a second dedicated vintage buyer (Fernanda), a dedicated production manager for new designs (Sarah), a new fit model (Aya), and a photo shoot assistant (Ria). People we knew came out of the woodwork, clamoring for work when their unemployment benefits ran dry. We did our best to place people in need in positions that worked for them. Our ragtag team grew, taking on people who struggled to find employment at other places.

The Statue of Liberty proclaimed, "Give me your tired, your poor, your huddled masses yearning to breathe free." Tunnel Vision acted on it. Our new hires were people with chronic mental and physical illnesses, neurodivergent people with unconventional working schedules, people of color who'd experienced discrimination in other workplaces, women who'd grown weary of misogyny in the tech industry, people who'd spent time in prison, people who were in recovery for addiction, people who did sex work, and people who had the types of tattoos that usually make you "unhireable" in traditional settings. We became the place you went to work when there was nowhere else to go. We weren't perfect, but we worked towards it. Our goal became accommodation. Wherever you were, Tunnel Vision would try to meet you there. The result was a group of dedicated and loyal workers who each cared about the business as though it was their own. As our team grew, it became obvious that for our workplace to function, we needed something other workplaces often claimed to have in theory, but rarely implemented in practice: unlimited paid time off.

Unlimited paid time off has been something of a buzzy term in recent years. Tech companies and the like have come under fire for offering "unlimited paid time off" but creating a work culture that actively discouraged workers from using it. At our business, the emerging culture seemed to be one based on our needs as workers. The unofficial rules that emerged were simple: take all the time you need for whatever you need. If you can manage your workload, there's no issue. If you need people to cover your workload while you're gone, let us know and we will make it happen. If people begin to think they've been covering your workload too much, they'll let you know and we'll troubleshoot from there. It was an informal system, but it worked well in our office. People with chronic physical and mental health issues could take whatever time they needed without fear of repercussion.

Sick days, mental health days, emergency days, and vacation days all blended together. It became a place where you could wake up feeling just not well, and you didn't have to hyper-analyze why or give a report. Sometimes, people took weeks or even months off. We all understood. When someone got antsy about how productive they thought they were compared to everyone else, we took it as a sign that maybe they needed to take some breaks, too. We began forcing each other to go home whenever someone got cranky. Like the shorter workweek, forcing people to take paid time off just because they're in a funk seems counterintuitive. In practice, though, we found it raised our productivity overall. To new hires, it was a hard transition. I explained it like this:

If you stayed home from work today, you'd be taking one person's productivity away from the team. Not ideal, but not a big deal either. If you come into work in a funk and create a weird vibe in the office, you might reduce the productivity of the eight people who work closest to you by, say, 25 percent. We're intuitive and sensitive to each other's experiences, right? We all feel it when someone is having an off day, and no matter how much we try to ignore it, it's going to affect our ability to focus on our own work at least a little. Twenty-five percent of eight workers is the equivalent of losing two people's whole day of productivity, plus your own productivity, which has surely been compromised too. You've effectively just traded losing one worker for losing two. "Toughing it out" is seldom the right answer. The right answer from a productivity standpoint is staying home so that the people who are in the office are in their best place to work and get things handled. The office is a working zone. If you're not in work mode, stay home.

It sounds rational enough because it is. Just like productivity has been proven to be contagious, a lack of productivity or a generally bad attitude can be contagious in a workplace, as well. Researchers at the University of Washington published a study in the journal *Research in Organizational Behavior* where they found negative workers can be a catalyst for an entire team's downward spiral. Where traditional business models recommend weeding "bad apples" out during the hiring process, we took on a different model. Instead, we assume that everyone is a bad apple sometimes. Life is hard, and dealing with stress can weigh on anyone. By assuming that all people go through rough spots once in a while, we create a space where people are allowed to stay home on days when they're feeling particularly negative. To accommodate the lack in personnel, we simply overstaff by roughly two bodies and cross-train rigorously. That way, the remaining team is always available and able to cover a missing body's workload. We covered one another's work with pleasure, knowing the next time we need a break for whatever, the team would be there to have our back, too. It became a workplace culture of mutual care.

How did we afford to overstaff by two full people? Well, quite easily—I, the official owner, just refused to take an egregious salary and instead paid myself the same as every other worker at the company. It's amazing how much extra cash flow is freed up when one person isn't hoarding all the money at the top. To really understand the impact of unequal pay distribution, you need to understand how much I could be earning as the owner of the business if I paid every other worker minimum wage, which in Los Angeles in 2022 for a business our size was just $14 per hour. Our total payroll obligation that same year was $807,300. Were I to pay the workers at Tunnel Vision minimum wage, our workers would each be earning just $20,384 per year, meaning I could be paying myself an annual salary of $601,276 per year without increasing *any* costs to the company. This is what most business owners are doing: minimizing their payroll expenses as much as possible to maximize their own earnings. By choosing instead to pay all workers the same—focusing on what is "enough"—revenue is freed up to bring more workers on board, creating more "good jobs" for our community. The average CEO pay in the United States in 2022 was $805,107, compared to an average worker pay of $57,043. That means the average CEO represents 14 regular workers on payroll, and earns over $200,000 more than I would be earning even in the aforementioned scenario.

Sometimes, people ask me how equal distribution of payroll can be sustainable for our business. I always have the same answer: the business might fail at any moment— businesses have a tendency to do that—but if it does, it won't be because our payroll was overlarge. Given the bloated salary of the average American CEO, our total payroll costs are actually lower this way.

I don't view my decision to distribute payroll this way as a choice. I view it as the only possible way I could ever run a business. I think back to working with Camila in that tiny home office in the house we rented, while the exploitative entrepreneurs advised me to cut her pay and keep the leftover profit for myself. I couldn't do it then, with her. How could I do it with anyone? How could I ever look a person in the eyes and tell them they deserve to have a worse life than I do? To me, there was never a choice to do it any other way. We all come up together. Punk rock taught me that. The business as it exists today is a vehicle through which we can bring people up with us. If the business grows in the future, bringing up even more will be the only goal.

How to Run an Equitable Business

Running an equitable business means seeing the humanity in everyone in a workplace. It's easy in theory, but there are some tips and tricks I've learned along the way.

1. Instead of acting like a manager all the time, try to act more like a mediator to help work through interpersonal conflict when it arises among employees in the workplace who feel someone is or isn't pulling their weight. The best use of a leadership role is as a diplomat. Emotional labor is a part of the job; factor it into your management style.

2. When something seems unfair in the workplace, practice balancing by giving rather than taking away. If someone is upset that someone else has had more time off, for example, problem-solve by having the angry party take more time off themselves, rather than limiting how much time everyone else can take.

3. Assume everyone will have bad days. Remember that in a workplace, everyone doesn't have to love each other. They just have to not kill each other long enough for everyone to get a paycheck! De-escalation is the name of the game.

4. Be radically transparent about all things financial. Ask people how aware they want to be of the company finances. Schedule optional sit-ins where those who want to know about the money can hear the nitty-gritty details. Be aware that not everyone will want to know, and that's okay. Some people just want to show up, get a paycheck, and go home.

5. Practice workplace democracy, but don't force people to make uninformed decisions. Practice acknowledging certain people's expertise in certain fields. Take votes for major decisions, but try assigning delegates for smaller decisions. Be open to trying out new systems of democracy and group decision-making; what works best might vary from one workplace to another. Don't be rigid—flexibility will allow you to tailor the workplace to suit everyone's needs.

6. Pay everyone equally for their labor. This one is pretty obvious, but for some reason it seems the hardest for most businesses to comprehend! If you have a workplace where some people acquired college degrees, practice paying everyone the same rate for their work, but allowing the business to repay employees' student loans. If you have a worker-owner who also was the primary investor in the business, repay the initial investment clearly and separately from payroll in a way that everyone can see and understand. Similarly, if an owner-worker has back-owed wages from before the business was able to comfortably pay everyone to be there, set up a visible repayment structure for those hours worked where the owner did not get paid. Make sure everyone knows why this is happening and when the debt will be repaid in full.

7. If you opt not to structure your business as a legal co-op, build in an equity agreement for all workers if the business were to be sold. Not every worker may want to be a full legal owner for a variety of reasons (at my workplace, some people feel it would adversely affect their mental health). However, they can reap the benefits of ownership with an equity agreement. If the business is ever sold, the workers and owner all earn an equal portion of the proceeds.

CHAPTER 15

And the Money Will Roll Right In

I walk into the office one day, on a mission.

"Everyone's getting houses," I yell as I hang my jacket up on the coat hooks by the front door. The coatrack is wonky, barely hanging on for dear life. I installed it myself the first week we rented the space—back when there were only three of us. Now it's hardly sufficient. There are between ten and thirteen of us there on any given day. If Kelsey and I both wear our heavy-duty leather motorcycle jackets into work at the same time, that coat hook is coming straight out of the wall—I can sense it.

Everyone looks up from their computer, quizzical looks on their faces.

"Maybe one day," Story says with a laugh.

"Maybe today," I say, walking to my desk and slamming my laptop on the table.

I open my laptop to a house listing still open in my web browser from the night before. It's a strange, small house covered in spray paint, set next to two burnt-down structures—the only three residential plots of land on an otherwise industrial block. It's $429,000—an unheard-of deal in Los Angeles, where the median house price is up to $999,000. I copy the link to the listing and send it to our work group chat. Everyone looks at their phones.

"What is this?" Story asks.

"A house," I reply, matter-of-factly.

"I don't understand," Kenna says, looking at the listing. "Could we afford this?"

"Yep," I say, smiling. "Look."

I open up a new tab—an online home affordability calculator. The first thing it asks for is income. Our current gross annual income sits at $73,060 each. I plug it into the screen. Next, it asks for monthly debts. Only a few of us have student loans. The rest never went to college. They were smart for that, I think. Earlier in the year, everyone managed to pay off their lingering credit card bills and medical debt and whatever random money they'd owed to friends and family members from when times were tougher. What other types of debt do people usually have? Car payments, maybe.

A few months back, when there were only eight full-time and two part-time workers at the business, nearly everyone's car broke down the same week. I had the Kia that I'd haggled my way into a good deal on. It was red, and the miles on it were too high for being only three years old. Nobody wants a red car, and especially not with 100,000 miles on it in just three years. It took me a whole day to negotiate that price. Everyone else at the office had old, shitty cars they'd been driving for years—some of their cars were older than me, and to be honest, I was surprised they'd been running at all. Sarah's car broke down in the middle of a bridge. Story's had the keyhole in the handle slashed so someone could break in. Fernanda's only ran half the time, and at any rate, the entire ceiling lining had fallen down into the car, making it hard to see anything while she drove. Kenna was driving her boyfriend's dead grandfather's car and it wasn't even registered in her name. When the registration expired, nobody quite knew how to get it up-to-date. The sideview mirror was missing on it anyway.

I learned about their car situations one day at work, while everyone sat around comparing their vehicular drama. "Wait, wait, wait," I said, taken aback. "Raise your hand if you have a reliable mode of transportation." Kelsey and I both put our hands up and looked around the room. She drove a used Prius that she loved, and I drove my Kia with no complaints. We were the only ones.

"Okay," I said. "Gimme a second."

I opened my computer search engine and typed in *Can my company buy employees cars?* I scoured the countless pages of internet search results. The internet's general consensus was yeah, kinda, with some stipulations for taxes. "Great," I thought. "My tax guy will love dealing with this next year." Every year is a new challenge.

"All right, dudes, look," I said to the room. "We just had a really successful sale, we've got some profit lying around—should we use it to get everyone a new car? Vote please."

The answer was an overwhelming yes. We set a budget based on the random tax notices found on the internet and went shopping. We bought seven cars in two months. The salesmen all condescended to me—a five-foot-tall girl with blue hair wearing ripped jeans and beat-up boots—in their offices. I took extra pleasure in plopping down the AmEx Platinum on the table. It's heavy, that card. It's made of metal. "Oh," they'd all say with a look of surprise. Sometimes, they wouldn't take credit, so we'd just plop down a debit card instead. "Do you need to call your bank to make sure it will go through?" they asked. "Nah," I said, and laughed. "Run it." I get why people like having money. It feels powerful sometimes. We were Pretty Woman. Big mistake being rude to us. Huge.

When all of the cars were purchased, we paid off the rest of Kelsey's loan on her Prius. One of our part-time workers doesn't drive, so we bought her furniture for her apartment instead. She'd been sleeping on a mat on her floor for years before coming to work for us.

Back in the office, I stare at the "monthly debts" box on

the home affordability calculator, smiling. I take delight in typing out the "0." Next is the down payment.

"You guys have savings, right?" I shout out to nobody in particular in the room.

"Yeah," everyone replies—a confused half-hearted jumble of affirmative responses.

I pull out the calculator on my phone and type in an equation: $429,000 × 0.035. I hit Enter and out spits a number: $15,015—the 3.5 percent down payment for the $429,000 house on an FHA loan.

"Who has less than fifteen K in savings?" I ask the room loudly. At any other workplace, the question might seem invasive. At our workplace, though, where finances are all radically transparent, it's just another day in the office. Nobody speaks. I look up from my computer to see a few of them shaking their heads back and forth as if to say "Not me."

I plug $20,000 into the home affordability calculator as the down payment. Interest rates are low, around 2.5 percent. That's going to help. I hit Enter and out spits a result:

"You can afford a house up to $436,535."

I screenshot the result and send it to the group chat.

"So," I ask, beaming, "who is going to buy this house?"

"Is this real?" Story asks, looking around. "Like, we could afford to buy a house?"

"The computer says yes," I reply. "Anyone wanna go look at it? I'll drive."

Story and Kenna and I pile into my car and drive the fifteen minutes or so down the street to where the house sits. It's a weird street, full of sheet metal and brick buildings. The three residential plots are at the very end of the road, near a big park that's been closed to the public for months. Two of the houses are burnt to a crisp. The one from the online listing sits at the end, largely unscathed. There's a corner of the building where the stucco has all broken away to expose the rotting wood of the crawl space below, and there are broken bars swinging from the windows, plus strange electrical cords scattered around.

"It's rough," I concede. "But it's a house."

Kenna and Story look at each other, then at me. They're skeptical. Being able to afford a house at all feels like a lie to them, and this house barely seems like a house at all. We drive back to the office—them: deep in thought, me: determined.

The next day, Camila comes into the office. She'd been off the day before—a mental health day, I think, but we try not to pry when people miss work. We just want everyone to be well. What's the point of having a business, I often wonder, if it can't be the kind of business you'd want to work at?

Camila is hanging up her bag on the sketchy coat hooks as Story says, "I don't think this is the year for me to buy a house. Maybe next year. I just need a little time to settle."

"Same," Kenna says. "I just don't know if I'm ready."

The office erupts in a series of *ahhh*s and *yes*es, but secretly, I'm a bit heartbroken.

"Wait," Camila says, sitting down at her desk. "There's a house we can afford?"

The thing about us all earning the same wages is that we're all in the same boat. What one of us can afford, all of us can afford, and we know it.

I smile at Camila. "Wanna go for a ride?" I ask.

Fifteen minutes later, Camila and I are standing in front of the weird little house with the broken bars swaying gently in the breeze.

"It's rough," I say, trying to pre-empt her concerns.

"But it's a house!" she replies.

Camila and I have been on the same money journey, together, for years. By this point, she sees the house for what it is: guaranteed shelter, yes, but also an appreciating asset that could be her gateway to a financially stable future. I call the number on the sign, pretending to be Camila. She's too anxious to do it herself.

The man on the other end of the phone says, "I'm just down the street. Are you around now?"

So, we wait.

The real estate agent arrives, the listing agent. He's a big man with a huge smile who grew up in this neighborhood. The three houses, all there in a row, were owned by a friend of his—been in the family for years.

"I'm from Los Angeles originally, too," Camila tells the agent.

"Is that right?" he asks, looking at her like he can't quite believe it.

"Yep," she says. "Born and raised. I never thought I could afford to buy a house here."

"Well," he says. "The price is right on this one. It needs some work."

"I like work," Camila says. She's right.

Once, years ago, Camila showed up to my house to work still drunk from the night before. She was early—a few hours early, even. I was still in my pajamas when I heard the doorbell ring. I opened the door, rubbing my eyes, and Camila was there—ready to work, still dressed in her going-out clothes from the night before. She had huge black eyeliner on and glitter on her cheeks.

"Hi," she said, smiling. "I know I'm early. Is it okay if I just start work now, though? It felt easier to come straight here from the after-party rather than go home."

About then is when she must have realized she was still drunk, because next she asked if she could use my bathroom to throw up. I told her to take a shower too, and got her some clean clothes to change into. The only thing I could find in her size, though, was a one-piece swimsuit with a ruffle at the waist. She emerged from the shower, dressed in the swimsuit, and took a nap at my place for the rest of her shift. No work today.

"Man," I told Kennedy later. "She was drunk as hell and the only thought on her mind was 'I gotta get to work.' That's dedication. She's got a job at Tunnel Vision for life."

Kennedy looked skeptical, but Camila's been with the

company now for eight or so years, and I trust her with my debit card, my house keys, and my life.

Back in the car, I give Camila the number for the mortgage broker we used to buy our house. Less than twenty-four hours later, she's put an offer in and just like that, it's accepted. In the office the next day, we're all invested. She steps outside to take a phone call, and we overhear her say the word "escrow." She comes back in and hangs up the phone looking dazed.

"Are we in escrow?!" I ask.

"We're in escrow!" she yells like she can't quite believe it herself, and the whole office jumps up and down and shrieks a bit.

Of course it's not "we," not really. Camila's in escrow, but it feels like a team effort. Camila's success is the whole office's success. It means anyone in that room could buy a house. Maybe it's not a pipe dream after all.

I've always kind of thought that money just makes people more of whatever they already are. Like, if you give an asshole a bunch of money, are they going to suddenly become a good person? No way; they're just going to use all of that money to become an even bigger asshole somehow. They're going to use that money to buy up foreclosed houses at discount rates when the economy collapses, then rent those same houses back to the people who used to own them at skyrocketing rents that leave them so house-poor they can never get back on their feet again. They're going to use that money to build giant rocket ship phalluses to propel them into space so they can colonize the moon because they ran out of places here on earth to pillage, and human rights watchdog groups have been hounding them for years about the conditions in their Earthly factories and warehouses—there aren't any human rights watchdog groups in space, though. At the very least, they are going to use that money to buy their yacht its own cuter tinier baby yacht. I think, anyway. I'm not sure how yachts work but I assume it's kind of like having guinea pigs—you need two or the first one will get depressed or something.

It turns out if you give money to a broke, scrappy, loud-mouth punk kid from Fresno, she wants to use that money to take care of her community in whatever way possible, including getting them into stable housing. It shouldn't be shocking, but for some reason it is. The business isn't a get-rich-quick scheme. It's not even a get-rich-slow scheme. It's still just a way to earn a living for me and for my friends. Wage labor is all exploitation in the end. We're coerced into accepting employment because we'll die if we don't. There's no choice there. There's barely even an illusion of choice.

Profit is a funny thing, the extra gunk left over after a business has paid all of its bills and everyone has taken their paycheck and all of the reinvestments into the business have been made. Profit is how the owning class gets paid, through draws or distributions from profit. It's not like a regular paycheck, and some owners don't even work in the business, meaning they aren't eligible for a paycheck anyway. It's not like repayment of start-up capital or investments; those would be business operating expenses. It's just extra money, sitting there, for the business owners to take as a fun little bonus. It feels evil to me. That money should belong to the workers; their labor produced it. They worked for it. They earned it. We try to just break even at Tunnel Vision, to pay ourselves and our operating expenses and call it a day. When there is a little extra, though, we distribute it among everyone. That's what the cars were: profit sharing. What would the houses be, then? The result of people being actually paid enough to live, I guess. It feels revolutionary, which is sad in its own right. It shouldn't be revolutionary that people who work are paid enough to have shelter.

At night, after work, Sarah and I make plans to go out. She was my friend long before she ever became an employee, and we meet up at the same old bar we've been going to for the

better part of a decade. We're determined to make it our version of Cheers. One night, a new friend of hers is there, too.
He stares at me through squinting eyes as if he's trying to
figure out how to place me.

"I know who you are," he says to me, finally. "You're that
chick that pays her employees the exact same wage as you!
You're fucking sick!" He high-fives me.

"Yeah." I laugh. "Wait, did you not know Sarah is one of
those employees?"

He looks at her, shocked, and she nods. "No way!" he
says.

Word gets around, apparently, in ways I wouldn't even
expect. That's how novel a concept it is. People talk.

"We work the same number of hours in the day, it just
seems fair," I tell him, and he agrees.

We all know it's fair, deep down in our kindergarten brains,
where we learn the difference between right and wrong, and
all about how sharing works, but that doesn't stop it from
being shocking. People tell themselves quiet lies to normalize
the suffering. By some calculations, income inequality in the
United States today is worse than it was in France in 1789.
They cut people's heads off for that one.

After the bar, we head to a house party. I'm talking with
Sarah and a man overhears.

"You own a business?" he asks me, without waiting for an
answer. "You should really incorporate it." I roll my eyes. I
did that a decade ago.

"You own a business too?" I ask, taking a sip from my drink.
It's strong and I'm small. I'm a bit tipsy and feeling rowdy.
I might be looking for a fight. You can take the girl out of
Fresno, but you can't take the Fresno out of the girl apparently.

"Yeah," he says. "I own a landscaping company."

"Oh," I respond. "So, you do landscaping?"

"Well, not me personally, no," he says. "I own the company. I've got guys, they do the landscaping."

I take another drink. "So, what do you do, then? Manage
the office? Keep the schedule?"

He laughs. "No, the receptionist does that. I just own the company."

"Ah," I reply, pretending not to get it. "So, you do the marketing? You get the clients?"

"Nah." He shakes his head. He feels comfortable, I can tell—one business owner talking to another, casually discussing the exploitation of the working class. "Mostly I just show up now and then to make sure they're actually working. I've got a lot of free time. It's more like passive income."

"Oh, your employees don't work without you there? That's weird. What are you, like, not paying them enough or something?" I'm starting to push back now.

"Well, they work, you know, a little. But they're lazy," he says, looking a little uncomfortable.

"Huh," I say. "How much are you paying them? Maybe it's not enough."

He pauses for a second, taken aback by the question. "I mean, it depends," he says finally.

"You're not paying them, like, minimum wage, are you?" I ask, then laugh and take another drink. His body language is closed off now; he's defensive. I pretend not to notice.

"You know what you should do?" I continue. "You should try paying them what you make. That's what I do—works great. You don't have to micromanage anyone. When you pay people well, oof, they will treat that business like their own, man."

"What I make?" he asks, shocked. "You can't be serious."

"I am," I tell him. "I think we need a universal wage. Equal pay for equal hours worked."

"But there's no such thing as equal work," he says. "Some work is more important than others."

"All work is equally important," I tell him. "If the job wasn't important, it wouldn't need to exist. Why pay someone to do a job that's not important? You'd fire them and save the money for yourself if you didn't need them to do the job, right?"

"So, let me get this straight," he says. "You think someone working at McDonald's should make the same amount of money as the president?"

I shrug. "Well, if you're really asking me, I guess I don't think McDonald's or money or the president should exist."

He doesn't know what to make of that one, I can tell. "Why would I pay my employees what I make when I do all of the hard work?" he asks, searching for clarity.

"Do you?" I ask. "I thought you said you had a lot of time off? Passive income, right?"

"I mean, I do," he says, getting tripped up in his own words. "But it's harder work. It's mental work. They can't do the work that I do."

"Sounds like you can't do the work they do either," I tell him. "You're not a landscaper, right?"

"No," he responds. "But my job is more important. Anyone can learn to be a landscaper. Not everyone can learn to run a business."

"Ah," I say. "So, it sounds like you need each other, then, for the business to operate, them to do the work and you to— what—manage the money or something? Whatever it is that you actually do. It's a symbiotic relationship, only you're not paying them like you need them, and it sounds like you need them a lot more than they need you. Their hard work and long hours are funding your lifestyle. I can see why they're not so keen on working and why you've gotta check up on them so much."

"All business owners have to keep their workers in check," he says. We're really fighting now, he can tell.

"Weird," I say calmly. "I don't. They just kinda manage themselves. If anyone's the boss at my office, it's probably Kelsey." I laugh. "Maybe you're just bad at hiring. Want any tips?"

"Well," the man says, "as the owner you deserve to earn more because you're taking on all the risk." He's pivoting now.

"What risk?" I ask.

"Start-up money, time," he says.

"I don't know about you, but I was already paid back for my start-up money—it was two hundred bucks. And anyway, that's not paid in owner wages, that's paid like you're repaying a loan. Otherwise, the company is paying extra payroll tax on it for no good reason. As for unpaid time I spent working on the business when it started? Yeah, those are back-owed wages. Pay yourself those, sure, but it doesn't pay back exponentially forever. That doesn't make sense. Just pay yourself for the hours you didn't pay yourself for originally, done deal."

"Well, what if the business goes bankrupt?" he asks. "Your assets are at risk."

"Not if I don't personally guarantee the debt," I say, "or do anything illegal or sketchy. You should know that. Weren't you the one telling me to incorporate my business? Surely you know that's what incorporating businesses is for, right? To legally separate the owner from the company and establish it as its own separate entity? It would be illegal to pursue a business owner for the debts the company took out."

The man looks at me, annoyed, then just walks away, presumably to go terrorize someone else at the party with his passive-income stories. It's probably for the best. I'm not above getting into a fistfight with a man twice my size to prove a point, even if I lose.

Another guy walks up to me. "Hey, I overheard your conversation with that dude," he says. "It's cool what you're doing, with your business and all, but aren't you still technically the owner? Like, you're still profiting from their labor, right?" He's read Marx, I can tell.

"We're not really profit motivated," I tell him. "It's more . . . break-even motivated. When there is profit, we just split it up among everyone."

"But the business," he says. "It has equity and value, and you're the owner."

"Businesses are usually valued at their net profit actually," I tell him. "Since we don't post huge profit, nah, the business isn't really worth anything to anyone but us."

I tried to sell the business once, on a whim. I was over running it. First, I tried to pass the ownership around the office, though, like a hot potato.

"Anyone wanna be the boss from now on?" I asked.

"No," they all yelled back at me, disgust in their voices.

That might be an oversimplification. Kelsey actually yelled "I don't want to own a business!" while doing the "suck it" motion with her hands at her crotch.

"What if we sold it?" I asked. "We could divide the sales price up among us all based on the total time we've worked here."

Everyone agreed that seemed fair.

"But only if it's enough money that we all get to retire!" Story said.

I pitched it to a few agents that week. They have agents for that, apparently—just to buy and sell small businesses. All of them got back to me with the resounding answer that my weird little business wasn't worth anything to anyone but me.

"You don't profit," one guy said. "Try paying yourself more, maybe a million bucks a year or so, and then we'll talk."

Business bros don't care about people, they just care about money. They all want that passive income, apparently. So much for that.

Back at the party, the man looks confused. "Well, you should really be a co-op still. Why not just take the final plunge and do it right?"

"If you wanna come by the office and see Kelsey do the suck-it motion with her hands while yelling 'I don't want to own a business,' be my guest," I tell him, shrugging.

Not everyone in the office wants to own a business, it's as simple as that. Millennial girlboss hustle culture destroyed generations of us. Besides, we're all too mentally ill for this shit.

"You'll have to be a co-op maybe one day," I tell them, though, in private. It's the reality. "If I die before the busi-

ness does, it's going to all of you. You'll have to figure it out."
They make stressed-out noises when I say it. "You'll be ready
by then," I try to assure them.

Back at work the next day, Camila fills us in on her house.
Inspections and appraisals come and go.

"Can I take a break to look for more houses?" I ask the
office. "Yes!" they yell back, enthusiastic.

"Everyone's getting houses," I say, and now they believe it.

Inside of our weird little office, the outside world feels
like a bad nightmare. We drive our reliable cars into work.
We drink our iced coffees. We earn our equal pay for equal
hours. We split our profit. We work our four-day workweeks
instead of five. We take our mental health days. We set up
our 401(k)s. We save our down payments for our houses and
put money into our retirement accounts. We talk about how
good things are, how we feel at peace, many of us for the first
time in our lives. There's the shaky feeling, though, that at
any moment, it could all go away. Maybe something unfore-
seen will happen. Maybe it will all fall apart.

"We'll just start another business," I say, and everyone
agrees.

Maybe next time, Kelsey really will be the boss, or maybe
Kenna, or maybe Fernanda. We know how to do it now—how
to run a business in a way that makes us all feel like everything
is fair. We could do it again if we needed.

There was this song, in the '90s, by that band called Cake.
You know the band—the singer has that monotone voice and
the songs all sound like they could be jokes you're not in on,
but you're not quite sure? Anyway, in this one song, the lyrics, they say it: excess ain't rebellion. These "passive income"
business owners and these corporate CEOs, with their egregious paychecks and piles of money that they can't possibly
even hope to spend in their lifetimes, it's all just that: excess.
They cut costs, they raise prices, they maximize productivity,
they increase profits, then they take those profits for themselves to buy a new vacation home or whatever and they repeat

the cycle, over and over again. Those costs they cut, though, they're usually people—people's wages, people's hours, people's jobs, people's livelihoods. They cut from them, and they give to themselves with their giant "profits" left over, all while patting themselves on the back for being good at "business." What they're actually good at is taking. At a certain point, you have to say "Nobody gets seconds until everyone has had a plate." You have to know when you have enough.

In my little old house with the green paint on my bedroom walls that I got from the "oops" section at the hardware store, with my elderly dachshund who's missing a quarter of her teeth and the pit bull we rescued on the day she was supposed to be put down, with my bills all paid and my credit card debt gone and my savings account growing, slowly but surely, into a nice little nest egg for my retirement, I think I have finally found enough. It strikes me that most people aren't asking for much; they're asking for just this. They're asking for a place they can safely call their home, food they can reliably eat, medical care they count on, care for when they're unable to work, and free time to spend with one another—the simple things it takes to have a good life.

Outside of the black-tiled walls of our office, one of the neighborhood guys—Charles with the missing teeth—sits drunk by the door cracking jokes. He tells me I don't need to wear my platform shoes.

"I'll build you a platform so you're always standing tall," he tells me.

"You already have," I tell him with a smile. This neighborhood, the people in my life, the support I receive from my community—this is the platform on which I stand.

Inside our office, Crass blares on the stereo. They're an anarcho-punk band from the 1980s—one of Drew's favorites. He stayed at their farm—a commune, really—once when his punk band was on tour in England. Now, decades later, it's the soundtrack to our daily work. Punk might be dead, or it might be more alive than ever—growing like weeds through the cracks of the concrete that is our daily lives struggling to get by in a system of capitalism.

"Do they owe us a living?" the speaker asks. "Of course they do, of course they do!" Kelsey and Kenna and Story and Chris and I all chant back in tune with the track.

'Course they fucking do.

How to Build a Better World

1. Start with revolutionary optimism. Believe a better world is possible. It's the first step to getting there.

2. Don't be afraid to imagine. Creativity is an essential part of imagining a more equitable, just, and fair future.

3. Fight for what you believe in. The world needs more fighters.

4. Aim for progress, not perfection. Start where you are, use what you have.

5. Don't listen if anyone ever tells you it's a dog-eat-dog world. Dogs are pack animals. We're stronger together.

Epilogue: My Life Online

I've always been active on the internet. In the early days of dial-up, I spent my time on message boards or the Craigslist ride-share section, meeting up with strangers from nearby towns like Bakersfield or Visalia to take miniature road trips to Los Angeles to see our favorite bands play. The more people you could fit in a car, the cheaper your share of the gas. We met up in McDonald's parking lots, sizing each other up, hoping the other person wouldn't rob us or—worse—make us listen to bad music for three hours straight. For broke sketchy weirdos, the internet was a place to find real-world community. As technology became more advanced, I found myself joining early subculture-based social media websites with edgy names like Make Out Club and Lipstick Party and Mad Rad Hair. I was on MySpace; I had a Xanga online diary. As time wore on, I had a fashion blog where I chronicled my daily outfits, and then eventually an Instagram where I posted selfies and memes, some of which I made myself. When TikTok became the platform du jour, I joined that, too, and amassed a bit of a following.

On TikTok, I told strangers stories about my life—everything from my thoughts about the cost-effectiveness of my college education to how I coped with grief and loss. I told stories about my childhood with my father and about working horrible minimum-wage jobs. I gave my tips and tricks for getting hired quickly at temp agencies when you're in between gigs, and how to pawn things from around your house if you're short on rent. The audience I gathered on the platform seemed to be a lot of people like me—Generation Z or Millennials who were struggling to piece together a good life in the middle of the dumpster fire of capitalism and labor exploitation. So many of us were broke and tired, and my account was a place where we could commiserate about our struggles.

The internet has always been somewhere people could go to feel a little less alone, I guess. Today, the algorithms know us better than we know ourselves, pushing us into other like-minded people at lightning-fast speeds, creating feed-back loops and insular communities that lull us into a sense of comfort and safety while also making it increasingly hard to relate to people who don't share our opinions 100 per-cent of the time. In my small corner of the internet, it was a given that you loathed the political and economic system that controlled our day-to-day lives. And if you didn't? Well, you were probably just an internet troll who'd stumbled onto what we called the "wrong side" of the algorithm. One day, though, I received a comment from a stranger who was nei-ther a lost troll from the wrong side of the internet tracks nor a like-minded person from the feedback loop. The com-menter seemed to see me not as an avatar of anti-capitalism but as a person. It was an oddly humanizing experience to have on the internet. The comment read: "I don't hate capi-talism, but the more I learn about your life, the more I under-stand why you do."

It hit me hard. Of course, I knew my ideological con-tentions about capitalism were rooted in the experiences I'd had in my life. However, it wasn't until I read that com-ment that I truly grasped just how direct the cause-and-effect actually was.

And now, having spent a year writing this book, reliving those experiences, I realize how it was inevitable that my frustrations would grow to become so pointedly directed at capitalism itself. Even a proponent of capitalism could see the ways in which the system had failed me—from my chaotic childhood with broke and struggling parents, to a series of dead-end jobs that compromised my safety for the sake of making billionaires even richer, to the horrific trauma of losing my partner, to the two major catastrophic economic collapses I'd experienced in my adult years.

The thing about capitalism is that it is fiercely individualistic. There are winners and there are losers, and from what I can tell there are a hell of a lot more losers than winners. As of 2023, poverty is the fourth leading cause of death in the United States, and here we are once again, hearing constant talk in the news of an impending nationwide recession. At Tunnel Vision, we've cautiously battened down the hatches to make sure nobody loses their job. We collectively voted to temporarily suspend our company-sponsored gym memberships and free lunches. We'd rather pack a lunch than see a member of our team struggle with unemployment. We share the spoils in the boom years and work together to get through the bust years.

The story of my life and of the weird little business that I've made isn't a fairy tale. It's real life, and in the real world there's no perfect ending. We have good months and bad months just like any other business. We juggle financing and inventory, tallying marks on spreadsheets of our assets and liabilities. We get confused by government websites and agencies and new regulations. We struggle to stay up-to-date with ever-shifting algorithms and organic marketing techniques. The business isn't perfect, but it's been eleven years now and it's still standing—in a country where 65 percent of small businesses fail within the first ten years. We're not able to escape capitalism, but somehow—despite all odds—we've managed to stay afloat within it. I'm not here to tell you that creating the job you wish existed in the world is easy. Nothing in capitalism is easy. What I can say, though, is that running a business where you view every worker as an equally essential asset to the company and compensate them accordingly is not any more difficult than running a business in the traditional way.

Now, years into sharing my life online, when I talk about my work on the internet I've started to see a certain type of comment slowly pop up here and there. It's nothing major, but it's the promise of something more to follow. Sometimes they say "I started a business that runs like yours! We're going into our second year of operation next month." Other times they say "You inspired me to restructure the pay at my small business! Everyone is earning the same rate now." When I see those comments, I smile. I'm not starting a movement. I'm too disorganized for that. I'm just a blue-haired girl on the internet telling you that if you want to do things differently, maybe you can. I'm proof of concept, for the time being anyway.

If you like what I do, though, if we share the same values, if you want to work together to build a less individualistic, less greed-motivated world, something tells me the algorithm will bring you to my social media accounts if it hasn't already. You'll find me there—telling stories about my strange little house and my weird little workplace. Maybe one day, I'll get a comment from you, too. But if you find me, be nice, okay? The world is a stressful place, and I'm still just trying to survive.

Madeline Pendleton
2023

Acknowledgments

I'd like to thank Brit for helping me create this weird little business all those years ago. Thanks also to Fat Jerry for always giving me a place to go when I needed it most—rest in peace. The Tower District isn't the same without you. I'd also like to thank my friend David, who helped me remember my teenage years as accurately as possible. I still don't understand how your memory is so good, but I'm grateful for it (and grateful that even though you remember so much about me, you're still somehow my friend). Last, I'd like to thank Drew for being an endless source of inspiration. I miss you every day. Hopefully somewhere in another universe, we're together right now on a beach lying in the sun.

Notes

INTRODUCTION

2 leading predictor in instances of depression: Joseph D. Wolfe, Elizabeth H. Baker, Jalal Uddin, and Stephanie Kirkland, "Varieties of Financial Stressors and Midlife Health Problems, 1996–2016," *Journals of Gerontology*, series B, 77, no. 1 (January 2022): 149–59.

CHAPTER 2: WORKING FOR THE WEEKEND

28 The average life span for an unsheltered homeless person: Jerzy Romaszko, Iwona Cymes, Ewa Dragańska, Robert Kuchta, and Katarzyna Glińska-Lewczuk, "Mortality Among the Homeless: Causes and Meteorological Relationships," *PLoS One* 12, no. 12 (2017), https://www.ncbi.nlm.nih.gov/pmc/articles/PMC5739436/.

29 approximately 40 percent of unsheltered unhoused people have jobs: Bruce Meyer, Angela Wyse, Alexa Grunwaldt, Carla Medalia, Derek Wu, "Learning About Homelessness Using Linked Survey and Administrative Data," BFI Working Paper (June 1, 2021), https://bfi.uchicago.edu/working-paper/learning-about-homelessness-using-linked-survey-and-administrative-data/.

CHAPTER 6: FUNEMPLOYMENT

128 those who graduated during the recession: Hannes Schwandt, "Recession Graduates: The Long-Lasting Effects of an Unlucky Draw," Stanford Institute for Economic Policy Research, April 2019, https://siepr.stanford.edu/publications/policy-brief/recession-graduates-long-lasting-effects-unlucky-draw.

CHAPTER 9: CAPITALISM KILLED MY BOYFRIEND

194 43 percent of people experiencing hunger: Mary Babic, Theresa DelVecchio Dys, Monica Hake, Meghan O'Leary, Elaine Wax-

man, and Andrew Yarrow, "From Paycheck to Pantry: Hunger in Working America," Oxfam, November 18, 2014, https://www .oxfamamerica.org/explore/research-publications/from-paycheck -to-pantry-hunger-in-working-america.

CHAPTER 13: HOME IS WHERE ~~THE HEART IS~~ YOU CAN AFFORD THE MONTHLY PAYMENTS

254   "A mortgage broker is an intermediary": The full definition: "A mortgage broker is an intermediary who brings mortgage borrowers and mortgage lenders together, but who does not use their own funds to originate mortgages. A mortgage broker helps borrowers connect with lenders and seeks out the best fit in terms of the borrower's financial situation and interest-rate needs. The mortgage broker also gathers paperwork from the borrower and passes that paperwork along to a mortgage lender for underwriting and approval purposes. The broker earns a commission from either the borrower, the lender, or both at closing." Julia Kagan, "Mortgage Broker: Definition, How They Work, and Responsibilities," Investopedia, https://www.investopedia.com/terms/m/mortgagebroker.asp.

CHAPTER 14: WHOA, WHAT HAPPENED?

280   35,000 people per year were dying in factories by the year 1900: Robert Samuelson, "Work Ethic vs. Fun Ethic," *Washington Post*, September 3, 2001.

EPILOGUE: MY LIFE ONLINE

307   As of 2023, poverty is the fourth: David Danelski, "Poverty Is the 4th Greatest Cause of U.S. Deaths," *UC Riverside News*, April 17, 2023, https://news.ucr.edu/articles/2023/04/17/poverty-4th-greatest -cause-us-deaths.

Madeline Pendleton is the CEO and founder of Tunnel Vision, an L.A.-based clothing company with a progressive, employee-centered approach to business. In addition to her entrepreneurial success, Madeline has garnered a massive following on TikTok, where she shares stories and advice based on her experience growing up in California's punk scene, escaping poverty, and building a community-minded company.

Instagram: @madelinependleton

TikTok: @madeline_pendleton

A NOTE ON THE TYPE

This book was set in Janson, a typeface long thought to have been made by the Dutchman Anton Janson, who was a practicing typefounder in Leipzig during the years 1668–1687. However, it has been conclusively demonstrated that these types are actually the work of Nicholas Kis (1650–1702), a Hungarian, who most probably learned his trade from the master Dutch typefounder Dirk Voskens. The type is an excellent example of the influential and sturdy Dutch types that prevailed in England up to the time William Caslon (1692–1766) developed his own incomparable designs from them.

Composed by North Market Street Graphics
Lancaster, Pennsylvania

Printed and bound by Berryville Graphics
Berryville, Virginia